CHRISTIANITY
THE ILLUSTRATED HISTORY

CHRISTIANITY
THE ILLUSTRATED HISTORY

CHURCH AND SOCIETY
†
CULTURE AND CIVILIZATION
†
SACRED ART AND ARCHITECTURE

GENERAL EDITOR:
HANS J. HILLERBRAND

DUNCAN BAIRD PUBLISHERS
LONDON

Christianity: The Illustrated History
General Editor: Hans J. Hillerbrand

Distributed in the USA and Canada by
Sterling Publishing Co., Inc.
387 Park Avenue South
New York, NY 10016-8810

This edition first published in the UK and USA in 2008 by
Duncan Baird Publishers Ltd
Sixth Floor, Castle House
75–76 Wells Street
London W1T 3QH

Managing Editor: Christopher Westhorp
Editor: Peter Bently
Managing Designer: Daniel Sturges
Picture Research: Julia Ruxton

Library of Congress Cataloging-in-Publication Data

Christianity : the illustrated history : church and society, culture and civilization, sacred art and architecture / general editor, Hans J. Hildebrand.
p. cm.
Includes bibliographical references and index.
ISBN 978-1-84483-717-5 (alk. paper)
1. Church history. I. Hildebrand, Hans J.
BR145.3.C46 2008
270--dc22
2008020628

ISBN: 978-1-84483-717-5

10 9 8 7 6 5 4 3 2 1

Typeset in Minion Pro
Color reproduction by Scanhouse, Malaysia
Printed in Singapore by Imago

For information about custom editions, special sales, premium and corporate purchases, please contact Sterling Special Sales Department at 800-805-5489 or specialsales@sterlingpub.com.

Abbreviations used throughout this book:
CE Common Era (the equivalent of AD)
BCE Before the Common Era (the equivalent of BC)

Note about Bible quotes:
All the Scripture quotations contained herein are from the New Revised Standard Version Bible, copyright © 1989 by the Division of Christian Education of the National Council of the Churches of Christ in the U.S.A., and are used by permission. All rights reserved. Exceptions are those marked KJV, which indicates King James' Version, courtesy of the Crown's Patentee, Cambridge University Press.

Captions to illustrations on pages 1–3:
Page 1: Fan tracery on the vaulting, York Minster, England.
Page 2: St. Knuds Kirche, Odense, Denmark.
Page 3: A detail of the outer container of a reliquary of the True Cross, an elaborate Byzantine enamel that survived the sack of Constantinople in 1204. The detail shows the enthroned Christ at the centre of the piece.

CONTENTS

INTRODUCTION

In the opening years of the twenty-first century, some two billion people around the globe call themselves Christians. In so doing they pledge allegiance to Jesus of Nazareth and to his life and work. Christianity is the largest of the world's religions, and Jesus stands alongside the Buddha and Muhammad as one of the foremost religious figures of humankind.

The beginnings of the Christian religion were more modest. Two thousand years ago Jesus of Nazareth, a Jew, walked the Palestinian countryside preaching and teaching. He had followers, male and female, propounded a striking message, ran into conflict with the religious and political authorities of his day, and eventually died an ignominious death as a criminal outside Jerusalem.

While this might well have been the end of the story, his followers, convinced that he had risen from the dead thereby vindicating his mission, followed his exhortation to go into all the world and make disciples. Though they promptly encountered the malevolence of the political authorities, the small group of disciples and followers turned

The Sermon on the Mount *and the Healing of the Leper (before restoration), by Cosimo Rosselli (1439–1507), a fresco on the walls of the Sistine Chapel in the Vatican. The challenging demands contained in Jesus' Sermon on the Mount (Matt. 5–7) and in the related Sermon on the Plain (Luke 6.20–49), lie at the heart of Christian ethics.*

into a movement that was found, within a couple of centuries, in all corners of the Roman empire. By the early fourth century, Christians had endured and survived intermittent oppression and persecution at the hands of the Roman state, but their church was a dynamic, well-organized movement.

DYNAMISM AND DIVERSITY

In 313 the emperor Constantine declared Christianity a recognized and privileged religion in the Roman empire. The subsequent decline, and eventual disintegration, of this mighty empire hardly affected Christianity, which continued its expansion beyond the boundaries of the empire until, by the end of the millennium, virtually all of Europe had formally become Christian. For over a millennium the Christian faith formally united the peoples of Europe. And when, beginning in the fifteenth century, the Europeans explored new continents and cultures, the Christian religion expanded with it to all four corners of the globe, so much so that in the early twenty-first century Christianity is liveliest and most dynamic not in its traditional European and North American locales, but in Africa and Asia.

Crucifix *by Margaritone d'Arezzo (fl. 1260–1290). The climactic event of Jesus' career was his execution by crucifixion ca. 30CE. This scene, so common in later centuries, was absent from early Christian art, partly because it was regarded in the Roman world as a shameful death. The earliest known depictions date from the fifth century, several decades after the emperor Constantine I abolished the penalty.*

The story of Christianity is thus a multicolored fabric with a richness of vibrant hues. It is the story of the development of Christian self-consciousness, what it means to be a Christian, and what is Christian teaching and living. It is the story of how this church organized itself, worshipped, and prayed. It is the story of saints and martyrs and heretics, of the splendor of soaring Gothic cathedrals and of St. Peter's in Rome no less than of St. Catherine's monastery in the desolation of the Sinai peninsula and of the simplicity of a Quaker meeting in Lincolnshire, England. It is the story of monks and nuns chanting their praise and adoration in countless monastic houses according to time-honored ritual, even as it is the story of Calvinists singing the 100th Psalm put to rhyme and music, of Lutheran congregations resounding *A Mighty Fortress is Our God,* or of African slaves in North America evoking the biblical stories of bondage and liberation with haunting melodies that they had brought with them from Africa.

In the process, Christian theologians delineated an impressive intellectual edifice that addressed the issues the religions of humankind have addressed—the existence of God; the reality of evil; divine providence and human freedom; sin; the end of history. Not all Christians agreed on all of these topics. It has therefore become fashionable to talk about "Christianities" in the plural to denote this diversity. Nonetheless, it is assuredly possible to speak of a common core of Christian beliefs through the centuries.

At the same time, Christians also addressed the sundry manifestations of what constitutes the "good" and "moral" life—how Christians must behave, personally and

The International Reformation Monument, *Geneva, Switzerland, built 1909–1917 to commemorate the city's role in the 16th-century Protestant Reformation. Some 325 feet (100m) and 30 feet (10m) high, it centers on the statues of four leading lights of what came to be known as Calvinism: Guillaume Farel, John Calvin Theodore Beza, and John Knox. Protestantism never had a uniform doctrine, and Martin Luther and Huldrych Zwingli, with whom Calvin differed on certain questions, are represented on the wall only by their names. Smaller statues and reliefs depict other figures and events in Protestant history, such as Roger Williams, Oliver Cromwell, the Pilgrim Fathers, and England's 1689 Bill of Rights.*

collectively. The Christian Bible is full of laws, exhortations, counsels, mandates, which moral theologians through the centuries sought to turn into systematic values. In varying ways, Christian moral reflection resulted in the creation of an ethos, a distinct Christian way of talking about the moral life.

FAITH AND SOCIETY

At the same time, the Christian faith has affected its surrounding society in a myriad of ways so that the story of Western culture cannot be told apart from the story of Christianity. Much of this story found artistic expression in architecture, paintings, sculpture, and music. Indeed, the history of Western art and music is to a large extent at once the story of Christian iconography: of the unknown builders of Gothic churches; of Giotto, Michelangelo, El Greco, and Bernini; of Palestrina, Byrd, Praetorius, and J.S. Bach. Alongside the arts, Christianity has influenced just about every other field of human endeavor—from education to concern for the poor and sick, the brewing of beer, and the invention, in Italy toward the end of the thirteenth century, of reading glasses.

The story of Christianity is also, unfortunately, the story of Christian intolerance toward other Christians whose interpretation of the gospel differed; of yielding to the dictates of society and those in power as identical with the message of Jesus; of churchmen jealously vying for supremacy with those in power. This dark side of Christian history has been much dramatized by the critics and despisers of Christianity through the centuries, and thereby much overstated; that it is part of the Christian story, however, must not be doubted.

A thoughtful account of the history of Christianity must embrace all of these facets, and at the same time note the persistence of certain themes, or motifs, that can be found throughout the centuries. The relationship to its surrounding societies is assuredly one of these themes, because Christianity has always been not only of another world but also of this world.

The quest for reform has been another basic motif in the history of Christianity. It has reflected the tension between Christian ideals and actual practice. Through the centuries sensitive souls invoked biblical ideals and found their church and their fellow believers wanting. The call was then for reform, sometimes modest, sometimes radical. The notion of *reformatio in caput et membris* (reform from the top and from below) made the rounds. Some advocates of such reform were committed to the monastic ideals and sought to reform and revitalize the church through old or new monastic orders. Francis of Assisi, with his radical commitment to Christian poverty, serves as a vivid illustration (see page 45). Others sought to engage the church at large, most dramatically when Martin Luther, an Augustinian monk and professor of biblical studies, issued the call for radical reform in the second decade of the sixteenth century. Finally, reform has also been the great watchword of Christianity in the modern world, when theologians and church reformers have argued that the coming of modernity called for abandoning traditional notions in favor of a new vision of the Christian faith.

ABOUT THIS BOOK

Christianity: The Illustrated History aims to introduce the religion that, in the opening years of the twenty-first century, continues to command the loyalty of thousands of millions of men, women, and children. The first part ("Origins and History") presents a broad survey of Christian history, from the time of Jesus to the present day. Part Two ("Principles and Practices") begins with an outline of the central tenets and practices of the Christian faith, together with its ethics, which have played such an important role in the development of "Western" culture and civilization. It goes on to look at the Christian faithful as a single community, as communities, and as individuals, from the early saints and martyrs to the active laypeople of today. Part Two concludes with surveys of the main branches of Christianity, beginning with Roman Catholicism, the group with numerically the largest number of adherents, and continuing with an overview of the multiplicity of groups that are collectively, and conventionally, grouped under the heading "Protestantism." The final chapter of Part Two looks at Eastern Orthodoxy, which in its various forms demonstrates a remarkable continuity from late antiquity to the present day.

Part Three ("The Christian Bible") looks at the scriptures of the Old and New Testaments, which form the basis of the Christian faith in all its many manifestations, and also noncanonical texts that have influenced Christian thought and culture. Part Four ("Christianity Today") concludes the book with a survey of the key issues and themes of the faith as it embarks upon its third millennium.

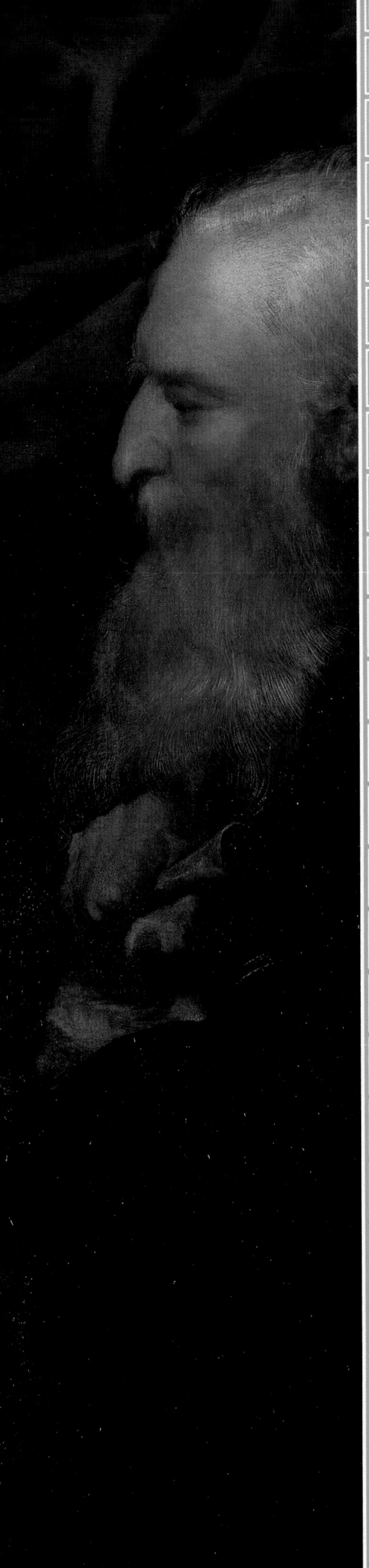

PART 1

ORIGINS AND HISTORY

Virgin and Child with Saints (Madonna delle Rose, detail) *by Titian (ca. 1480–1576). Depictions of the infant John the Baptist meeting his relative, the infant Jesus, were popular in the 16th century, although they have no scriptural basis. John carries a cross of reeds, prefiguring the crucifixion, and roses were symbols of Jesus' mother Mary, the sinless "rose without thorns." Mary's husband Joseph looks on.*

ROMAN PALESTINE: LAND AND RELIGION

In 63BCE the Roman empire took control of what is traditionally called Palestine, or the Holy Land, when its troops captured Jerusalem and ended the rule of the Jewish Hasmonean dynasty. Subsequently, in 37BCE, Rome entrusted Palestine to a client king, Herod the Great (see box), but after his death the major part of his kingdom (Judea, Samaria, and Idumea) came under the direct rule of Roman prefects, of whom the fifth is the most famous: Pontius Pilate (governed 26–36CE). Luke calls Pilate ruthless (Luke 13.1) and other first-century authors depict him as inflexible and even incompetent. On several occasions he came into violent conflict with the Jews under his rule, and the gospel accounts of Jesus' career reflect this uneasy relationship with the Roman authority. Jesus

HEROD THE GREAT AND HIS SUCCESSORS

The gospels of Matthew and Luke record that Jesus was born near the end of the reign of King Herod the Great (37–4BCE). Herod was an astute ruler who was careful to conciliate Jewish religious factions in his realm, while also fostering Hellenistic culture and building Greco-Roman-style cities such as Sepphoris in Galilee. He also rebuilt the Temple of Jerusalem, the center of Jewish religious life (see main text). But Herod also utterly ruthless in preserving his throne, even executing several of his own family. The gospel story of the massacre of the children of Bethlehem certainly reflects Herod's increasingly paranoid character in old age.

On Herod's death the Romans divided his kingdom into an "ethnarchy" and two "tetrarchies," each ruled by one of his sons. The ethnarchy of Judea, Samaria, and Idumea fell to Herod Archelaus, a tyrant who was deposed by Rome in 6CE for misrule; his domains were then placed under direct Roman rule (see main text). His brother Herod Antipas (ruled 4BCE–39CE) was tetrarch of Galilee—Jesus' home territory and the scene of much of his ministry—and Perea, a region across the Jordan. The most prominent Herodian ruler in the gospels, Antipas is the "Herod" who executes John the Baptist and, in Luke, is involved in Jesus' condemnation (see page 22).

Ruins of Herod the Great's palace *near Jericho, a winter resort of the Herodian dynasty and of their Hasmonean predecessors. Like the Jerusalem Temple and many of his other monumental building projects, Herod's palace was destroyed during the First Jewish War of 66–70CE.*

The Pilate Stone *was discovered in 1961 at the site of Caesarea Maritima, the seat of the Roman prefect of Judea, and is the only known ancient inscription bearing the name of the Roman prefect who condemned Jesus. Now partly erased, it records the dedication of a "Tiberieum" (a building in honor of the emperor Tiberius) by "[Pon]tius Pilatus [Praef]ectus Iudae[ae]" (Pontius Pilate, Prefect of Judea). Seen here is a replica* in situ*; the original is in a museum.*

and his followers would have been suspect merely because they came from Galilee, where there had been rebellions (see, for example, Acts 5.36–37). Pilate ruled not from Jerusalem, the Jewish holy city, but from Caesarea Maritima on the coast, travelling to Jerusalem with troops on major Jewish festivals, when thousands thronged the city and trouble was feared. It was at the most popular festival, Pesah (Passover), that Jesus was arrested and executed.

The day-to-day internal government of the Jews was entrusted to the high priest: the gospels mention two incumbents, Annas (in office 6–15CE) and his son-in-law Joseph Caiaphas (18–36CE). The high priest headed the Temple establishment and its large body of priests, and presided over the Jewish council, whose basic function seems to have been to oversee the operation of the Jewish law. It is likely that the Romans expected the high priest and his associates to prevent unrest among the Jewish population: it is the council which, in the gospels, initially tries and condemns Jesus.

SYNAGOGUE AND TEMPLE

The various Jewish groups of Jesus' day (see sidebar) shared many fundamental tenets and practices, including belief in one God, who had chosen Israel as his people, and adherence to the Torah, the law of Moses set out in the Pentateuch, the Bible's first five books. The Torah included laws on Sabbath observance, diet, and circumcision, practices that clearly marked out Jews from their pagan neighbors. Sabbath worship for most centered on the synagogue, in this era primarily a place where the law was taught and read. It also served as a local law court. At Passover and other great festivals the law required all male Jews to go to Jerusalem for sacrifices and other rites at the Temple, the focus of Jewish life and faith until the Romans destroyed it in 70CE. The Temple precincts occupied a vast raised platform, the Temple Mount, which Herod the Great had lavishly rebuilt in Hellenistic style.

THE PHARISEES

Jewish groups in Jesus' day included Pharisees, Sadducees, Essenes (see page 18), and Herodians. From deductions based on the evidence of the New Testament, the Pharisees (the dominant group) shared with Jesus a belief in resurrection and apparently in angels and demons. Sadducees (Mark 12.18–27) accepted only the Pentateuch as scripture, as did the Samaritans, an ancient offshoot of Judaism in Samaria. But Pharisees also accepted the Prophets and probably at least some of the Writings (see page 196). The Pharisees were scrupulous interpreters and observers of Jewish law. The gospels accuse them of being excessively rule-bound and even hypocritical (Matt. 23.3), but also record that Jesus was friendly with some Pharisees. The apostle Paul was a Pharisee before his conversion (Phil. 3.5, Gal. 1.14).

SOURCES FOR THE LIFE OF JESUS

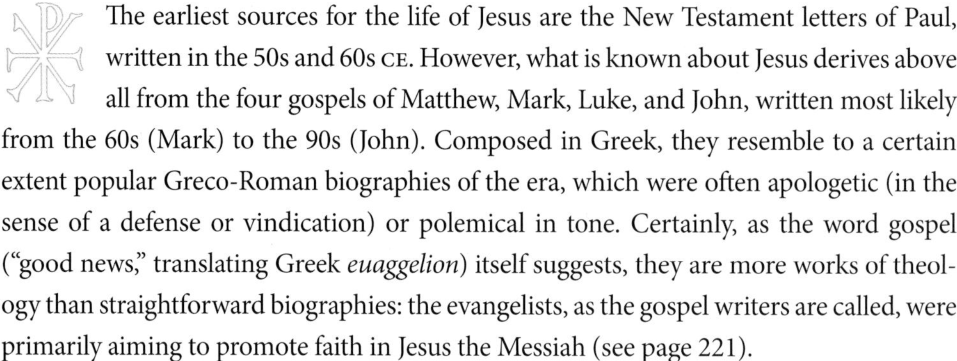

The earliest sources for the life of Jesus are the New Testament letters of Paul, written in the 50s and 60s CE. However, what is known about Jesus derives above all from the four gospels of Matthew, Mark, Luke, and John, written most likely from the 60s (Mark) to the 90s (John). Composed in Greek, they resemble to a certain extent popular Greco-Roman biographies of the era, which were often apologetic (in the sense of a defense or vindication) or polemical in tone. Certainly, as the word gospel ("good news," translating Greek *euaggelion*) itself suggests, they are more works of theology than straightforward biographies: the evangelists, as the gospel writers are called, were primarily aiming to promote faith in Jesus the Messiah (see page 221).

Hence many scholars would assert that the gospels' accounts of Jesus' career and message reveal more about the early congregations for which they were written than they do about Jesus himself. But this point can be exaggerated. Christianity has always claimed to rest on the life and teachings of a real person who lived in a certain place at a certain time, and it seems very unlikely that what the early Christians believed about Jesus was entirely unrelated to his actual life and teachings. It was usual for the sayings and deeds of Jewish teachers (*rabbis*) to be remembered by their disciples for the benefit of later generations, and Jesus' first followers may well have done likewise. It is possible that the gospel writers also drew on written and well as oral accounts.

St. Mark the Evangelist *from the 6th-century Rossano Gospels, written in Greek on purple-colored parchment and one of the world's oldest extant illuminated manuscripts. It contains the entire gospel of Matthew and most of Mark. Here Mark is shown in the posture of a Classical scribe, his words inspired by the figure of Sophia (divine Wisdom).*

The gospels are at times inconsistent (giving the same deeds or utterances of Jesus in different versions or contexts), and also contain what are probably legends as well as words that Jesus is unlikely to have spoken. But the same is true of most other ancient biographical writings: for example, there are also four surviving accounts of the life of Jesus' contemporary, the Roman emperor Tiberius (ruled 14–37CE), which vary widely in detail (two of them are hostile). But historians have little difficulty in constructing from these sources a broadly agreed biography of the emperor.

OTHER EARLY SOURCES

There are numerous references to Jesus in sources outside the gospels, some Jewish and pagan (see box and sidebar) but most of them Christian. Particularly significant are the *agrapha*, sayings of Jesus not found in Matthew, Mark, Luke, or John but recorded elsewhere. In the New Testament, for example, the apostle Paul cites Jesus as saying "It is more blessed to give than to receive" (Acts 20.35), an utterance that does not appear in the gospels. There are also *agrapha* in the writings of the Church Fathers (see page 30) and other sources, notably the Gospel of Thomas (see page 203). Such sayings may represent an oral tradition distinct from the gospels and at least some may be authentic.

Other Christian sources include various "apocryphal gospels" of the second to fifth centuries. Written to fill gaps in the gospel stories (for example, the evangelists contain only one incident from Jesus' childhood; see page 16) and inspire popular devotion, they are clearly works of imagination of probably negligible historical value, although the second-century *Protevangelium of James* feasibly contains authentic traditions about Mary, Jesus' mother. Other works include a large body of Gnostic Christian texts and writings that reflect a Jewish-Christian viewpoint and which are known only from citations in later Christian authors. (See also pages 202–203.)

JESUS IN PAGAN WORKS

The Roman historian Tacitus (ca. 55–ca. 120CE) wrote that the emperor Nero blamed the great fire of Rome in 64 on the "Christians," named for "Christus," who he says was executed in the reign of Tiberius by the procurator Pilate. The "mischievous superstition" had spread to Rome from Judea. Suetonius (ca. 69–ca. 140CE) refers to the emperor Claudius expelling "Jews" from Rome in 49—whether all Jews or just the followers of Jesus is unclear—following unrest instigated by "Chrestus." The event is mentioned in Acts 18.2.

DID JOSEPHUS WRITE ABOUT JESUS?

The earliest reference to Jesus outside the New Testament may be a passage in the *Antiquities of the Jews* (ca. 90CE) by the Jewish historian Flavius Josephus: "At this time lived Jesus, a wise man (if one may rightly call him a man), a worker of miracles and a teacher of people who receive the truth with pleasure; as followers he gained many Jews and many Greeks. He was the Christ, and when by the accusation of our chief men Pilate condemned him to the cross, those who first loved him did not cease from doing so; for he appeared to them, alive again, on the third day, since the divine prophets had foretold this as well as countless other marvels about him. Up to the present the tribe of Christians, named after him, has not disappeared." (*Ant.* 18.63–64.)

Josephus, a devout Jew, could hardly have written the most overtly Christian parts of this passage and hence scholars question its authenticity. Elsewhere, Josephus writes of John the Baptist and of Jesus' brother James, so it is possible that he did mention something about Jesus, which was later expanded by a Christian scribe.

The Beheading of John the Baptist, *by Hans Memling (ca. 1433–1494). This detail shows Salome receiving the head: it is from Josephus that we know her name.*

THE BIRTH AND CHILDHOOD

The traditional "Christmas Story" of Jesus' birth is a harmonization of two accounts, one in Matthew 1–2 and the other in Luke 1–2: the rest of the New Testament is entirely silent about Jesus' nativity and childhood. On Jesus' birth, Matthew says only that he "was born in Bethlehem of Judea" (Matt. 2.1) before relating how Jesus came to live in Nazareth in Galilee, starting with the story of three wise men (magi) who follow the star to the newborn Jesus. On the way they visit King Herod, who fears that the child will be the king-Messiah prophesied in scripture, so orders the slaughter of all the infants of Bethlehem. The holy family flees to Egypt and after Herod's death they return not to Judea, now ruled by Herod's despotic son Archelaus (see page 12), but to Nazareth in Galilee.

Christ and the Temple Teachers *by Duccio di Buoninsegna (ca. 1260–1318). This depicts the New Testament's sole episode from the childhood of Jesus (Luke 2.41–52) when, aged 12, he goes missing during a visit to Jerusalem for Passover. His parents find him in the Temple—in the precincts, where rabbis would teach, rather than the sanctuary—debating with religious teachers, who are "amazed at his understanding." Jesus' age may be significant because 13 is the usual age of religious maturity in Judaism. In the Synoptic Gospels, Jesus does not return to the Temple until the last week of his life.*

Matthew sets Jesus' birth in the context of the fulfillment of biblical prophecy, but Luke's version establishes Jesus within the wider Gentile world to which his message is carried in Luke's sequel, Acts. Joseph and Mary travel to Bethlehem to register for a census of the Roman empire decreed by the emperor Augustus and overseen by Quirinius, governor of Syria (Luke 2.1–5). In fact, there was never a census of the whole empire, and Quirinius's Judean census took place in 6 or 7CE, a very unlikely date for Jesus' birth. Moreover, Luke 1.36 suggests that Jesus was born within six months of John the Baptist, in the reign of Herod the Great (died 4BCE). However, as well as providing an international context, the census explains why Jesus was born in Bethlehem and not Nazareth, where he was raised (see sidebar).

It is Luke who gives the familiar details of Jesus' birth in a manger, presumably in a stable, at an inn that has no spare room, and describes the visit of the shepherds to the newborn Messiah. After Jesus is circumcised and named according to the Law (Luke 2.21), Luke concludes his birth story with Jesus' presentation in the Temple of Jerusalem, dedicating him to God his future mission (Luke 2.23). After this the family returns peacefully to Nazareth, where Jesus grows up with God's favor and "filled with wisdom" (Luke 2.40).

BETHLEHEM

Scholars have long asked whether the tradition, as recorded in the gospels, that Jesus was born in Bethlehem has a historical basis or a theological one—according to prophecy it was the place where the Messiah would be born (Matt. 2.6). On the other hand, the tradition is both consistent and very early. Luke says that Joseph's family was from Bethlehem (2.4), and attests to another strong early tradition, that Mary too had family ties in Judea (1.36).

RECONCILING MATTHEW AND LUKE

It is not always easy to reconcile the Nativity stories in Matthew and Luke. A prime example is their accounts of how Jesus came to be born in Bethlehem: Matthew implies that Mary and Joseph lived there (2.11) and says that they only moved to Nazareth later (2.23); Luke says they lived in Nazareth (1.26–27), moved to Bethlehem for a census (2.4–5), then returned to Galilee (2.39).

However, the two narratives share enough important similarities to suggest that both drew on the same basic traditions. Both gospels contain the names of Jesus' parents (Joseph and Mary); the description of the couple as betrothed (in Judaism, the first stage of marriage); the claim that Jesus descends from King David; an angel's annunciation of the birth of a son (to Mary in Luke, to Joseph in Matthew); the angel's message that Mary has conceived by the Holy Spirit and that the child should be named Jesus (Yeshu or Yeshua, "God saves"); the claim that Mary is a virgin; and the assertion that the birth took place in Bethlehem (see sidebar).

The Adoration of the Magi *by Jaume Ferrer II. The story of the wise men, or magi, from the East is recounted in Matthew, and the setting of the stable comes from Luke. In Christian tradition the magi are often portrayed as kings, who bow down, as here, in acknowledgment of an even greater king. Catalan, 1432–1434.*

THE MINISTRY

The three Synoptic Gospels agree that Jesus' public career began in Galilee and ended in Jerusalem, where he died. They also agree that, at the start of his ministry, Jesus was closely associated with John the Baptist, who baptized him in the Jordan River (see box). Jesus then spent a period of solitude in the Judean wilderness, where he was "tempted by Satan" (Mark 1.12–13). In Matthew and Luke the temptation becomes a dramatic dialogue between Jesus and Satan, who fails to persuade Jesus to misuse his powers (Matt. 4.1–11, Luke 4.1–13).

In the Synoptic gospels, most of Jesus' ministry takes place in Galilee, mainly in a small area around the western shores of Lake Galilee, in the territory of Herod Antipas

JESUS AND JOHN THE BAPTIST

The New Testament records that Jesus was linked, at the start of his ministry, with John the Baptist, an ascetic teacher who is also mentioned by Josephus (see page 15). The gospels state that John exhorted people to be cleansed of sin before the imminent coming of the Messiah. This cleansing John accomplished by immersing people in the Jordan River in a rite called baptism (Greek *baptizein*, "to immerse"). Before beginning his own ministry, Jesus was very likely one of John's followers (John 1.28ff., 3.22), and one gospel honors John as the new Elijah (Matt. 11.14) who heralds the coming Messiah, as prophesied in Malachi 4.5. The gospels and Josephus record John's popularity, and his execution by Herod Antipas.

Both John and Jesus are said to have spent time in the wilderness and it has been speculated that John, at least, may have had links to the Essenes, an exclusive sect that rejected the Temple. It was almost certainly the Essenes who lived in the desert at Qumran and produced the so-called Dead Sea Scrolls.

The Baptism of Christ *by Piero della Francesca (ca. 1412–1492). John baptizes Jesus by the banks of the Jordan as the divine Spirit descends in the form of a dove. For the evangelists, this act marked Jesus' formal designation as Messiah and his own realization of his mission.*

A fishing boat at sunrise *on Lake Galilee, the setting for much of Jesus' ministry, according to the gospels. Fishing was central to the lives of those living on the lakeshore, and two fishermen—the brothers Andrew and Peter—were the first of Jesus' twelve leading disciples to be called (see sidebar below).*

(see page 12), with occasional visits to the eastern shores, a more mixed Jewish and Gentile area ruled by Herod Philip. The chief aim of all the gospels was to demonstrate that Jesus was the savior-Messiah and it does not seem likely that Mark, Matthew, or Luke was interested in strict chronology. Hence it is quite common for a particular saying or miraculous healing to appear in different gospels in entirely different contexts.

The Synoptists also agree that the main part of Jesus' ministry ended when he and his disciples travelled through the Jordan valley to Jerusalem for Passover. This follows an episode near Caesarea Philippi, in Herod Philip's lands, in which Peter makes a special confession, or avowal, of faith in Jesus' messianic character. This episode, also found in John (6.67–69), is followed in the Synoptics by the Transfiguration, when Jesus appears bathed in light on a mountain with Moses and Elijah. Near the end of the journey, Jesus heals one or two blind men in Jericho (Mark 10.46–52 and parallels), where he is hailed as "Son of David," anticipating the cry that will greet his entry into Jerusalem.

Luke makes the journey to Jerusalem into an extended travel narrative (Luke 9.51–19.28) that brings together traditions of Jesus' teaching in such areas as prayer, wealth, and forgiveness. Luke also includes some famous parables (see page 22) found nowhere else in the gospels, such as those of the Good Samaritan and the Prodigal Son.

THE MINISTRY IN JOHN

On the whole, John presents a distinctly different picture of Jesus' public career. In John, the ministry begins in Judea and neighboring Perea across the Jordan, and moves regularly between there and Galilee. However, the greater part of Jesus' ministry takes place in and

THE DISCIPLES

The gospels state that Jesus had many disciples (literally "pupils"), from whom he chose a select group of twelve men with authority to exorcize, heal, and preach the kingdom of God. The names of the Twelve—whose number parallels the tribes of Israel (Matt. 19.28, Luke 22.30)—are recorded as: Simon (Peter, Cephas) and his brother Andrew; James and John, sons of Zebedee; Philip; Bartholomew; Matthew (Levi); Thomas Didymus; James, son of Alphaeus; Simon the Zealot (the Cananean); Judas Iscariot; and Judas (Jude), son of James (also named Lebbaeus or Thaddaeus). After the death of Judas Iscariot (see page 23), the disciple Matthias was chosen to make up the Twelve (Acts 1.16, 1.26).

around Jerusalem. The Synoptists may seem to imply a ministry lasting only a year, since they mention one visit by Jesus to Jerusalem, at Passover. In contrast, John describes Jesus as visiting the city on three Passovers, and also on other important festivals. These accounts may not be incompatible. The Synoptists' single Passover is important mainly because it was the occasion of Jesus' death. If they record no other visits to Jerusalem by the adult Jesus it need not imply that he did not make them, as these were required by Jewish Law.

THE KINGDOM OF GOD

The notion of the "kingdom of God" (or "kingdom of heaven") is of central importance in Jesus' teaching. "The good news of the kingdom" (Matt. 4.23, Luke 8.1) is a repeated theme in the Synoptics, and Jesus urges hearers: "Repent, and believe in the good news" (*euaggelion*, or gospel; Mark 1.15). The kingdom of God is not an earthly realm, like the Roman empire, but embraces the whole universe. One much-debated question is whether Jesus regarded the kingdom as a hoped-for future phenomenon or as a present reality, but the two notions are not incompatible: many contemporary Jews saw the

JESUS THE HEALER

In the gospels Jesus can heal people by exorcizing them of "unclean spirits." These stories tend to be highly dramatic, as when Jesus sends the "legion" of evil spirits tormenting a man into a herd of pigs that career downhill into the sea (Mark 5.1–20 and parallels). Other stories focus on the power of Jesus' word as well as the recipient's faith, as when he heals a paralytic by declaring his sins forgiven (Mark 2.1–12). At other times Jesus' healings are tactile, as when he places his fingers in the ears of a deaf man (Mark 7.31–37; Matt. 15.29–31).

Jesus Heals the Paralytic *from a 3rd-century church excavated at Dura-Europos, Syria, and one of the earliest known depictions of Jesus. He cured a paralyzed man saying: "Take up your mat [or bed] and walk" (Mark 2.9, 11 and parallels; compare John 5.11–12).*

kingdom as present but locked in a struggle against the world of evil; for his followers, Jesus' success as a healer (see sidebar), especially his mastery over demons, were signs that the kingdom was about to triumph, establishing God's universal rule and transforming the present world of evil, sin, sickness, and imperfection.

In the gospels, Jesus' announcement of the kingdom includes radical reversal—the roles of rich and poor, powerful and humble, oppressor and oppressed were overturned. In Luke's Sermon on the Plain (Luke 6.20–49), for example, Jesus blesses the poor and condemns the rich, and all the normal expectations are subverted. Jesus' most famous teaching, though, is in Matthew's Sermon on the Mount (Matt. 5–7), a collection of reflections and injunctions about the Law, relationships, and religious practices; its most famous section is the Beatitudes ("Blessed are the meek" for example; see pages 214–215). Jesus tells his hearers that those hoping to enter the kingdom must follow God and show universal mercy and love, even toward enemies; indeed they must "be perfect" (Matt. 5.43–48). Jesus' ethical teaching is essentially one of love, memorably encapsulated in his summary of the Law: you shall love God above all, and love your neighbor as yourself (Mark 12.29–31 and parallels).

THE PARABLES

Matthew, Mark, and Luke record that Jesus frequently used "parables" to illustrate his teaching. The term (from Greek *parabole*) most often refers to a short allegorical narrative, but also embraces metaphorical sayings (as at Mark 7.14–15) and proverbs (as at Luke 4.23). As well as conveying moral lessons, parables help to explain the apocalyptic nature of the coming kingdom of God. Parables also feature royal imagery and judgment scenarios, with the righteous rewarded and the wicked punished, as in the story of the Wedding Banquet (Matt. 22.1–14; Luke 14.15–24). Many draw on images of rural life, like the parables in Mark 4.

All three Synoptics share a number of narrative parables, but also include some that are unique to each gospel. Luke's are stories with real human interest and include famous ones such as the Good Samaritan (Luke 10.25–37) and the Prodigal Son (15.11–32). In contrast, John's gospel has only two passages that resemble the Synoptic narrative parables (see pages 214–215).

Christ Preaching *by the anonymous 15th-century Master of the Low Countries. In the right foreground is Mary Magdalene, traditionally said to have been converted from sinner to saint on hearing Jesus teach.*

THE PASSION

It cannot have been long before those in power took notice of Jesus. The tetrarch Herod Antipas had recently executed John the Baptist, who had attracted large crowds, and accounts of similar crowds around Jesus—coupled, perhaps, with his rumored teachings about a coming kingdom and an end to the current world order—must have made the authorities nervous when Jesus and his disciples travelled toward Jerusalem one fateful Passover, sometime ca. 30CE.

All four gospels have an account of Jesus' arrest, trial, and death, traditionally known as the Passion (from Latin *passio*, suffering). There are differences in detail, but the evangelists concur on the basic events to a remarkable degree. The Synoptics and John disagree

THE LAST SUPPER

The Last Supper is the name given to Jesus' final meal with his disciples before he was arrested. It is likely, as reported in Matthew, Mark, and Luke, that this was the traditional Jewish Seder, the meal eaten on the night of Passover, and all three gospels record the preparations, which included the sacrifice of lambs (Mark 14.12-16 and parallels).

For Christians, the meal marks the institution of the rite of Eucharist. But whether Jesus intended to found such a new regular rite is debatable. It is only in Luke that he explicitly does so; in Matthew and Mark he implies that the meal will be repeated only in the final age, when the Messiah returns. At the same time, the earliest account of the meal, written by Paul just twenty years after the event (and no doubt verified by disciples such as Peter) suggests that Jesus understood his approaching end as momentous. Paul writes: "On the night when he was betrayed [Jesus] took a loaf of bread, and when he had given thanks, he broke it and said, 'This is my body that is for you. Do this in remembrance of me.' In the same way he took the cup also, after supper, saying, 'This cup is the new covenant in my blood. Do this, as often as you drink it, in remembrance of me.' For as often as you eat this bread and drink the cup, you proclaim the Lord's death until he comes" (1 Cor. 11.23–26).

The Last Supper *(detail) from a 12th-century fresco in the Collegiate Church of San Isidoro, León, Spain. It shows the apostles' shock at Jesus' declaration that one of them will betray him. Shown in this detail are (left to right) James the Greater, Thomas, Matthew, and James the Less.*

about the precise date of Jesus' death (Passover in the Synoptics, the eve of Passover in John), but the idea that he was arrested around Passover time is historically compelling. Passover was a great pilgrim festival, at which Jews celebrated their liberation from Egypt, and all male Jews were obliged to visit Jerusalem. The pilgrims swelled the population of the holy city hugely and the Roman prefect, Pontius Pilate, came up from Caesarea on the coast with extra troops to prevent disorder.

The Kiss of Judas, *ca.1442, by Fra Angelico (1387–1455). As Christ and the disciples left the garden of Gethsemane, an armed party seized him when Judas identified Jesus by kissing him: "The one I will kiss is the man; arrest him and lead him away under guard." (Mark 14.44)*

In this volatile setting, Jesus arrived in Jerusalem with his followers and (in the Synoptic gospels) was hailed by crowds with nationalistic fervor as he entered the city (Mark 11.1–11 and parallels). Almost immediately on his arrival, Jesus apparently caused a scene in the Temple (Mark 11.15–18 and parallels; John also records this incident, but places it at the start of the ministry). It was a prophetic demonstration that spoke of the restoration of Israel, and it is little surprise that Jesus' arrest occurred not long after.

Jesus was apprehended in the garden of Gethsemane, a grove on the Mount of Olives outside the city, where, according to the Synoptics, he prayed in agony, conscious of his impending fate. When the arresting party arrived, Jesus was picked out by Judas Iscariot, an enigmatic figure whose largely unexplained act of betrayal has been the invitation to writers of fiction from the second century to the present (see sidebar). In so far as the gospels explain why he did it, it is because Satan had entered into Judas (Luke 22.3), but beyond this, it is difficult to guess what motivated a character who was later so filled with remorse that, according to Matthew, he committed suicide (Matt. 27.3–10; compare Acts 1.18–19).

THE TRIALS OF JESUS

According to the Synoptic Gospels, the high priest Caiaphas tried Jesus before a gathered council (see page 13; it is sometimes called "the Sanhedrin," though this name may be anachronistic), and having pronounced sentence, handed him over to Pilate. According to Mark, this was because Jesus admitted to being "the Messiah, the Son of the Blessed" and spoke of a future when he would be "seated at the right hand of God," a confession that caused Caiaphas to tear his garments and declare "blasphemy" (Mark 14.55–65).

Whatever Caiaphas's role in Jesus' arrest and trial, it is clear that historically the key role in his execution must have been taken by Pontius Pilate, since it is likely that only the Romans could, in most instances, impose or authorize the death penalty, as John claims (John 18.31–32). Pilate was a ruthless man who at times rode roughshod over Jewish sensi-

THE GOSPEL OF JUDAS

The Gospel of Judas, a Coptic manuscript from Egypt not published until 2006, portrays Judas Iscariot as Jesus' closest disciple, who does his master's bidding in handing him over, despite the warning: "You will be cursed." The gospel is likely to be the one named ca. 180 by Irenaeus of Lyons as the product of a heretical sect that revered "the traitor" Judas.

bilities. The gospels tend to play down his desire to have Jesus crucified, but it is likely that he played the key role since crucifixion was a Roman punishment. Most scholars agree that Pilate condemned Jesus for claiming to be "king of the Jews"—as reflected in the inscription affixed to the cross on which Jesus was hung (Mark 15.25 and parallels)—and this fits with the judgment of the high priest and council that Jesus claimed to be the Messiah, a national liberator widely expected to be a descendant of King David. When Pilate asks Jesus if he is "king of the Jews," Jesus is evasive, much as when the high priest asks if he is the Messiah. In Roman trials the accused had three opportunities to defend himself. When, after repeated questioning, Jesus gives no direct answer, Pilate has no choice but to find him guilty.

The gospels characterize Pilate as wishing to let Jesus off with a warning flogging (Luke 23.16, 22). But the prefect changes his mind when the crowd, incited by the Temple authorities, threatens to riot (Matt. 27.24). The gospels' portrayal of Pilate may be motivated by their inclination to stress the responsibility of the Jewish leaders and to depict Jesus as innocent of any crime—not least because crucifixion was a shameful punishment and the idea of a "crucified Messiah" would have sounded absurd to many ancients (see box).

The gospels also narrate an incident in which Pilate offers the crowd a choice between freeing Jesus and an insurgent called Barabbas, supposedly according to an annual Passover custom for which there is no other evidence (Mark 15.6 and parallels). There is plenty of evidence, though, for public floggings in antiquity, and it is likely that this was often a prelude to crucifixion, as the gospels record in Jesus' case.

THE PASSION AND SCRIPTURE

The Passion narratives often directly cite, echo, or allude to the Hebrew Bible, especially Isaiah and the Psalms. Thus Jesus' silence at his trials fulfills Isaiah 53, in which the suffering servant is silent before his accusers; and his cry of abandonment from the cross (Mark 15.34) comes directly from Psalm 22.1. Some see this as evidence that the gospel writers knew little about the historical events of the Passion, and filled in the gaps in their knowledge by scouring the Jewish scriptures for clues. Another view is that the traditions led the evangelists to the scriptures, which in turn helped them to interpret and express these traditions creatively.

For the earliest Christians it was important, above all, to show how Jesus' crucifixion was not some random tragedy but God's will, foreordained in scripture.

A 1st-century tomb *at Khirbet Midras, 19 miles (31km) southwest of Jerusalem. As in the gospel accounts of Jesus' burial, this tomb was sealed by rolling a large circular stone across the entrance.*

CRUCIFIXION AND BURIAL

Jesus is crucified alongside two men described as "bandits" or insurgents, and this may be another sign that he too was executed as a political rebel. He is mocked and taunted as a would-be "king of the Jews" or "king of Israel" and he is given a crown of thorns. The whole event appears darkly ironic, with those in the drama unaware how true their words appear to the readers of the gospels, for whom Jesus' exaltation to heaven and return in glory are cosmic realities. The evangelists do not dwell on the details of the crucifixion, but focus on demonstrating how Jesus' last hours fulfilled scripture (see sidebar). They use remarkable, apocalyptic imagery, as darkness comes over the earth at noon and lasts until Jesus' death at 3pm (Mark 15.33), when the veil of the Temple is torn in two (Mark 15.38), and there is an earthquake with bodies rising from tombs (Matt. 27.51–53).

John and the Synoptics differ on whether the crucifixion took place at Passover or on the day before Passover, but they agree that it was a Friday, and that Jesus' body was taken down from the cross before nightfall in time for the Sabbath. It was placed in a tomb by Joseph of Arimathea, a member of the council before which Jesus was condemned.

THE HORROR OF CRUCIFIXION

Crucifixion, in which the victim was bound or nailed to a large cross or pole, is little covered in ancient writing because it was regarded as so horrific. Cicero (106–43BCE) says that "the executioner, the veiling of the head, and the very word 'cross' should be far removed not only from the person of a Roman citizen but from his thoughts, his eyes, and his ears." (*Pro Rabirio* 16). Seneca (4BCE–65CE) wrote: "Can anyone be found who would prefer wasting away in pain dying limb by limb, or letting out his life drop by drop, rather than expiring once for all? Can any man be found willing to be fastened to the accursed tree, long sickly, already deformed, swelling with ugly weals on shoulders and chest, and drawing the breath of life amid long drawn-out agony?" (*Epistle 101 to Lucilius.*)

The punishment was as much about humiliating and shaming the victim, and providing a warning to others, as it was about torture. It is significant that the crucifixion, the climactic event of the Passion, is absent from very early Christian art. The reasons are complex, but they include the fact that the nature of Jesus' execution was so dishonorable. The first known representations date from the fifth and sixth centuries, over a century after the penalty was abolished ca. 313 by the emperor Constantine I, by which time memories of its shameful nature had no doubt begun to fade.

Good Friday procession *at San Fratello near Messina, Sicily, where Holy Week—the week leading up to the crucifixion—is marked by parades and other popular events commemorating the Passion, culminating on Good Friday with the procession of the crucified Christ.*

THE RESURRECTION AND ASCENSION

It is a central tenet of Christianity that, three days after his death and burial, Jesus rose from the dead and subsequently made numerous appearances to his followers before ascending to heaven. The first account of an empty tomb is found at the end of Mark's gospel (Mark 16.1–8), when the women who witnessed Jesus' crucifixion and burial are now witnesses at his tomb, where the stone has been rolled away and a young man tells them about Jesus' resurrection.

The gospel then, probably, comes to an abrupt end (16.8, "and they said nothing to anyone, for they were afraid")—so abrupt that it used to be common to think that Mark's original ending had been lost, though contemporary scholars are more inclined to think that Mark intended to end it there. Later scribes provided Mark with a longer ending (Mark 16.9–20) that integrates the empty tomb story with traditions of the appearance of

THE ASCENSION

At the end of his gospel, Luke says that Jesus was "carried up to heaven," (24.51) and begins his sequel, the Acts of the Apostles, where he left off, with the story of the Ascension (Acts 1.3–11). Jesus is transported to heaven from the Mount of Olives after commissioning the disciples and promising that the Holy Spirit will descend at Pentecost (Acts 2). The event provides the impetus for the birth of the church and its mission in Acts. The gift of the Spirit is also in John (20.22), who also mentions the Ascension (20.17), as does the longer ending of Mark (16.19; see main text). However, it does not appear in Matthew.

There is little detail of the Ascension itself, either in the gospels or Acts. In the latter, the disciples watch as Jesus is "lifted up; and a cloud took him out of their sight."

The Ascension, *a 14th-century Coptic icon from the church of St. Barbara in Cairo, Egypt. As the apostles look on, Jesus ascends to heaven on a cloud (Acts 1.9–10). Following an early tradition, the Virgin Mary is also represented (center, with an angel).*

Doubting Thomas. *Unable to comprehend that Jesus has risen from the dead, the disciple Thomas thrusts his finger into the wound in Jesus' side. A relief carving from the monastery of Santo Domingo de Silos, Spain, 11th century.*

the risen Jesus. Matthew, Luke, and John all have fuller endings that include accounts of the resurrected Jesus appearing to his followers.

RESURRECTION APPEARANCES

The conclusion of Matthew's story continues where Mark's stops, with Jesus himself appearing to the women as they flee from the tomb (Matt. 28.8–10). Similarly, in John, Jesus appears at the tomb to just one of the women, Mary Magdalene (John 20.10–18). Appearances to the disciples follow in each of the three later gospels. In Matthew, Jesus issues his great commission to "the eleven" (the original core disciples minus Judas Iscariot) on a mountain in Galilee before promising that "I am with you always, even to the end of time" (Matt. 28.16–20).

John too has an appearance in Galilee in a story based around a great catch of fish (John 21), but he also has appearances in Jerusalem, most famously involving the "doubting" apostle Thomas (John 20.24–29), an incident that underlines the physical nature of the resurrection appearances in John's gospel, a feature he shares with Luke. Luke's appearances take place in Jerusalem and, in one of the finest pieces of storytelling in the New Testament, Jesus appears as the anonymous traveller who engages his followers in conversation on the road to Emmaus, recognized only when Cleopas and his companion break bread with him (Luke 24.13–35).

PAUL AND THE RESURRECTION

The earliest account of the resurrection is in Paul's first letter to the Corinthians, written in the 50s CE: "For I handed on to you as of first importance what I in turn had received: that Christ died for our sins in accordance with the scriptures, and that he was buried, and that he was raised on the third day in accordance with the scriptures, and that he appeared to Cephas [Peter], then to the Twelve. Then he appeared to more than five hundred brothers and sisters at one time, ... to James [the brother of Jesus], then to all the apostles. Last of all ... he appeared also to me." (1 Cor. 15.3–8.) It is striking that Paul includes himself at the climax of this list of those who had seen the resurrected Jesus. Since Paul's conversion came several years after the crucifixion, this claim was controversial (1 Cor. 9.1–2).

2 OUT UNTO ALL LANDS

Jesus instructed his followers to "Go therefore and make disciples of all nations" (Matt. 28.19). As recorded in Acts, on the Jewish festival of Pentecost following the death and ascension of Jesus, they experienced a remarkable outpouring of the Holy Spirit, enabling them to tell of God's mighty deeds in many languages (Acts 2.1–5). Thus began the worldwide dissemination of the Christian message. The first Christians were Jews, but very quickly Gentiles were received into the church through baptism. Acts records that the Jewish authorities in Jerusalem persecuted the followers of Jesus, and created the first Christian martyr, Stephen (Acts 7; see page 134). Among the chief persecutors was Saul, or Paul, a rabbinically-trained Greek-speaking Jew and Roman citizen from Tarsus in Asia Minor. While travelling to Damascus to hunt down

HOUSE CHURCHES AND EARLY CHRISTIAN WORSHIP

From the earliest days of the church, Christians gathered together to worship on Sunday, the day of Jesus' resurrection. They met in private homes, from small apartments to more elaborate residences. Such "house churches" were often identified with their owner who, presumably, presided at the services and communal meals held there, such as Prisca and Aquilla (1 Cor. 16.19) and Nympha (Col. 4.15).

Two key elements of worship were the reading and interpretation of scripture and the eucharist. Justin Martyr describes a second-century service: "The memoirs of the apostles or the writings of the prophets are read [then] the president in a discourse urges and invites [us] to the imitation of these noble things. Then we all stand up ... and offer prayers.... Bread is brought and wine and water, and the president similarly sends up prayers and thanksgivings ... and the congregation assents, saying the Amen; the distribution and reception of the consecrated [elements] by all takes place, and the deacons send them to the absent."

The churches were also centers of missionary endeavor, patronage, hospitality, education, and social service.

A Christian family at prayer *is depicted in this fresco of ca. 500 in the San Gennaro catacombs, Naples, Italy. The deceased bishop Theotecnus (right) with his wife Hilaritas and daughter Nonnosa are praying in the "orant" posture, a feature of early Christian worship.*

A Palm Sunday procession *in Axum, Tigray, Ethiopia. Christianity came to Ethiopia in the 4th century under the influence of Frumentius, a Syrian Christian who became Ethiopia's first bishop in 328 and baptized Ezana of Axum as the first Christian Ethiopian king.*

Jesus' followers there, Paul underwent a remarkable conversion to Christ (Acts 9). From that point, he became an important early evangelist to both Jews and Gentiles, travelling around the eastern Mediterranean establishing and supporting churches. The New Testament includes several of Paul's letters to these churches, such as those at Corinth, Ephesus, and Philippi (see pages 218–219).

SPREADING THE WORD

The well-developed infrastructure of the Roman empire, together with the *Pax Romana* (the empire's relative internal peace), were vital to the spread of the message. Jews were exempt from Roman emperor-worship and synagogues often became local centers for the new religion. Evangelism was done by travelling preachers as well as local converts talking with their neighbors. North Africa was an early stronghold of the faith: reputedly founded by the evangelist Mark, the Coptic Church in Egypt dates from the first century. Indeed, the Roman province of Egypt may have been the first land with a Christian majority.

The gospel soon reached such remote areas as Britain and Spain, and also spread outside the empire. Tradition has it that the apostle Thomas travelled to India in the first century and was martyred there; many Indian churches bear his name. Churches with enduring ties to the Syrian Church were certainly established in southern India by the fourth century. Having adopted the faith as its official religion in 303, Armenia prides itself on having been the first Christian state, before even the Roman empire (see pages 38–39).

Farther south, Christianity spread in the kingdom of Axum (Ethiopia) in the fourth century. Located between Egypt and Ethiopia, the Christian kingdom of Nubia flourished from the sixth century through the Middle Ages.

PAGAN VIEWS OF CHRISTIANITY

The early Christians often met with hostility and confusion from their pagan neighbors. For the Roman historian Tacitus (ca. 55–ca. 120), Christianity was a "pernicious superstition," while Pliny the Younger (ca. 62–ca. 113) told the emperor Trajan it was an "absurd and extravagant superstition" that was spreading its "infection" from cities to the countryside. Christians were rumored to be cannibals (a misunderstanding of the eucharist); incestuous (they called one another brother and sister); and atheists (they had no visible gods). To correct such ignorance and to argue for tolerance, Christian writers produced "apologies" (literally "speeches for the defense"), such as that by Justin Martyr (ca. 100–ca. 165).

HERESIES AND HERETICS

CHURCH FATHERS

The early church produced many influential writers and theologians. They include Irenaeus of Lyons, Clement of Alexandria, Origen, Tertullian, Athanasius of Alexandria, Ambrose of Milan, John Chrysostom, Basil of Caesarea, Gregory Nazianzen, Gregory of Nyssa, Jerome, Augustine of Hippo, Isidore of Seville, Gregory the Great, and John Damascene.

The titles of Doctor ("teacher") and Father were applied to those who refuted heresy, elaborated orthodox doctrine, and demonstrated holiness of life. The Fathers gave Christianity much of its theological language, liturgy, commitment to various modes of discipleship, and models of preaching.

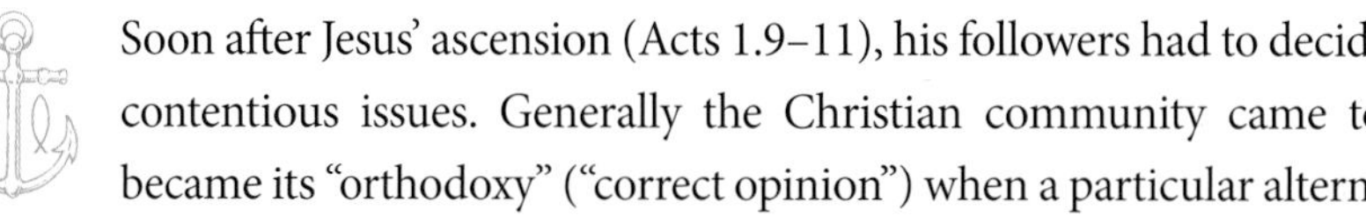

Soon after Jesus' ascension (Acts 1.9–11), his followers had to decide a number of contentious issues. Generally the Christian community came to adopt what became its "orthodoxy" ("correct opinion") when a particular alternative teaching brought an issue to a head. The alternative was then labeled as false or "heretical." Among the first issues was Christianity's relationship with Judaism. The first followers of Jesus were Jews, but the council of Jerusalem (Acts 15.1–29) decided that Gentile converts did not need to be circumcised. Subsequently, Marcion, a second-century Christian teacher in Rome, rejected the Old Testament on the grounds that its God was petty and vindictive, while the Christian God was loving and good. The Christian community did not accept this position, a decision that shaped the interpretation of the Old Testament as Christians sought the continuity of God's purposes and the fulfillment of God's promises.

Another key issue was leadership. By the early second century, a threefold pattern of bishop (*episkopos*, "overseer"), presbyter (*presbuteros*, "elder"), and deacon (*diakonos*,

Doctors (or Teachers) of the Church, *a detail of the vault in the upper basilica of St. Francis, Assisi. It shows St. Jerome (ca. 347–420, wearing red), translator of the Latin Vulgate Bible. (Another Western Doctor, St. Ambrose, is depicted in blue, top right.) Attributed to Giotto, ca. 1290.*

"servant") had become common (see page 137). The bishops' collective power increased in the wake of a movement that arose in Asia Minor around this time. Known as Montanism, it was led by the self-proclaimed prophets Montanus, Priscilla, and Maximilla, who announced the coming of a new age. They veered into extreme asceticism and questionable doctrines, apparently claiming that Christ's death and resurrection did not alone accomplish salvation. Regional bishops responded by asserting their corporate authority over the church and declared the Montanists heretics. After this, church leadership was more "institutionalized" and there were fewer self-appointed charismatic leaders.

A Nestorian cross *from Tang China. In 431, Archbishop Nestorius of Constantinople was condemned as a heretic for asserting that Christ's human and divine natures were separate rather than unified. Nestorius' supporters split from Byzantine orthodoxy to become the Assyrian Church, which exists to this day. The Assyrians (also called Syrians or Nestorians) were active missionaries, notably in China. Bronze, 7th–10th centuries.*

CHRIST AND SALVATION

Issues such as the Montanist heresy brought into focus the question of what constituted true Christian teaching; in particular, who is Jesus and how does he provide salvation? Docetists (from Greek *dokeo*, to seem) said that Jesus was God masquerading as a human being; others said that he was a simply a human being with a particularly close relationship with God. Ebionites, a Jewish-Christian group, held a version of the latter position; a related view (Adoptionism) argued that Jesus was "adopted" as God's son at his baptism. However, the greatest threat to early orthodoxy were Gnosticism and Arianism (see box).

Christians taught that salvation was available to all believers. The question of what God does and what the Christian must do came to a head in the early fifth century. Pelagius, a layman from Britain teaching in Rome, argued that God called Christians to live morally perfect lives; indeed, to live free from sin was within human power and was therefore obligatory. However, Augustine of Hippo argued that God must free believers from sin since human will is unable to do so on its own. The church sided with Augustine, but Pelagian teaching has often been heard from the pulpit down the ages.

GNOSTICS AND ARIANS

Gnostics and Arians accepted the widely held notion that the spiritual world was valuable and real; the material world was inferior, less real and evil. According to Gnosticism, human beings are fundamentally parts of the spiritual realm entrapped in the material world; Gnostic Christians claimed that Jesus was a teacher of the secret knowledge (*gnosis*) required to escape from this material realm. Orthodox writers such as Irenaeus of Lyon (late 100s), countered such teaching by asserting the public nature of apostolic tradition, the goodness of creation, and the reality of the incarnation.

Arius, a fourth-century Alexandrian priest, claimed that Jesus was not fully God but the most exalted of God's creations. For Arius, Christ had to be changeable, able to grow in virtue; he became the Son of God as a reward for responding to grace and advancing toward God. As such, Jesus could be an example to individuals in their search for salvation. But Arius' opponents taught Christ's full divinity, articulating the doctrine of the Trinity (see pages 68–69), and that Christ provided salvation by uniting God's full being with humanity's full being, taking on death and rising from the dead.

CREEDS AND COUNCILS

As heresies prompted the church to refine its teachings and practices (see pages 30–31), creeds and councils became its distinctive modes of articulating orthodoxy. Creeds (from their opening word, Latin *credo*, "I believe") were short statements of belief used both to instruct new believers and to praise God and confess the church's shared faith in worship. The Apostles' Creed, one of the earliest creeds, was in use in Rome in the second century, and creeds played a key role in baptism (see box).

As important summaries of orthodoxy, it is unsurprising that creeds were used to disseminate the decisions of early church councils, meetings of church leaders to discuss matters of faith and policy (see sidebar). Acts 15 describes such a meeting in Jerusalem, probably ca. 50, to decide whether Gentile Christians needed to follow Jewish requirements

CREEDS AND BAPTISM

Creeds played an important role in baptism, the ritual of Christian initiation (see page 96). The third-century *Apostolic Tradition* of Hippolytus, a presbyter at Rome, describes one threefold question-and-answer creed used in the baptismal rite: The baptizer asked three questions: "Do you believe in God the Father Almighty?" "Do you believe in Jesus Christ, the Son of God, who was born of the Holy Spirit and the Virgin Mary, who was crucified under Pontius Pilate, and died, and rose on the third day … and ascended into heaven, and sat down at the right hand of the Father, the one coming to judge the living and the dead?" and "Do you believe in the Holy Spirit and the Holy Church and the resurrection of the flesh?" To each question the candidate answered "I believe" ("*Credo*").

Creeds also formed a syllabus for catechesis, an education in the basics for adults preparing for baptism.

The Baptism of Constantine. *On the verge of death, the emperor is baptized by Pope Sylvester. From the Stavelot Triptych, a gold and enamel reliquary produced at Stavelot abbey, Belgium, ca. 1157.*

The first council of Nicea *(detail). Constantine (in red) and Christ preside over the assembled bishops. Held in 325 to discuss Arianism, the council devised the first version of what came to be called the Nicene Creed. A Russian icon of the Novgorod School, ca. 1750.*

such as circumcision. It soon became customary for regional bishops to confer together on local policy. The first ecumenical council, or council of the whole church, was held at Nicea (Iznik, Turkey) in 325 to discuss Arius' view of Christ (see page 31) and other matters. The council was called by the Roman emperor Constantine I (ruled 303–337), who had legalized Christianity (see page 36) and believed Christian unity would promote political stability.

The bishops at Nicea decided that Jesus' divine nature was the same as that of God. Finalizing the creed issued at Nicea, the first council of Constantinople in 381 further affirmed the divinity of the Holy Spirit, thus articulating orthodox Christian faith in God as the Trinity of Father, Son, and Holy Spirit. The new statement of faith became known as the Nicene Creed, Christianity's most ecumenical document outside the scriptures, being used by Roman Catholics, Orthodox, and many Protestants.

THE CHALCEDONIAN DEFINITION

Further questions about how the divine and the human were related in Jesus were taken up at the council of Chalcedon (Kadiköy, Istanbul) in 451. At one extreme were those who stressed the unity and divinity of Christ; at the other, those who stressed his dual nature and full humanity. In the orthodox view, each extreme denied something fundamental about Christ. The bishops at Chalcedon affirmed that Jesus has two natures, divine and human. His divine nature is the same as God's while his human nature is the same as ours, but without sin. However, Jesus is just one *person*. The bishops did not resolve this apparent contradiction; on a fundamental level, the incarnation of God in human nature is left a mystery.

CHURCH COUNCILS

Church councils became an important means of guiding the church as a body. Beginning with the first council of Nicea, there are seven councils commonly held by the churches of both East and the West (including many Protestants) to be ecumenical, or binding on the whole church. The last of these was the second council of Nicea in 787, which affirmed the practice of venerating icons following the Iconoclastic crisis (see page 192). The Roman Catholic Church considers fourteen further councils to have been ecumenical, the most recent being the Second Vatican Council (Vatican II, 1962–1965).

ART AND ARCHITECTURE

EARLY BASILICAS

OPPOSITE *Santa Sabina, Rome (422–432), retains the simplicity and sense of spaciousness of the early basilicas. It is now the seat of the Dominican order.*

BELOW *Old St Peter's, Rome, by Giovanni Battista Ricci (ca. 1540–1625). Constantine's basilica of 326–333 began to be demolished in 1505 to make way for the present St. Peter's (1506–1626).*

The legalization of Christianity under the emperor Constantine I in 313 (see page 36) inspired the creation of monumental Christian architecture. The best known churches are Constantine's own foundations (St. John Lateran and St. Peter's in Rome, the Holy Sepulchre in Jerusalem, and the church of the Nativity in Bethlehem), but individual patrons, the clergy, or groups of the faithful also began to sponsor large-scale churches. Many of these adopted the form of the Roman basilica, a large columned hall used for a variety of official functions, often serving as the local mercantile exchange and law court. The choice of the secular basilica as a model for churches undoubtedly reflected a desire to avoid the pagan associations of Classical temples, relatively few of which were adapted for Christian use.

The Christian basilica differed from its secular model both in its sacred function and in the fact that it was covered with a wooden truss ceiling (the more monumental secular basilicas were sometimes vaulted) and had a more strictly axial emphasis. It was a longitudinal space, usually consisting of an aisled hall, or nave, culminating in an apse. By the sixth century it had become customary to place the apse in the east and the entrance in the west. The upper nave walls were often open with large windows, and the interior walls were covered with frescoes or mosaics, although few original decorative programs survive. The exterior, by contrast, received little or no decoration.

The church itself was part of a larger complex of buildings, which often included the bishop's residence, a baptistery, and spaces for the training of catechumens (sometimes a hall as big as the church itself) and for various ancillary functions such as the dispensation of charity and hospitals. The excavations at Aquileia, Italy, and at Poreč, Croatia, reveal such clusters of structures, often lavishly decorated with mosaic paving and liturgical furniture. The best surviving buildings are those of the late fourth and early fifth centuries, such as Santa Sabina and Santa Maria Maggiore in Rome.

PATRIARCHS, POPES, AND EMPERORS

In 313 the emperor Constantine I (ruled 306–337, sole emperor after 324) and his co-ruler Maxentius issued the Edict of Milan, legalizing Christianity in the Roman empire. Constantine and many of his successors vigorously upheld the church, giving it material support and using its leaders as civic authorities.

In 330 Constantine founded a new imperial capital in the eastern empire, Constantinople (Istanbul), which became the seat of government for the Roman empire, and its eastern successor, the Byzantine empire, until it fell to the Turks in 1453. In 325 Constantine called the first ecumenical council at nearby Nicea (see page 33), and established the close ties between ruler and church that became the norm in the East, with the emperor

POPE GREGORY I "THE GREAT"

Pope Gregory I was among the towering ecclesiastical figures of the period following the fall of the western Roman empire. Indeed, he is identified as the father of the medieval papacy, having helped to consolidate the church and forge close relations between Rome and more distant parts of western Europe, as well as greatly increasing the temporal power of the Holy See. His writings synthesized earlier teachings and were studied throughout the Middle Ages.

Gregory came from a leading Roman family and served as Roman prefect as a young man. After some time in a monastery and several years in the eastern empire as papal legate, he became pope (590–604) amid crisis: the Tiber was flooding, food stores were destroyed, and plague was rampant. As pope he negotiated treaties with the Lombards, the Germanic rulers of northern Italy, paid soldiers' wages, ransomed refugees, and fed the poor—all with church funds. Gregory also wrote a life of St. Benedict (see page 43) and encouraged monastic values through his book *Pastoral Care*. In 597 he sent the monk Augustine to Canterbury on a successful mission to convert the king of Kent, an event which marks the founding of the English Church.

Pope Gregory I "the Great", *from a 14th-century fresco in the abbey church of Vezzolano, near Turin. The collapse of Roman infrastructure meant that churchmen such as Gregory took on temporal leadership, negotiating with invaders and mustering resources during social crises.*

The Virgin and Emperors. *The Virgin, regarded as the protector of Constantinople, is flanked by its founder, Constantine I, who holds a model of the city (right) and Justinian I, who holds a model of the church of Hagia Sophia (Holy Wisdom), which he rebuilt in 532–537. Byzantine society understood itself to be under the patronage of God and the Mother of God, with the emperor serving as God's viceroy in harmony with spiritual authorities. A mosaic over the south door of the Hagia Sophia, Istanbul, 10th century.*

often shaping church policy and controlling the election of the patriarch of Constantinople. It was from Constantinople that the emperor Theodosius I (ruled 379–395) decreed that Christianity should be the only official religion of the empire, outlawing paganism.

As the mother-city of the empire and the burial place of the apostles Peter and Paul, Rome remained the most influential city in the West, and its bishop was the *primus inter pares* ("first among equals") of the five patriarchs, the empire's senior bishops (see page 186). By the fourth century, however, Rome was beginning to claim supremacy not merely on account of the city's historical importance but by divine and apostolic right. Leo I, bishop of Rome, (or pope, 440–461), saw himself as having the authority of Peter, which ultimately came from Christ. By the time of Pope Gelasius I (492–496), claims of priestly superiority over royal power were also being made that would come to shape church-state relations in the medieval West.

COLLAPSE IN THE WEST, REVIVAL IN THE EAST

Such claims were influenced by the dramatic political events of the preceding decades, which had seen imperial authority in the West crumble in the face of incursions by Germanic armies. As the secular infrastructure of the western empire fell into chaos, the church remained the strongest institution, and its leaders, such as Pope Gregory the Great (see box), took on tasks of the former imperial secular government and social elites.

The eastern (Byzantine) empire rallied under Justinian I (ruled 527–565), who reconquered parts of Italy and other regions of the West. Justinian made the decrees of the ecumenical councils part of the law of the eastern empire and declared the Nicene Creed

THE DONATION OF CONSTANTINE

Ostensibly a letter from the emperor Constantine I to Pope Sylvester I (314–335), the *Donation of Constantine* granted the Pope and his successors supremacy "over all the churches of God in the whole world" along with "the city of Rome and all the provinces, districts, and cities of Italy or of the western regions." In the Middle Ages the *Donation* was considered an authoritative articulation of ecclesiastical supremacy and temporal power, but in 1440 the scholar Lorenzo Valla demonstrated it to be a forgery of no earlier than ca. 750 by some unknown supporter of papal claims.

THE BENEFICE SYSTEM

As the Roman infrastructure in the west crumbled, supporting the clergy became difficult. Gradually plots of land became attached to certain church positions, and these "benefices" provided an income for clerics. They ranged from small plots for village priests to vast estates of farmland or vineyards for bishops or monasteries, often donated by wealthy laity. While the benefice system helped to stabilize the early medieval church, it would present many opportunities for abuse in the more stable conditions of the central and late Middle Ages, when the church became Europe's biggest landholder. Thus some churchmen acquired multiple benefices (pluralism) and some used bribes and other influence to gain lucrative offices (simony).

(see page 33) the only creed of the church. He was active in attempts to reconcile other Christian groups with orthodox Christianity and rebuilt the great church of Hagia Sophia in Constantinople, while the divine liturgy took on many features of imperial ceremonial.

The fourth- and fifth-century controversies over the nature of Christ, as debated at various ecumenical councils (see page 33), continued to play out in the East more than in the West, as did the iconoclastic crisis of the eighth and ninth centuries (see page 192). Long divided culturally and politically, the Greek East and Latin West continued to drift apart. Eastern bishops resisted Roman claims to supremacy and criticized such Western practices as clerical celibacy and the use of the word *filioque* in the creed (see pages 186–187). The year 1054 has often been seen as marking the schism between the churches (see sidebar, right).

CHURCH AND EMPIRE IN THE WEST

From the seventh century, Islam spread rapidly from Arabia across former imperial and Christian areas from Syria to Spain. The geographical center of the Christian world shifted north and west as more of Europe was evangelized. Germanic rulers in England and Frankish territories converted and established strong ties to the papacy. The most remarkable ruler of this era was King Charles of the Franks (ruled 768–814), better known as Charlemagne or Charles the Great. His grandfather, Charles Martel, had halted the Muslim advance from

The imperial abbey of Corvey *in northwestern Germany was founded by Charlemagne's son Louis the Pious ca. 820. As defender and benefactor of the church, Charlemagne became the archetypal Christian ruler in the west. He forced baptism on conquered Saxons (see page 41); mandated Christian practices (such as keeping the Sabbath); brought to his court Christian scholars from all over Europe; and encouraged standardized liturgical and monastic practices.*

Iberia into France in 732, and Charlemagne succeeded in bringing much of western Europe under his rule. For this he was crowned "emperor of the Romans" by Pope Leo III on Christmas Day, 800. Leo owed his position to Charlemagne's military defense of the papacy; the emperor received church sanction for his position as ruler and conqueror. Thus came to a new fruition in the West a collaboration between church and state whose ideal had been set back in the time of Constantine. However, the relationship between Leo and Charlemagne also set a precedent for later tensions over supremacy; it was around this time that a supporter of clerical supremacy forged the *Donation of Constantine* (see sidebar on page 37).

A new chapter in church-state relations in the West opened with the "Investiture Controversy." Secular rulers had become used to appointing senior clerics in their realms, but in 1075 Pope Gregory VII (1073–1085) decreed that the papacy alone had this right, arguing that all power in this world flowed from God to the pope, who dispensed it to kings and churchmen alike. The issue came to a head when Gregory and Henry IV, the king of Germany and Holy Roman emperor (ruled 1056–1105), each appointed his own archbishop of Milan. With the Concordat of Worms in 1122, the papacy won the right to install senior clergy, with the secular ruler serving as advisor and receiving homage from bishops and abbots for the temporal holdings that went with their posts. Along with this came a commitment to clerical celibacy and a focus on the sacramental powers of the priest.

THE "SCHISM" OF 1054

In 1054, a dispute over the status of Byzantine Christians in southern Italy prompted Pope Leo IX to send a mission to Constantinople, where a series of misunderstandings led the papal legate, Cardinal Humbert, and Patriarch Michael Cerularius to excommunicate one another. This event traditionally marks the split between the churches of East and West, but it was less obvious at the time (the excommunications were personal, not against a whole church). The more profound rupture came in 1204 when Constantinople was sacked by western crusaders (see pages 46–47).

THOMAS BECKET

Medieval tensions between church and crown are famously exemplified in the life and death of Thomas Becket (ca. 1118–1170). He served as Lord High Chancellor (chief minister) for King Henry II of England (ruled 1154–1189) and in this role he sought to enhance the king's power in relation to the church. In 1162, at Henry's instigation, Becket was consecrated as archbishop of Canterbury, the most important position in the church in England.

Becket then began to promote the interests of the church over those of the crown. After years of contention, Becket was murdered in his cathedral on December 29, 1170, by four knights who believed they were carrying out the king's will. Becket was soon hailed as a martyr; he was canonized in 1173 and in 1174 the king performed a public act of penance at Canterbury. Until its destruction in 1538 on the orders of King Henry VIII, his shrine at Canterbury became the focal point of pilgrimages from all over Europe.

The Becket Casket *is a magnificent early example of the numerous shrines made to house relics of Thomas Becket. It depicts his murder and burial and the raising of his soul to heaven. Gilt copper and enamel on a wooden core, from Limoges, France, ca. 1180–1190.*

MISSIONS AND CONVERSIONS

By the year 600 Christianity was well established around the Mediterranean and known as far afield as India, Ethiopia, and Britain, though with many unconverted people in between. The faith was spread by a series of missionary endeavors. Patrick (Patricius), a fifth-century Romano-Briton, evangelized in Ireland, set up an enduring and distinctive Celtic Christian tradition that itself sent missionary monks all over Europe, including back to northern England. The Celtic Britons were largely Christianized by the fifth century, but the Anglo-Saxons, who occupied much of post-Roman Britain, were pagans. Their conversion was initiated in 597 by Augustine of Canterbury (see page 36), who first preached to King Ethelbert of Kent. Monks and nuns were vital to the spread of the faith. In the eighth century two English Benedictines, the monk Boniface (died 754) and nun Leoba (died 782), evangelized in Germany. The example of their lives, the stability of their new monastic foundations, the reputed power of their miracles, and their training of new leaders all contributed to the formation of the German Church.

THE "APOSTLES OF THE SLAVS"

In 862, King Boris of the Bulgars agreed to Christian baptism in the Roman Catholic tradition to cement an alliance with the Eastern Franks. In 863, his neighbor, Rastislav, king of Great Moravia, requested Christian teachers from Byzantium. The emperor sent two monks from northern Greece, the brothers Cyril (827–869) and Methodius (826–885), who became known as the "Apostles of the Slavs." The brothers devised a new alphabet—tradition has it that Cyril received the letters through divine inspiration—called Glagolitic (from *glagol*, word) for writing the local Slavonic language. Soon the gospels, psalms, liturgy, and catechetical works were available in the vernacular, a language now known as Old Church Slavonic. This alphabet was later widely adopted by other Slavic peoples, especially in its various simplified forms named "Cyrillic" for St. Cyril (see also pages 204–205). The Slavic church retained close relations with the Byzantine church.

A procession in Moscow *on May 24, 2007, to mark the "Day of Letters," a celebration of Slavic literacy and culture that honors saints Cyril and Methodius in several Orthodox countries of eastern Europe.*

A "stave church" *at Borgund in Norway, dating from the late 12th century. The distinctive design of these early wooden churches was once common in Scandinavia; most of the surviving examples are in Norway, where a number bear carvings of pre-Christian motifs.*

Both Rome and Constantinople sent missions to the Slavs (see box). Poland and Bohemia affiliated with Rome following the conversions of kings Mieczyslaw and Wenceslas (the "Good King" of the carol) respectively in the tenth century. The conversion of the Russian king Vladimir in 988 encouraged a Russian Christianity with close ties to Byzantine traditions. Under King Stephen (ca. 970–1038), the Hungarians, or Magyars, adopted Roman Catholicism.

The last regions of Europe to be evangelized were Scandinavia and the Baltic. In the eleventh century Christianity was broadly established in Denmark and Norway of under kings Knut I (Canute) and Olaf II (St. Olaf) respectively. Lithuania and other eastern Baltic lands were converted only in the thirteenth century; this was often done by force, as with the continental Saxons under Charlemagne (see sidebar).

THE HELIAND

In the wake of Charlemagne's conquest and forced baptism of the German Saxons (804), an anonymous monk sought to present the gospel in local cultural idioms. The *Heliand* ("Savior") relates Christ's life in Saxon alliterative verse. Christ is represented as a Germanic "*drohtin*" or warrior chieftain, the apostles as his loyal warriors who help God to keep peace in his kingdom. Jesus is born in the hill-fort of Bethlehem; Lake Galilee becomes the North Sea. As "Lord of the Runes," Jesus' teaching is more powerful than that of the pagan gods Odin or Thor. The poem ingeniously seeks to cultivate enthusiasm for the new religion, even as it expresses compassion for the conquered people.

MONKS AND NUNS

BASIL AND BENEDICT

In the mid-300s, St. Basil ("the Great," ca. 330–379) wrote the East's most influential rule for monastic communities. Moderate in its asceticism, it calls for communal obedience lived in poverty, chastity, prayer, labor, and social work. (See also pages 188–189.) In the West, the most influential rule was that of St. Benedict of Nursia (ca. 480–ca. 547), who took up the life of a hermit as a young man (ca. 500) and soon gathered a following. Still influential today, the "Benedictine" rule prescribed a daily balance of prayer, work, and rest. Monks were to cultivate humility through lifelong obedience to the abbot and mutual service within the community. Benedictine monastics gather seven times during the day and once at night for prayer (see page 140).

Asceticism—the disciplining of the body through practices such as prayer, fasting, and chastity—was used by early Christians to prepare for martyrdom and to remove barriers to spiritual vitality. This combination of spiritual and bodily discipline took on a new focus with the long life of St. Anthony (ca. 251–356), an Egyptian Christian known as the "Father of Monasticism." Inspired by the gospel words: "If you wish to be perfect, go, and sell your possessions" (Matt. 19.21), Anthony took up a solitary life in the Egyptian desert. He disciplined himself through prayer and fasting, overcame powerful inner struggles against pride, lust, and boredom, and became a teacher for other ascetics. The story of St. Anthony, as recounted by Athanasius of Alexandria (ca. 293–373), helped to promote the solitary spiritual life.

Following the legalization of Christianity in 313, many Christians took up ascetic lifestyles to demonstrate their total commitment to Christ. Many concluded that the best place to find God was away from the distractions and obligations of social life and family and headed to the desert, especially Egypt and Palestine. Gradually communities of such

A Coptic monastery *in the Wadi al-Natrun, Egypt, a desert valley that drew St. Anthony and other early Christians seeking a solitary life. The most important center of Coptic monasticism, the Wadi al-Natrun is home to some of the world's oldest Christian monastic sites.*

individuals (monks and nuns) formed, who vowed to live together under the direction of an abbot or abbess and supported themselves by basketmaking or other manual labor, developing in effect an alternative society. Influential rules, or sets of regulations, for monastic communities were devised by Basil of Caesarea and Benedict of Nursia (see sidebar).

WESTERN MONASTICISM

Benedictine monasticism became pervasive in the West, where the dissolution of the Roman empire made monasteries the backbone of many communities (see page 140). Because monks made lifelong vows and lived in self-supporting enclaves, monasteries were oases of stability in a chaotic world. Through their commitment to hospitality and education (see pages 104–105), they provided many of the services we now associate with hotels, clinics, and schools. Although not envisioned by Benedict, the copying of manuscripts became a characteristic form of monastic work, preserving the heritage of the ancient world.

From Pope Gregory the Great (see page 36) onward, many church leaders were nurtured within monasticism, disseminating its values as the ideal form of Christian life. Society at large often made pious gifts to local monasteries in recognition of their valued spiritual and temporal roles, and monasteries were vital to the Christianization of Europe (see pages 40–41). Toward the end of the early Middle Ages, Benedictine wealth and influence reached a peak at the monastery at Cluny in France, established in 909. For many years, its church was the largest in western Europe and its abbot was second only to the pope in influence.

LAY SPIRITUAL ORGANIZATIONS

Many laypeople unable to join a monastery still wanted a life inspired by New Testament models. From around the early thirteenth century communities of laypeople emerged, especially in the Low Countries, known as Beguines (women) and Beghards (men). They worked in secular occupations but took temporary vows to live together and cultivate a shared spiritual life. Dominicans and Franciscans (see page 45) also established lay "third orders" associated with the orders' work and devotion. St. Catherine of Siena was a famous "tertiary," as third order members are known. The later Middle Ages also saw the founding of confraternities, local lay associations devoted to religious and charitable purposes including reciting the rosary, praying for souls in purgatory, and engaging in the care and education of orphans.

The Spiritual Marriage of St. Catherine and Christ *by Michelino da Besozzo (fl. 1388–1450). The Dominican tertiary St. Catherine of Siena (1347–1380) tended the sick, served the poor, and offered spiritual counsel. After a series of ecstatic visions, she became more public in her ministry, travelling, speaking, and writing to leaders of the day.* .

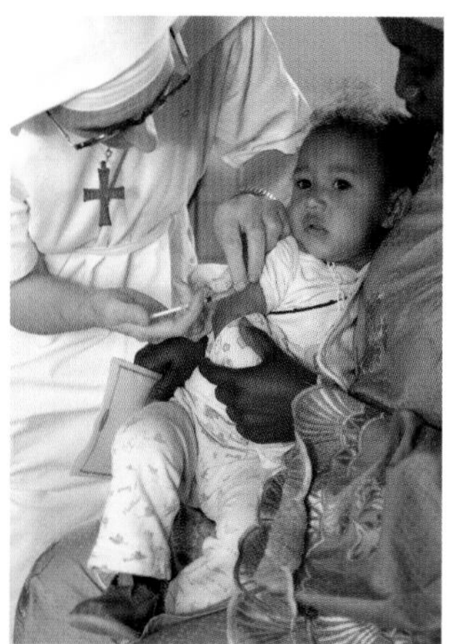

A Benedictine nun *vaccinates a baby girl at Keur Moussa, Senegal. In many regions of the world today members of religious orders provide essential social services to local populations.*

By the twelfth century social changes were underway (see box) and new modes of religious life came to the fore. Reacting against the wealth of Cluny, the Cistercians under St. Bernard of Clairvaux (1090–1153), one of the leading clerics of his age, launched a very influential return to the original austerity of the Benedictine rule. Named for their first monastery at Cîteaux, France (founded 1098), the Cistercians built plain churches, worshipped with a simple liturgy, and restored the balance between work and prayer. They built monasteries in remote areas, in the process bringing great tracts of land under cultivation.

THE MENDICANT ORDERS

Around this time many were inspired by the lives of Christ and the apostles—lives of poverty, itinerant preaching, and service to others—and this inspired new modes of religious life alongside traditional monasticism. While monks generally do not engage in public ministry and are supported by their corporate holdings, friars (from *frater*, brother) are in active ministry and are historically barred from collective support. Two of the most influential orders of friars, also known as mendicants because they supported themselves

CHANGING SOCIAL AND ECONOMIC PATTERNS

After the chaos of the ninth and tenth centuries, with waves of invasions by Vikings, Muslims, and Magyars, western Europe moved toward a new stability. By the twelfth century, there was new social and economic vitality, grounded in growing population, wealth, and infrastructure. New institutions such as banks and universities were forming. Great cathedrals began to rise (see pages 46–47 and 52–53). Trade was expanding. Wool produced in England was turned into cloth in Italy; the Hanseatic League traded fish and timber around the North Sea. The number of large towns grew rapidly where education was more readily available, and trade brought in new ideas and cultivated competition. The rise of wealth and the growing practice of lending money at interest (usury) aroused moral tensions leading some Christians to adopt voluntary poverty in the spirit of the gospel and as a potent critique of the papacy's power and material wealth. In the thirteenth century, many immigrants came to the burgeoning towns, often settling outside the walls, providing new urban contexts for ministry. In order to reach people who were no longer served by their home parishes, Franciscans and Dominicans frequently built their convents and churches in these areas.

Fountains Abbey *in Yorkshire, a Cistercian house founded in 1132, was England's wealthiest monastery during the 12th-century economic boom. Activities on its huge estates ranged from sheep farming and horse breeding to mining and quarrying.*

The Meeting of St. Francis and St. Dominic *by Benozzo Gozzoli, (1420–1497). The founders of the two great mendicant orders of friars may have met in Rome at the fourth Lateran council of 1215.*

by begging (Latin *mendicare*, to beg), are the Dominicans and Franciscans. The former were founded by the Spaniard Domingo de Guzmán (St. Dominic, 1170–1221) and authorized in 1216 with the express goal of fighting heresy, in particular the Catharism of southern France (see page 49). It was vital that they be learned in theology and scripture, and the order set up schools to give its aspiring members at least three years of theological training in preparation for preaching. Dominicans took a leading role in the new universities of western Europe (see page 50), and their intellectual spirituality is exemplified by the great theologian St. Thomas Aquinas (ca. 1225–1274).

The Franciscan order was similarly based on itinerant preaching and a commitment to poverty, but its animating spirit was quite different. Its founder, Francis of Assisi (St. Francis, 1181–1226), the son of a wealthy Italian cloth merchant, embraced poverty and humility as ways of ensuring that nothing would come between him and the love of God. His preaching was simple and charismatic, urging peace and repentance. Endorsed by the pope in 1209, the order grew very quickly. (See also box on page 128.) One of Francis's followers, St. Clare (1194–1253), began a parallel movement for women, the Order of Poor Ladies, or "Poor Clares." Contemporary culture precluded them from preaching or an itinerant life, but their devotion to poverty and prayer was tenacious.

In 1256 a number of small orders were merged as the Hermits of St. Augustine (Augustinians or Austin Friars), who followed a rule based on that saint's writings.

PREACHERS AND CONFESSORS

As part of the new cultural energy of the central Middle Ages, from the twelfth century on, there was a growing demand for more and better preaching. The mendicant orders (see main text) provided trained priests who were available to travel and preach. In the universities, a new style of preaching developed that suited the temper of the times. In an orderly way, it marshalled the authorities of the Bible, Church Fathers, liturgy, Classical authors, and the natural world to urge crowds toward conversion of life.

Christians were urged to repent, turning from the world, the flesh, and the devil, and to cultivate a life of virtue. Everywhere preachers explained how to make a good confession and begin this process. They frequently travelled with confessors in their entourage, although this often created competition with local clergy. Mendicants produced a vast amount of "how-to" literature, enhancing the pastoral work of clergy, especially in urban areas.

ART AND ARCHITECTURE

ROMANESQUE CHURCHES

ABOVE *The Ascension is depicted in the sculpted tympanum over the Porte Miégeville entrance to the basilica of St.-Sernin in Toulouse, France. Built 1080–1122 it is one of the largest of all Romanesque churches.*

In the late tenth and the eleventh centuries a wave of monumental church building swept throughout Europe. It reflected the ambitions of the clergy in the wake of the reforms initiated by Pope Gregory VII (see page 39), and was often sponsored by princely bishops and abbots, as well as ambitious secular patrons. This new architecture, called Romanesque, was to a large extent a monastic phenomenon, especially associated with the Benedictine order and therefore largely rural. Romanesque abbey churches set the general standard for our concept of the great medieval church, with grand sculptured entrances, high towers, and soaring interiors.

There were, no doubt, numerous reasons for the renewal of large-scale church building in the tenth century. Certainly the explosion of piety that characterized the high Middle Ages expressed itself in a new prominence of scale and complexity in the configuration of abbey churches. These were often now designed to facilitate the access of pilgrims to the shrine of a saint, as at St.-Sernin at Toulouse, and ambulatories and radiating chapels now became a common feature of church planning. In the twelfth century, increased economic well-being (see page 44) provided the financial resources for these enterprises, while the growth of population and the availability of specialized labor provided the manpower.

RIGHT *First erected by the Holy Roman emperor Conrad II from 1030 to 1061, the cathedral of St Mary and St Stephen in Speyer houses the tombs of eight German emperors and kings.*

OPPOSITE *The Benedictine abbey church at Vezelay in Burgundy, France. Dedicated in 1104, it claimed to hold the relics of St. Mary Magdalene, for whom the abbey is named. Rounded arches supported on massive piers are characteristic of the Romanesque style, which is characterized by a striking harmony and dignity of interior volumes, tempered by restrained light from small window openings.*

Romanesque churches are characterized by large scale, an increasingly refined use of materials (brick and ashlar masonry), complex exterior massing (frequently with high towers at the entrance and crossing), and often rich sculptural decoration over entrance portals or on capitals in the nave and chancel. Eleventh- and twelfth-century church interiors departed from the rigid typology of the early basilica (see pages 34–35) by utilizing piers, which could support articulated wall surfaces and the weight of vaults. Vaulting was not only a mode of fireproofing, but also provided a new kind of monumentality that recalled Roman antiquity.

The interior structures of Romanesque churches often tied the conception of the wall to that of the vault, so that the nave is defined by a series of vertical elements that continue across the vault as transverse arches, thus giving the interior spaces a striking sense of unity.

THE CRUSADES

The crusades were a series of military expeditions (traditionally numbered as nine) designed to ensure the access of Christians to pilgrimage sites in the Holy Land. Beginning under the strengthened papacy at the end of the eleventh century, they gave concrete reality to the idea of Christians united in the great cause of God's defense. Crusades were accompanied by liturgies, processions, fasts, and prayers, since they offered a strenuous form of penance for sin. Pope Urban II (1088–1099) preached the first crusade at the council of Clermont in 1095, urging Christians to liberate Jerusalem and put an end to the perceived sufferings of eastern Christians (see box). The crusader army, largely made up of French knights and their entourage, achieved an unlikely victory, capturing Jerusalem on July 15, 1099. In its wake, the Latin Kingdom of Jerusalem (1100–1291) and several other crusader states, such as Antioch and Edessa, were established.

St. Bernard of Clairvaux preached the second crusade (1147–1149) in response to the Muslim capture of Edessa. The crusaders' failure to retake Edessa and defeat in a bid to take Damascus were a setback for the papacy and many lost their zeal for crusading.

The third crusade (1189–1192) failed to regain Jerusalem, which had fallen to Salah ad-Din (Saladin) in 1187. Often called the kings' crusade, it was led by Philip II of France and Richard I of England ("the Lionheart"), and the Holy Roman emperor, Frederick I "Barbarossa," who drowned en route.

The last major crusade was the fourth (1202–1204). It aimed to invade the Holy Land through Egypt, but the crusaders got no further than Constantinople, capital of the Christian East, which they sacked in 1204. This devastating betrayal of Christian solidarity marked the final split between the churches of East and West. Subsequent crusades had little enduring success, and with the fall of Acre in 1291 crusader rule ended in the Near East. Nevertheless, the crusading ideal persisted up to the Reformation, when there were calls for a pan-Christian crusade against the Ottoman Turks.

Crusader spoils. *This Byzantine chalice in the Treasury of St. Mark's, Venice, was probably taken from Constantinople during the fourth crusade. Onyx, silver gilt, pearls, and enamel, 10th century.*

Within Europe itself, the 750-year Christian reconquest of the Iberian peninsula from Muslim control, ending in 1492, came to be understood as a crusade. In 1209, Pope Innocent III called the Albigensian crusade against the Cathar heresy in southern France. In the same century, the Teutonic Knights, a military order (see sidebar) joined in conflicts to defend Poland and subdue pagan peoples in Lithuania and other Baltic lands; these are sometimes called the "Northern crusades."

A BITTER LEGACY

The period of the crusades saw a growth in trading, cultural, and intellectual contacts between western Europe and the Near East. But these military exploits were a profound trauma for the Muslim world and worsened relations between western and eastern Christians. Fired by anti-infidel zeal, crusaders also directed violence against Jewish communities, as in the Rhineland on the first crusade; at the time of the second crusade, St. Bernard preached against such violence. One consequence of the persecution was the migration of many Jews to eastern Europe, taking their culture and dialect (Yiddish) with them.

MILITARY ORDERS

The crusades gave rise to a new phenomenon: military monastic orders. The Knights Hospitaller ran a hospital in Jerusalem from 1080. After the first crusade they developed an armed guard for pilgrims that became a regular force. From similar roots as pilgrim guards the Knights Templar were established ca. 1118 and played a key role in crusader conflicts. The Teutonic Knights arose after the third crusade out of a German hospital at Acre. All three orders were influential in subsequent European history.

PRELUDE TO CRUSADE: ISLAM AND CHRISTIANITY IN THE EAST

Although many Christians were long accustomed to living under Muslim rule, developments in the eleventh century inflamed tensions. In 1009 the Fatimid ruler of Egypt, Al-Hakim bi-Amr Allah, apparently annoyed by the number of Christian pilgrims at Easter, destroyed the church of the Holy Sepulchre in Jerusalem, which marked the traditional site of Jesus' burial and resurrection. The news caused widespread dismay in Europe, although the Byzantines were permitted partially to restore the shrine, and pilgrimages continued to grow as part of penitential spirituality for western Christians.

Meanwhile, the Seljuk Turks were advancing from Asia. The Byzantines lost territory to them and in 1071 suffered a great defeat at Manzikert (Malazgirt, Turkey). In 1077 the Seljuks took Jerusalem and soon restricted Christian access to sites. When the Turkish leader Malik Shah died in 1092, the Byzantine emperor Alexius Comnenus (1081–1118) sought to regain lost lands and in 1095 he sent a direct appeal to Pope Urban II for military assistance—resulting in the first crusade.

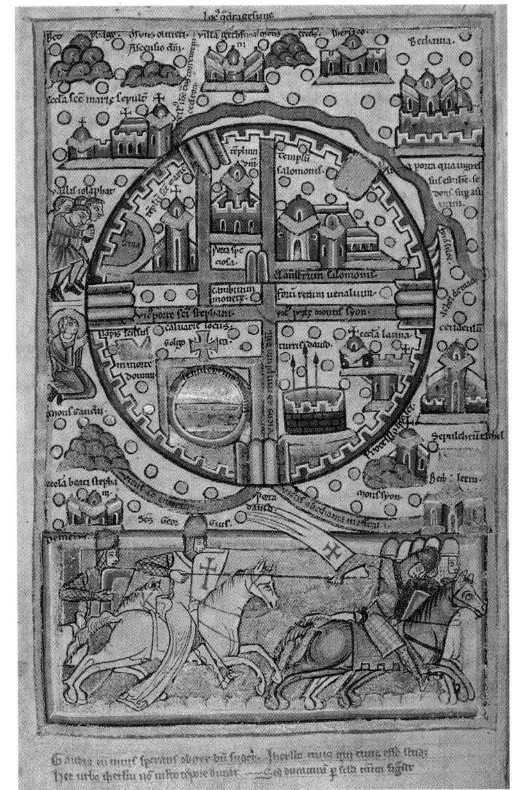

The Holy City. *A 12th-century plan of Christian-held Jerusalem and its environs, including Bethlehem (bottom right). The cross in the bottom left quarter, atop the circle denoting the rotunda of the church of the Holy Sepulchre, marks the site of Golgotha. In the bottom register, crusaders are shown driving off Muslims.*

SCHOLARS AND SCHISMS

OPPOSITE The Triumph of St. Thomas Aquinas, *by Benozzo Gozzoli, (1420–1497). The great Scholastic theologian stands between Aristotle and Plato and above the Arab philosopher Averroes. Below them is the assembled clergy with Pope Sixtus IV (elected August 1471).*

Throughout the early Middle Ages, most education in Europe took place in monastic settings where the focus was on cultivating the spiritual life through steeping oneself in scripture, the writings of the Church Fathers (see page 30), and the liturgy. In the twelfth-century West, education took a turn toward the outside world. Cathedrals developed their own schools with a view to training priests to work in local parishes. *Studia generales*, schools open to students from across Europe, grew rapidly as cities expanded. Soon universities—corporations or communities (*universitates*) of students or professors—were founded: Bologna (1088) was famed for its law faculty, Paris (ca. 1150) and Oxford (pre-1167) concentrated on theology, and Padua (1222)

WINDS OF REFORM: WYCLIFFE AND HUS

The Great Schism prompted many Christians to consider questions of church reform. The Oxford Scholastic John Wycliffe or Wyclif (1328–1384) argued that all rule was a form of stewardship; kings or priests who failed to exercise their offices well should be removed. He advocated clerical poverty and rejected transubstantiation. After his death, his followers, known as Lollards, were condemned as heretics. They followed Wycliffe's example of translating scripture into English and preached a devout faith purged of clerical pretensions and greed, as well as such practices as pilgrimages and the veneration of images and relics.

Wycliffe's ideas influenced Jan Hus (or John Huss, 1369–1415), rector of the university of Prague, Bohemia, who called for an end to such abuses as simony and pluralism (see page 38) and argued that Christ, not the pope, was the true head of the church. In fact, being a high cleric said nothing about one's salvation, since the latter lay fully in God's hands. Executed for heresy, Hus became a national hero. The enduring presence of Lollards and Hussites in the sixteenth century helped to shape the course of the Reformation by questioning the church's hierarchy and doctrines; advocating vernacular scriptures and expository preaching; and raising fears of nationalist movements.

The Death of Jan Hus. *Promised a safe-conduct to attend the council of Constance, Hus was arrested, tried as a heretic, and burned, a betrayal that inflamed the reform movement in Bohemia. From a 1484 manuscript of Ulrich Richental's chronicle of the council (1420).*

specialized in medicine. Later, in the fifteenth century, Europe witnessed a veritable flood of new universities.

A new educational method known as Scholasticism (from Latin *schola*, school) developed. It involved the systematic asking of questions, weighing of authorities, and logical framing of answers that could be integrated into a coherent body of natural and spiritual knowledge. Vital to this approach was the introduction, via Islamic sources, of works of Aristotle (384–322BCE) previously unknown in the West. The great Italian theologian St. Thomas Aquinas (ca. 1225–1274) synthesized Aristotelian philosophy with Christian theology. The Scholastic schools of thought shaped theological debates in the later Middle Ages on such topics as the freedom of God and the role of humans in their salvation.

THE GREAT SCHISM

Around the turn of the fourteenth century Western Christianity faced a crisis that had ramifications in centuries to come. Conflicts over clerical taxation and jurisdiction between Pope Boniface VIII (1294–1303) and King Philip IV of France (1285–1314) led to the papacy coming under such strong French influence that it moved from Rome to Avignon. Pope Gregory XI (1370–1378) returned to Rome, but the election of his successor was disputed, and soon there was a schism—two rival popes, one in Rome and one in Avignon. The council of Pisa in 1409 deposed the two popes and elected another—but since both popes refused to go, there were now three popes, with nations and principalities giving their allegiance to one or another.

Eventually the council of Constance (1414–1418) brought a return to a single pope, but the papacy had lost much of its spiritual prestige and worldly power. The "Great Schism" had shocked many Western Christians as thoroughly unseemly, and spiritual anxiety and uncertainty were rampant. Calls for church reform "in head and members," heard since the twelfth century, continued well beyond Constance. The experience of the Hussites (see box) and the reluctance of popes to call a reforming council served to feed the rupture of the Western church in the following century.

ART AND ARCHITECTURE

GOTHIC GLORIES

Flying buttresses *like these at Chartres cathedral, France, were a key feature of Gothic cathedral architecture, enabling larger windows and greater height.*

Toward the middle of the twelfth century increased episcopal wealth and authority and the growth of cities, led to the reconstruction of many cathedrals in the style known as Gothic (a term coined as a pejorative description in the early modern period). It was based on features introduced during the Romanesque period (for example large scale and vaulting; see pages 46–47), which were refined and elaborated by the introduction of new elements, particularly the pointed arch and rib vault. By the end of the twelfth century, the systematic adoption of the flying buttress on the exterior of churches permitted three related innovations: the reduction in the weight of the walls (thus reducing the amount of stone to support the vaults); the elongation of clerestory windows, now filled with stained glass; and ever-increasing scale, so that churches came to assume majestic proportions and tower over cities.

For over a century the myth has persisted that Gothic cathedrals were built as a spontaneous outpouring of faith by medieval townspeople. However, recent scholarship tends to suggest a different picture: that in spite of clerical rhetoric, cathedrals were built largely by the clergy and funded by the donations of wealthy patrons and indulgences. Church taxes and pilgrim donations were also among sources of revenue. These resources often did not suffice, and many cathedrals remained incomplete.

The lightening of structure permitted by the adoption of rib-vaults, pointed arches, and flying buttresses helped builders to produce more structurally efficient and larger buildings. At the same time, the large window openings filled with stained glass flooded the interiors of Gothic churches with a saturated and deeply colored light (see pages 76–77). The Gothic style is also characterized by a unified approach to sculptural decoration on portals and capitals. In France, sculptured portals now extended across the width of facades, often accompanied by further decoration high up in the building, as at Rheims cathedral.

To a large extent Gothic architecture is an urban phenomenon, although there were also rural monastic churches in this style, in which the use of colored glass and sculpture tended to be far more restrained.

RIGHT **King's College Chapel,** *Cambridge (1446–1547), has the world's largest fan vault, a feature of the English late Gothic style known as Perpendicular from its emphasis on soaring vertical lines.*

OPPOSITE **Cologne cathedral,** *Germany, was begun in 1284 but completed only in 1880. The basic plan of Gothic cathedrals (transept, ambulatory, radiating chapels) and exterior elevation (soaring towers), were also central features of Romanesque design. The principle innovations of Gothic churches were structural, permitting much greater scale.*

THE REFORMATION

Despite various theological and political challenges, the unity and cohesiveness of western Christendom remained intact throughout the medieval period. Then, on October 3, 1517, Martin Luther—an Augustinian friar and professor of biblical studies at Wittenberg university in Saxony—posted a set of ninety-five academic theses concerning the practice of indulgences (see box). Ideas expounded in these theses generated a theological controversy that soon involved all those who had been clamoring for reform, with ever more voices supporting Luther. In 1520, Rome decided that Luther's notions were heretical and gave him sixty days to recant. Luther defiantly burned the papal bull threatening him with excommunication outside Wittenberg city gates.

INDULGENCE AND PURGATORY

In 1517 Pope Leo X undertook to finance the new St. Peter's in Rome partly through the sale of indulgences. In return for a "good work," including a gift of money, the faithful received an "indulgence," or reduction, of the punishment for their sins. However, indulgence was popularly taken to mean complete forgiveness of one's sins, and such beliefs were not discouraged by unscrupulous indulgence-sellers such as one Johann Tetzel, whose activities in Germany were instrumental in prompting Luther's initial protest of 1517.

Indulgences were believed to reduce the soul's time in purgatory, where it would be "purged" of sin before entering heaven. While the idea has no clear biblical basis, there is a long Christian tradition of intercessory prayers for the dead. Purgatory has often been conceived as a subterranean torture chamber—another notion intensified by indulgence-sellers.

Souls in purgatory. *Protestants rejected the concept of purgatory mainly because of the abuses with which it was associated. In present-day Catholicism purgatory is no longer considered to be either a place of torment or a "waiting room" on the way to heaven, but rather a process of purification and growth after death. From a fresco by the Cagnola brothers at Holy Trinity oratory, Momo, near Novara, Italy, 1520s.*

Lutheran worship. *This altar front of 1561, from Torslunde, Denmark, is the earliest known depiction of Lutheran rites: baptism (left); Lord's Supper before the altar and crucifix (center); and preaching (right). The traditional vestments worn by the presiding clergy were still common in the early years of Lutheranism. King Christian II (ruled 1537–1559) established the reformed church in his territories of Denmark, Norway, and Schleswig-Holstein in 1537, with the monarch as leader of the church, much as in England. The Danish National Church remains one of the few established Lutheran churches today.*

Support for Luther, mixed with hostility to Rome, forced the Holy Roman emperor Charles V (ruled 1519–1556) to give Luther a hearing before the imperial diet (parliament) at Worms in 1521. Luther refused to recant and escaped burning for heresy only because his sympathetic ruler, Elector Frederick of Saxony, spirited him away to the Wartburg castle.

A NEW VISION

Luther and his supporters did not so much object to alleged abuses in the church as propound a new vision of the faith. In the Wartburg, Luther began his famous German translation of the Bible, believing that scripture should be available to all since it alone was the source of Christian truth, and not, as the Catholic Church taught, the Bible supplemented by church tradition. Luther also attacked the idea that salvation was a coming together of human effort and divine grace; salvation, he insisted, was by grace alone. (See also pages 156–157.)

The extent of popular support for reform should not be overestimated, but it was sufficient to prompt ever more states and cities, beginning in the 1520s, to replace the Mass with a new, "evangelical" communion and preaching service. These changes were effected by secular authorities, which thereby enhanced their power over the ecclesiastical realm.

After Luther's refusal to recant, Charles V issued an edict declaring him and his followers outlaws. In 1529, when the diet at Speyer demanded that rulers put the edict into effect, those who backed reform protested, and hence came to be dubbed "Protestants."

In 1529 the Ottoman Turks besieged Vienna, threatening central Europe with military subjugation. Charles needed the financial and military aid of Protestant rulers, who

SUPPORT FOR REFORM

It is not altogether clear what exactly prompted the widespread enthusiastic support for Luther in the early days of the Reformation, at least at the political level. Undoubtedly, aggrandizing political power over the church was a factor, as was hostility to a church that seemed far away and demanded ever new financial contributions. Contrary to much Protestant propaganda through the centuries, in the early sixteenth century the Roman Catholic Church was hardly in dire straits nor can it be said that there was a widespread yearning for reform, whatever that may have meant.

St. Bartholomew's Day Massacre, *by François Dubois (1529–1584), an eyewitness. On August 24, 1572, the feast of St. Bartholomew, a savage massacre of Huguenots (French Calvinists) began in Paris and soon spread to other regions of France. The massacre took place during the French Wars of Religion (1562–1598) and was almost certainly at the instigation of members of the Catholic ruling dynasty. It was among the worst of the 16th century's religious persecutions.*

used the threat of the Turks to exact religious concessions from the emperor. Thus Charles found himself unable to give his anti-Protestant policies any teeth, and Protestantism made steady and significant headway in Germany. Despite a successful war against the Protestants in 1546–1547, Charles was unable to force the Protestants back into the Catholic fold, and the 1555 Peace of Augsburg gave legal standing to the new faith. Rulers could determine which religion—Catholic or Lutheran—their subjects should follow, a doctrine summed up as *cuius regio, eius religio* ("whoever's domain, his religion"). It was meant to be a temporary arrangement, but proved to be the permanent solution to the Reformation in Germany.

DIVISIONS AND DIFFERENCES: ZWINGLI AND CALVIN

The reform movement was never a cohesive entity. Some reformers were mainly concerned about reforms in society; others in theology; yet others in church practice. A first division, over the Lord's Supper (Eucharist), involved Luther and Huldrych Zwingli (see sidebar), and there were others: Luther wanted the gospel message confined to religion, whereas Zwingli understood reform to apply to all of society in order to fashion a Christian commonwealth.

Zwingli's understanding of the faith was creatively recast two decades later by the Frenchman John Calvin (1509–1564), perhaps the most influential of all the reformers. Calvin had burst onto the theological scene aged 27 with a brilliant exposition of the tenets of the Reformation, *The Institutes of the Christian Religion* (1536). Calvin, whose center of activity came to be Geneva, envisioned four church offices—pastors, teachers, deacons, and elders—and an institution called the consistory, comprised of the pastors and elders and meeting weekly to monitor the faith and morals of the Genevan citizens. An intense emphasis on God's sovereignty led Calvin to insist not only on the centrality of grace but also of predestination: God has predestined who will be saved and who will be lost. More significantly, Calvin argued the importance of the Christian way of life. The Genevan consistory, comprised of laymen and clergy, became the model of Calvinist congregations everywhere. Some expected that the doctrine of predestination would lead to moral paralysis, but Calvinists soon distinguished themselves by their model conduct. (See also pages 158–159.)

A different sort of division occurred in 1525, when some of Zwingli's followers in Zurich rejected infant baptism, demanding that the church be comprised only of those who had been baptized upon confession of faith. Zwingli and the Zurich authorities promptly began to suppress these "Anabaptists" ("rebaptizers"), as they were dubbed, who also insisted that the Sermon on the Mount be taken literally (for example, they were pacifists). Despite persecution, Anabaptist sentiment spread throughout Switzerland, Austria, and South Germany, and later to North Germany and the Low Countries (see also page 141).

THE LORD'S SUPPER

Luther and Huldrych Zwingli (1484–1531) of Zurich disagreed over how to interpret Jesus' words of institution at the Lord's Supper, beginning "Take, eat, this is my body" (Matt. 26.26ff.). While rejecting the Catholic idea of transubstantiation, Luther affirmed a bodily presence of Christ in the bread and wine ("consubstantiation"). But Zwingli denied any real presence, holding that Jesus' words were only symbolic. The disagreement was perpetuated when Calvin appeared on the scene.

THE REFORMATION IN ENGLAND

The English Reformation was initiated by King Henry VIII (ruled 1509–1547). Questions about the legitimacy of his marriage to Catherine of Aragon (who had failed to bear him a male heir), as well as a new understanding of the nature of royal rule, set him on a collision course with the papacy. In 1527 Henry petitioned Rome to have his marriage annulled so that he could remarry. The pope refused, so Henry used Parliament to accomplish his purpose. Several statues not only dissolved his marriage but also, in 1530, separated the English church from Rome. A new "Anglican" church emerged, which, given the king's conservative stance, hardly differed theologically from the Roman Catholic Church.

Henry's young son Edward VI (ruled 1547–1553) brought a more overt manifestation of Protestant sentiment, but Edward's Catholic half-sister Mary I (ruled 1553–1558) persecuted Protestants in her vigorous attempt to return the country to Rome. Her successor, Elizabeth I (ruled 1558–1603), daughter of Henry's second wife Anne Boleyn, imposed a conservative form of Protestantism on the land. (See also pages 160–163.)

Henry VIII *gained the papal title* Fidei Defensor *(Defender of the Faith) for writing an anti-Lutheran treatise in 1521. Just 15 years later, when Hans Holbein the Younger painted this portrait, Parliament ended the last vestige of papal power over the English church.*

THE CATHOLIC REFORMATION

OPPOSITE The Glory of St. Ignatius of Loyola, *the founder of the Society of Jesus (Jesuits), by Antonio Balestra (1666–1740).*

The Roman Catholic Church responded to Luther with determination, but to the emerging movement of reform with hesitancy. While Luther himself was quickly declared a heretic, the church failed to sense the implications of the growing reform movement and the call for a general council to resolve the controversy. When a council eventually convened at Trent in northern Italy in 1546, the impossibility of undoing the split between Catholics and Protestants was obvious. Accordingly, the council confined itself to clarifying the salient Catholic positions on the controversial theological issues and to "modernizing" ecclesiastical practices, such as seminary education, episcopal residency, or the monitoring of theological books.

THE THIRTY YEARS WAR

In the wake of the Reformation, the attempt by the Catholic Habsburg emperors to exert influence over the disparate collection of German and other states of the Holy Roman empire—never easy at the best of times—was complicated by religious divisions. In 1618 one German ruler, the Elector Palatine—a Protestant—secured his own election as king of Bohemia in defiance of the Habsburgs, who saw Bohemia as their fiefdom. Thus began the devastating string of conflicts known collectively as the Thirty Years War and fought mainly in Germany.

The Elector Palatine was defeated by imperial forces in 1619, but other states took sides, religious motives blurring with political ones. Lutheran Denmark led the anti-imperial coalition from 1625 to 1629, followed by Sweden from 1630 to 1635, then Catholic France—arch-rivals of the Habsburgs—from 1636 to 1648. There were no clear military victors and no decisive triumph for any religious party. In the end, with much of central Europe utterly devastated, the main contenders began a weary four-year search for peace that ended in the Treaty of Westphalia of 1648. Needless to say, religious and political controversy did not end with the treaty, and demoralized European states did not recover for a century to come.

The Taking of Breisach, *by Jusepe Leonardo de Chavier (ca. 1605-1695), an imperial defeat over Swedish forces in 1633. Most major European powers were involved in the war at one time or another.*

If the council of Trent was the hallmark of the Catholic response to the Reformation, Ignatius of Loyola, Teresa of Avila, and John of the Cross (see pages 138–139) were telling illustrations of the ability of the Roman Catholic Church to marshal ever new resources for spiritual renewal. Iñigo, or Ignatius, de Loyola (1491–1556) embarked on a military career until it was cut short by an injury. Ignatius then experienced a conversion that eventually led to a vision of a new kind of monastic community, which took the name of the Society of Jesus, or Jesuits. It saw itself, under Ignatius's guidance, as an elite force of the Catholic Church. Before long, the Jesuits became a powerful agency for revitalizing the Catholic Church and enhancing its authority. By the first half of the seventeenth century, Jesuits were serving as spiritual guides to numerous Catholic rulers in Europe, and were in the forefront of Catholic missionary activity, notably in the Far East.

The sixteenth century brought dramatic challenges—and losses—to the Catholic Church: Scotland; England; Scandinavia, and much of Germany deserted Rome. France, Hungary, and Poland were battlegrounds. However, where the Catholic Church had retained its position, mainly in southern Europe, it assuredly manifested a dynamic vitality that made the seventeenth century a triumphant century in the history of the Catholic Church.

REFORMATION: THE AFTERMATH

The Christian religion weathered the storm of the Reformation controversies with considerable vigor. If anything, increasing self-confidence characterized Christianity, both Catholic and Protestant, in the opening decades of the seventeenth century—which found devastating expression, played on a political level, in the Thirty Years War (see box). At the same time, however, subtle changes were beginning to take place. No fewer than five new churches had emerged from the Reformation—Lutheran, Anglican, Calvinist, Anabaptist, and Antitrinitarian (Unitarian)—each with its own range of theological opinion and each claiming, as did the Catholic Church, to be in sole possession of Christian truth. Understandably, theology became the overriding consideration in the differentiation of these several churches, and the Christian faith toward the end of the sixteenth century was widely understood as a system of doctrine. The mandate for Christian living and piety, while not without advocates, such as Johann Arndt (1555–1621)—a popular Lutheran writer of devotional tracts, was considered secondary.

THE "THIRD ROME"

The Byzantine empire ended in 1453 when Ottoman armies captured Constantinople, but the Orthodox patriarchate continued to operate. In 1589, Patriarch Jeremias II raised the bishop of Moscow to the rank of patriarch of Moscow and All Russia. He thus became the head of the largest Orthodox church, and the only Eastern patriarch not subject to an Islamic ruler. Moscow came to be known as the "Third Rome," successor to imperial Rome and Constantinople.

THE AGE OF REASON

From the late sixteenth century western Europe witnessed a series of internal and international wars that had their roots in the Reformation: the Wars of Religion in France (1562–1598); the protracted Dutch war of independence from Spain (1562–1609, 1621–1648), which in its latter stages became part of the wider Thirty Years War (1618–1648); and the Puritan revolt and Civil War in England (1642–1649). Meanwhile, however, Europe was undergoing what has been termed the "Scientific Revolution" (see box). While intellectual activity remained confined to the examination of nature, it had little impact on Christian self-understanding, even if Galileo's discoveries challenged the traditional notion of the Earth as the center of the universe (see pages 122–123).

Increasingly, though, the argument was put forward that not only the world of nature should be critically scrutinized but also the founding document of the Christian religion, the Bible. Promptly, the supernatural aspects of the Bible—miracles and prophecies—were called into question, not only by agnostics but also by Christians, such as Isaac Newton (1643–1727), who believed that God's revelation had occurred in two ways—in the book of

The Managers of the Haarlem Orphanage, 1633, *by Jan de Bray (ca. 1626–1697). Newly independent from Spain, the Dutch Republic enjoyed a golden age of prosperity in the 17th century, and many merchants expressed their piety in donating to charitable foundations. The plain dress of these wealthy citizens was common at the time in Calvinist communities.*

nature and in the book of the Bible. The lawful regularity of the universe meant that revelation and human reason harmoniously combined to attain knowledge of God. The simple knowledge of God became the heart of the new understanding of the Christian faith.

THE DEISTS

John Locke's *The Reasonableness of Christianity* (1695) began a line of writers that culminated in the eighteenth century with David Hume's *Dialogues concerning Natural Religion* (1779) and included individuals such as John Toland, Thomas Chubb, and Matthew Tindal. Known as Deists, these men argued that authentic Christianity was simply a restatement of the original natural religion. While the Deist writers initially conceded the possibility of divine revelation to humankind (but only to confirm and strengthen the knowledge of the religion of nature), eventually most Deists rejected all notions of revelatory truth.

Deist sentiment became increasingly pervasive in the eighteenth century, first in England, then on the European continent and the North American colonies. In Germany this new understanding triggered an intense controversy incited by the posthumous publication of the *Wolfenbüttel Fragments* by one Hermann Reimarus (1694–1768), who reiterated the notions of the English Deists. At the same time, many in the Protestant churches continued to affirm the traditional Christian faith. In continental Europe, the Pietist movement's understanding of Christianity as pious living proved enormously influential (see box on page 62).

"NATURAL RELIGION"

In 1624 Edward Herbert, Lord Cherbury (1583–1648), published *De Veritate (On Truth)*, which proved to be enormously influential. Herbert argued that humans shared five common religious ideas: the existence of a Supreme Being; the worship of this being; the exercise of virtue; the repentance of wrongdoing; and a final judgment. This fundamental and natural religion was, in fact, the essence of Christianity, found among all peoples. Natural religion was all that was needed; following its precepts led to eternal salvation. Herbert has been called "the father of English Deism."

THE SCIENTIFIC REVOLUTION

In western European society, beginning in the later sixteenth century, nothing less than an intellectual revolution took place—the "Scientific Revolution," marked by remarkable new discoveries being made in the study of the natural world by Galileo, Kepler, Newton, and many others. Their investigations and discoveries elicited a fundamental change not only in the way Europeans understood the physical universe but also in the European mindset. Up until then, the old had been accepted and revered, while the new was considered dubious and questionable. The European mind was historically oriented; it focused on the past and on tradition. The incipient scientific revolution brought with it a relentless disparagement of the old and awe of the new.

The Library of Trinity College, *in Cambridge, England, where Sir Isaac Newton was professor of mathematics. Some of Newton's papers are on the lectern. The library was built (1676–1695) by Sir Christopher Wren.*

THE WESLEYAN REVIVAL

In England a similar turn to traditional religion is associated with two Anglican clerics, the brothers John and Charles Wesley. "Methodism," as their movement came to be called, seems to have been a preferred term for a gathering of pious Oxford students, among whom John and Charles stood out. Their "Holy Club" was serious about faith and piety, and its members disliked the relaxed forms of observance in the Anglican clergy as represented by many at Oxford, where every don was a cleric. They promoted a vital piety, given to fervent prayer, hymn-singing, and attempts to convert others.

On a voyage across the Atlantic to do missionary work among native peoples in Georgia, John Wesley (1703–1791) was deeply moved by the piety of Moravian immigrants, who pointed out to him that his faith was intellectual and lacked personal commitment. When, upon his return to England, he attended a Moravian meeting in London and heard a reading from Luther's commentary on Romans, his "heart was strangely warmed." This conversion changed his life; his passion became to preach a practical Christianity for Christians who had experienced a conversion as he had. For John Wesley and the Wesleyans, instinctively orthodox though they were, doctrine and dogma meant less than the "warmed heart;" this for Wesley meant "to promote vital, practical religion." Wesley wanted to evangelize, or "save souls."

SPENER AND PIETISM

Breaking with the dominant emphasis on doctrine, Philip Jakob Spener (1635–1705), a Lutheran pastor in Frankfurt, Germany, published in 1675 a slender book that became the manual of Protestant Pietism, *Pia Desideria* (*Pious Wishes*). Its message was simple: Christianity demonstrated itself in everyday living. Spener called for Bible study, commitment to a devotional life, and an overhaul of clergy education. His appeal found no fault with traditional Lutheran theology, and since this agenda minimized doctrine, his summons to Christian living was easily embraced by Lutherans, Calvinists, and Anglicans alike. Spener's book dominated German Protestantism for generations. In the German town of Halle, Spener's disciple, August Hermann Francke, undertook a set of practical initiatives—orphanage, boarding school, publishing house, hospital, newspaper—that gave the Pietist impulses a structural embodiment. These "Francke Foundations" exist to this day.

August Hermann Francke. *A statue in Halle, central Germany, where Francke (1663–1727) secured the support of the Prussian monarchy for the implementation of Pietist impulses in practical and charitable ways.*

The Open-Air Preacher *by Alexander Carse (died 1838) depicts a typical Methodist outdoor gathering, following the example of John Wesley, who preached to crowds numbering in the hundreds and even thousands.*

John Wesley's preaching mission took him from parish to parish in England with ever greater resonance among the common people. When the Church of England labeled him a rabble-rouser and made his preaching in churches difficult, John followed George Whitefield's practice of preaching in open fields to increasingly huge crowds. His brother Charles (1707–1788) followed his lead but became best known as a writer of hymns in the English language (see page 90). John Wesley astutely recognized the importance of continued nurturing of those converted by his preaching. He organized his followers into small conventicles that met weekly to pray and study the Bible, and admonish one another to proper Christian living. These "classes" were a far cry from a new church, and while John Wesley initially insisted that only ordained Anglican clergy preach in meetings organized by his Methodist society, the hostility of the Anglican establishment prompted him to allow others to preach and lead the Bible classes that became the hallmarks of the Wesleyan revival. While in Germany the Pietists remained members of the "Reformed" churches, in England the Wesleyan revival led to the establishment of local gatherings that the eventually broke with the Church of England and formed the new Methodist church.

In the broader sweep of Christian history, the eighteenth century exhibited an intriguing diversity. On the one hand, the challenge of the Enlightenment (see sidebar) and its advocacy of natural religion meant a softening of longstanding Christian beliefs, such as the belief in the resurrection. On the other hand, traditional Christianity persisted and not only retained its vigor but also attained, through the Pietist movement on the continent and the Wesleyan revival in England, a new dynamic.

THE ENLIGHTENMENT

A climate of opinion and expression of values that developed in the eighteenth century, the "Enlightenment" colored religious life in western Europe and America. Stressing human reason as the force in which to invest for a humane and progressive future, the thinkers of the Enlightenment cherished science, rationalist philosophy, "religion without revelation," and ethics. This movement tended to be most radical in Catholic France, but the French Enlightenment also influenced Protestant thinkers in Germany and in Britain and the American colonies. In Europe the Enlightenment often took more vehement anti-Christian forms than it did in America, where a characteristic exemplar was Benjamin Franklin (1706–1790), who believed that some sort of force, personal or impersonal, did govern the universe and that rewards and punishments, in this life or a life to come, were part of this divine government. Enlightenment thinking continued to have influence in the new United States, but it was eclipsed by Protestant revivalism early in the nineteenth century.

THE MODERN AGE

A GLOBAL FAITH

From the late 1400s Europeans began to make contact with continents and peoples previously unknown. The missionary efforts of succeeding centuries often occurred in the context of European imperialism, and the new churches established were European outposts. But after the Second World War, indigenous Christian churches and congregations came into existence. At a time when the hold of Christianity in Europe and North America appeared to be waning, Christian churches outside these regions were dynamic and flourishing; at the beginning of the twenty-first century more Christians lived south of the equator than in Europe and North America.

Up until the end of the eighteenth century, most European states supported one official church, politically and financially; other churches were either illegal or variously restricted. The idea of "state churches" was challenged by the thinkers of the Enlightenment, and began to crumble altogether in the closing decades of the century with the revolutions in American and France (see page 113). In the nineteenth century, in spite of efforts by individuals, the churches had difficulty responding to social and economic problems. A process of alienation took place, especially among the new industrial working classes, which found socialist ideas more relevant to their lives than the Christianity proclaimed by upper-class clergy. However, Christians (such as Methodists in Britain) were sometimes at the forefront of political radicalism, while the church loyalties of most people, especially in rural areas, remained largely unchanged throughout the century.

In the wake of Enlightenment attacks on Christian teachings, many theologians

Dr. John Sentamu *after his enthronement as 97th archbishop of York on November 30, 2005. Ugandan-born Dr. Sentamu is the first person of non-European origin to hold the second highest office in the Anglican church. British colonialism spread Anglicanism to Africa, which today is home to some of the Anglican Communion's most vigorous churches.*

had responded by reinterpreting traditional Christian theology. A shared factor of these efforts was to spiritualize what had been previously understood as historical facts, such as the resurrection of Jesus. The nineteenth century also brought world-views hostile to Christianity from such thinkers as Marx and Nietzsche, while Darwin's *The Origin of Species* sparked renewed tension between religion and science (see pages 122–123).

The French Revolution prompted a conservative reaction in church and society that remained strong in the first decades of the nineteenth century. Most Protestant churches swiftly abandoned this disposition, while Anglican conservatism was expressed in the Oxford Movement, which sought a return to Catholic roots; indeed, some adherents converted to Catholicism, such as John Henry Newman (1801–1890), later a cardinal. The Catholic Church was a bulwark of conservatism—underlined by the new dogmas of the immaculate conception and papal infallibility (see pages 145 and 151)—until the "modernizing" second Vatican council of the 1960s (see sidebar). The rise of Catholic "liberation theology" in the same period emphasized the societal responsibility of the Christian faith.

Two additional developments left their mark on modern Christianity: the encounter with hostility from the secular state and the globalization of the faith (see box and sidebar). A by-product of globalization has been the ecumenical movement, which has striven, both practically and theologically, to promote Christian unity (see pages 228–229).

TWO MODERN POPES

Among several remarkable twentieth-century popes, John XXIII (1958–1963) and John Paul II (1978–2005) stand out. John XXIII called the Second Vatican Council (1962–1965), which promulgated a series of "modernizing" acts, from expressing regret for historic antisemitism to approving vernacular languages in the Mass. John Paul II travelled incessantly to cement global Catholic cohesiveness, while taking conservative positions on issues plaguing all churches in the later century, such as female ordination, abortion, and homosexuality.

THE HOSTILE STATE

Christianity's first encounter with a hostile secular ideology was in France, where the revolution of 1789 not only dissolved the ties between church and state, but also led to active and at times brutal persecution of the Catholic clergy. Anticlericalism—the opposition to church influence in public life—became a running theme in French republicanism, and also characterized revolutions in Central and South America, but found its most radical expression in Russia after the 1917 Bolshevik Revolution. Far from being neutral, the USSR (and later its eastern European satellites) made atheism the state doctrine, and persecuted those loyal to the church. The situation was similar in Fascist Italy and Nazi Germany; although neither actively persecuted Christian churches as a whole, traditional privileges were curtailed, and these states' demands of total loyalty and obedience triggered conflicts of conscience (see pages 112–113).

Murder in the Papal Palace. *On October 16, 1791, sixty adherents of the papacy were slain in the Palace of the Popes in Avignon by revolutionaries demanding the papal territory's unification with France.*

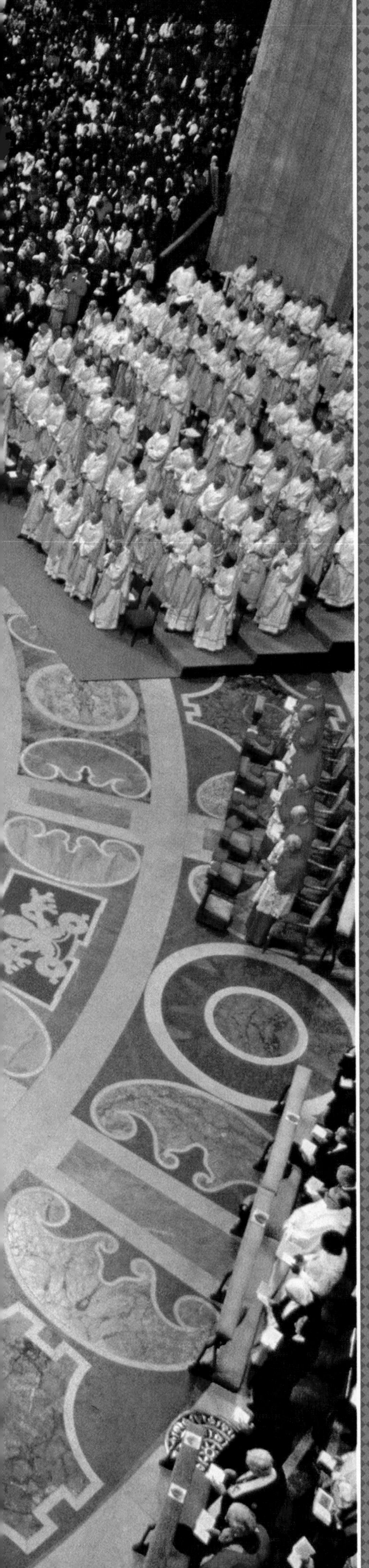

PART 2

PRINCIPLES AND PRACTICES

At the heart of St Peter's basilica *in the Vatican is the papal altar, or Altar of the Confessio. Lying directly beneath the dome, it is surmounted by Gianlorenzo Bernini's bronze-gilt baldacchino, or canopy (1624–1633), which stands on four marble pedestals. On the feast of Ss. Peter and Paul (June 29), the pope celebrates the Eucharist at this altar and presents a band of wool, or pallium, to every archbishop appointed in the previous year, reminding them of their duties as shepherds to Christ's flock. The Confessio itself is a chapel beneath the altar and contains St. Peter's tomb.*

1

THE TRIUNE GOD

Christians believe in a God who is the creator, sustainer, and redeemer of humankind and the world. But this one God is in three persons. Belief in a triune God, or Trinity, sharply distinguishes Christianity from other monotheistic religions. Some groups, such as the Jehovah's Witnesses, denounce this belief as unbiblical. Indeed, the Bible never mentions the Trinity; Renaissance scholars recognized the following passage as a later addition: "There are three that testify in heaven, the Father, the Word [Christ, the incarnate "Word" of John 1.14], and the Holy Spirit, and these three are one" (1 John 5.7).

While there is no explicit biblical reference to the Trinity, there is ample mention of the spirit of God in the Old Testament. The spirit (*ruach*) is the difference between life and death: "If [God] should take back his spirit … and gather to himself his breath, all flesh would perish together…" (Job 34.14). Israel anticipated the abundant outpouring of God's spirit, forever ending the dominion of death. God's *ruach* bestows wisdom (Job 32.8) and power (Gen. 41.38). The Psalmist identifies *ruach* with God's creation of the world: "By the word of the Lord the heavens were made, and all their host by the breath of his mouth" (Ps. 33.6).

A Vision of the Trinity, *from the* Rothschild Canticles, *a manuscript collection of sacred writings. Golden suns shine from the wings and tail of a haloed dove, its body a triple-framed portrait of Christ, flanked by haloed beings. Two mortals are astonished at the vision. French, 13th or 14th century.*

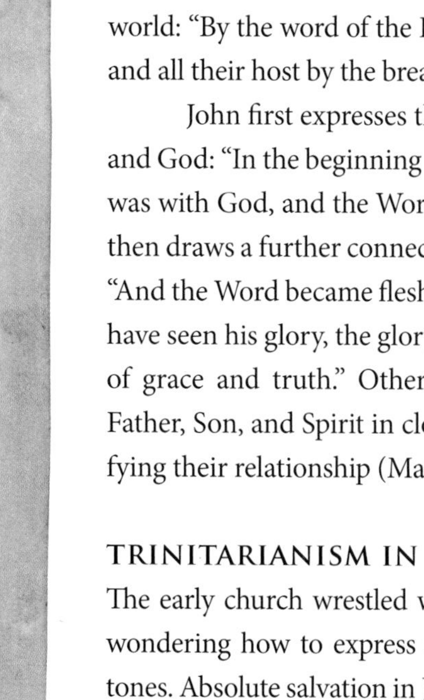

John first expresses the unity of the Word (Spirit) and God: "In the beginning was the Word, and the Word was with God, and the Word was God" (John 1.1). John then draws a further connection between Spirit and Son: "And the Word became flesh and lived among us, and we have seen his glory, the glory of the father's only son, full of grace and truth." Other triadic formulations name Father, Son, and Spirit in close proximity without specifying their relationship (Matt. 28.19; 2 Cor. 13.13).

TRINITARIANISM IN THE EARLY CHURCH

The early church wrestled with the Trinitarian concept, wondering how to express it without polytheistic overtones. Absolute salvation in Jesus distinguished him from the host of Hellenistic demigods with limited power; yet in bringing salvation to humankind, Christ had to be truly human, too. But most Christians of the very early church had Jewish roots and therefore abhorred the idea of admitting more than one divine being. Consequently, what is termed "dynamistic monarchianism," a belief professing only one dynamic power, was widespread in the early church. Its proponents tried to safeguard monotheism by denying Jesus' pre-existence, claiming that such a notion would lead to the belief in two Gods, the Father and the Son. Only through his baptism, so they claimed, was the human Jesus given divinity. The concept known as "modalistic monarchianism" was only slightly different: it claimed that the same power exists circumstantially in different modes of existence, that is, as Father or Son. A variety of this belief called "patripassianism" held that the one eternal and invisible God is born and seen, suffers and dies.

Over time, these proposals were considered deficient. The matter was finally resolved by Origen (died 254), who asserted the unity of Father and Son. While the Son is a second being and not part of the Father, he eternally "proceeds from" the Father. Arius (280–336), a presbyter of a church in Alexandria, Egypt, emphasized that God the Father does not owe existence to anyone else. The Son, however, is a creature, a created being, and therefore did not proceed from the Father. This development (Arianism) endangered Christ's divinity (see page 33), and Arius' bishop, Athanasius (died 373), reiterated that the Son eternally proceeds from the Father. He declared Father and Son to be the same being (*homoousios*), over against the idea that they are of similar being (*homoiousios*).

The council of Nicea (325) cemented Athanasius's distinction as doctrine, declaring all else heretical. The inclusion of God's Spirit in the Trinitarian formula was therefore logical, given John's association between Word (Christ) and Spirit. The council of Chalcedon (451) finally decided that Jesus Christ is truly human and truly divine, his two natures inseparable and incapable of being transformed into each other.

ANTITRINITARIANS

Radical Italian scholars such as Fausto Sozzini (1539–1604) questioned the legitimacy of the doctrine of the Trinity. Persecuted by Roman Catholics and Protestants alike, sixteenth-century Italian Antitrinitarians sought refuge in Poland and Romania, where some remain today. Modern Antitrinitarian groups (Unitarians and Universalists) arose in England in the seventeenth century, from where Unitarian beliefs were subsequently carried to North America. Unitarianism today is a very broad term: some churches retain a distinctly Christian and biblical focus; others, while honoring Christian roots, are open to a wide range of spiritual paths.

THE TRINITY TODAY

Trinitarian scholarship abounds today. The noted German Reformed theologian Jürgen Moltmann (born 1926) sees in the three-in-one interrelation a paradigm for communal social interaction without exploitation. For John Zizioulas (born 1931), the premier Greek Orthodox theologian, the unbreakable relationship between the three persons of the Trinity means that their essential otherness as Father, Son, and Holy Spirit is no threat to their unity; on the contrary, the very precondition of their community, since community is by definition a unity of separate elements.

The German Lutheran theologian Wolfhart Pannenberg (born 1928) understands the three persons of the Trinity as both different ways of being of the one divine subject and independent centers of activity.

Some feminist theologians refer to the persons of the Trinity in gender-neutral terms such as Creator, Redeemer, and Sustainer (or Sanctifier). However, since, all three persons of the Trinity are involved in the external acts of creation, sustaining, and redemption, some theologians see this terminology as a new form of modalistic monarchianism (see main text). The general view is that God as Father and Son expresses a special relationship rather than an emphasis on gender. Current Trinitarian scholarship encompasses ethics, creation, and many other Christian affirmations.

THE NATURE OF HUMANKIND

Christianity has always affirmed God as sole creator. Biblical theology recognizes two creation narratives in Genesis: the "Priestly" narrative (Gen. 1.1–2.4a) and the "Yahwistic" or "Jahwistic" narrative (Gen. 2.4b–24), abbreviated respectively to "P" and "J" (see sidebar). The P narrative begins: "In the beginning when God created the heavens and the earth...." The subsequent seven-part narrative declares that all cosmic reality owes its existence to God's power. The idea is often promoted that God's creation culminates with humanity. However, the creation of humanity in P falls on the sixth day, and this narrative culminates with the establishment of the Sabbath: God rests from his creative labours on the seventh day and hallows it as the day of rest.

GOD AND HUMANS IN AN EVOLUTIONARY UNIVERSE

Since Charles Darwin published *The Origin of Species* (1859), a battle has ensued between those who recognize God as absolute creator and those who claim that evolution categorically excludes that possibility. Darwin himself was reticent on the subject, admitting only that more divine guidance yields less likelihood for natural selection.

Despite a few militant evolutionary atheists such as the British biologist Richard Dawkins (born 1941), there has been a recent cosmology-centered rapprochement between faith and science. This newfound harmony emphasizes the fine-tuning of universal constants without which life as we know it could not have evolved. If, as physicist Paul Davies claims, "we are truly meant to be here," what is humanity's task as God's representatives? Should we take evolution into our own hands? It can be argued that we have done so all along: in animal husbandry, in horticulture, and even in selecting marriage partners. But should we go so far as to change the genetic makeup of ourselves and other species? In the Christian view, as long as such actions alleviated hunger, suffering, and pain, they would fall under the task of being God's caretakers of creation; but once we do things for selfish purposes, or to achieve "heaven on earth," we overestimate our powers and abandon our obligation to God.

The quest for cosmic knowledge *is symbolized in this depiction of a medieval pilgrim lifting the veil of the sky to peer at the workings of the universe. A French wood engraving of 1888 in 16th-century style.*

The Creation of Adam and Original Sin. *Adam eats from the Tree of Knowledge (right), the first human act of sin (disobedience to God). Catalan, 12th century.*

The current text probably originated in the sixth or fifth century BCE, around the time of the Babylonian Exile of the Jews, but individual segments may reach far back into Israel's history. An argumentative defense of Israel's faith is noticeable throughout: Israel confesses its own God to be creator and Lord of the whole world.

The J narrative (Gen. 2.4b ff.) deals not with cosmic creation but with human beings only. While P places humanity at the end of the creative process, J makes humanity central, with everything created around it to make it feel at home. Genesis clearly illustrates that God acts without preconditions. Nothing can influence or resist God's creative power. Creation was neither necessity nor accident: it occurred because God wanted it so.

The same is true of humanity. No special day or food is reserved for it. Human life is a gift of God, participating in God's spirit and closely associated with the rest of creation. Humans have sexual differentiation, male and female each made for the other and from the same stuff. Women are not inferior to men: both bear God's image (Gen. 1.26, 1.27) which denotes a special function rather than a certain quality. Human beings are not replicas of God, but rather created to represent God in their actions. In this respect, humans are God's caretakers on earth (see pages 128–129).

SIN AND EVIL

In the Christian view, human beings as a whole and as individuals have accomplished the task to be God's administrators rather badly. While the creation narrative in Genesis 1 asserts that whatever God created was good, the story of the Fall in Genesis 3 tells us that the first humans, Adam and Eve, succumbed to sin by disobeying God's instruction not to eat from the Tree of Knowledge in the garden of Eden. Why they came to sin—for which they were permanently exiled from the paradise of Eden—remains unexplained.

WRITING THE CREATION

The creation narratives at the start of Genesis mainly derive from two earlier source texts, known respectively as "P" and "J." The first of these, the "Priestly" text (P), usually uses the Hebrew *el* for God and is ascribed to an anonymous priest of ca. 500BCE. P reveals a preference for exact numbers and wants to show that there is a hidden order to the world established by God. The "Yahwistic," or Jahwistic, text (J), so named because it usually uses the Hebrew *Yahweh* for God, is probably the oldest source text in the entire Bible, dating to ca. 950–750BCE and perhaps in parts even earlier. J depicts God with surprisingly human characteristics.

The Expulsion from Eden *by Michelangelo (1475–1564). According to Augustine, humans are born directly into sinfulness and alienation from God. We become children of God and gain access to God's kingdom through baptism; only then can we call upon God's aid in the struggle with sin. Sistine Chapel, Vatican.*

PELAGIUS V. AUGUSTINE

The Romano-British monk Pelagius (ca. 350–418) caused controversy in the early church by stressing personal accountability and the possibility of human sinlessness. According to Pelagius, the Fall did not organically damage humans, but sin spread further through imitation. Therefore one can always refrain from sin and seek to avoid it. St. Augustine vehemently challenged this view. He conceived of humans as communal beings caught in the quagmire of sin and incapable of extricating themselves from it. Sin, he said, is not an individual, avoidable act but an attitude that shapes our lives. Therefore even the virtues of the pagans, since they occur within the context of human striving in this world instead of being informed by God's will, are merely "splendid vices." Baptized persons still live within this world's sphere of influence, but they can overcome their sinful desires with God's help. Humans have no free will with regard to salvation, only with regard to earthly matters.

But the Fall is not an isolated event. From it radiates a whole series of sin stories: Genesis 4 reports the fratricide of Cain and Lamech's unrestrained threats of revenge, and Genesis 6–8 tells of the marital union of human women with disobedient angels (the source of the legend of the fall of the rebel angels: see box), the rampant wickedness of humankind, and the destructive waters of the flood. The primal history concludes with the account of the tower of Babel (Gen. 11).

Each of these accounts sheds light on the mysterious breach between humanity and God, as well as on God's response. The initially intended childlike trust of Eden has been changed to distrust toward God and thereby distrust of one human being toward another. Idealist philosophy claimed that these acts of disobedience (against God) were actually steps to human freedom. Yet the Swiss psychologist Carl Gustav Jung (1875–1961) reasoned that "the emancipation of the ego-consciousness was a Luciferian deed." Asserting their ego, humans immediately distanced themselves from God, like the rebel angel Lucifer, or Satan.

The human inclination to evil actions cannot be likened to a genetic defect, because then it could be eliminated. Neither is it only socially conditioned (as claimed by Jean-Jacques Rousseau, 1712–1778), because then a different environment could amend such inclination. Immanuel Kant (1724–1804) reasoned that in humanity the origin of evil cannot be explained. There is a natural inclination toward evil which humans willingly follow. Evil can also be an external phenomenon that is often inexplicable. Martin Luther (1483–1546) mused that such evil is part of the mystery of the divine; it cannot be explored, only adored. Therefore, we must not, or simply cannot, seek to discover why evil exists.

As a former Augustinian monk, Luther largely followed his great teacher, Augustine (354–430), the most influential Christian theologian to reflect on the power of sin and the extent of human corruption (see sidebar). While initially humans had the ability not to sin, they lost this faculty through disobedience in Eden and are therefore inherently sinful. Humans are corrupt entities whose main sin is pride. Sin is not just a deficiency of the good but a human inclination and desire to do bad things.

Pursuing Kant's notion of radical evil, the German Lutheran theologian Albrecht Ritschl (1922–1989) and the German-American Baptist theologian Walter Rauschenbusch (1861–1918) spoke of a kingdom of evil, stressing evil's corporate nature. However, the great Swiss Reformed theologian Karl Barth (1886–1968), called evil "nothingness", a void overcome by God's triumph of Grace: through God's gracious will shown to us in Jesus Christ, the "kingdom of nothingness" is already destroyed.

THE ORIGIN OF EVIL

In the Christian view, the world was created good but not perfect, hence there are natural evils or calamities such as earthquakes, floods, and so on. But this does not explain the intentional evil acts that humans inflict upon nature and each other. Since the origin of such evil cannot be located in God's good creation and thereby in God, Genesis 3 introduces a serpent without saying either why it became the tempter or whether it too was created by God.

A nonbiblical Jewish work, the First Book of Enoch, ascribes the origin of evil in the world to disobedient angels (1 Enoch 6–11). In the Second Book of Enoch, God says that an archangel arrogantly conceived "that he might become equal to my power. And I hurled him out from the height, together with his angels" (2 Enoch 29.4ff.). The New Testament (Jude 14–16, Rev. 12.9) also features this influential legend, with Satan as the chief of the rebel angels (see also page 202). But while these evil powers were believed to tempt humans to evil actions, humans must bear the responsibility for their own deeds.

The Fall of Satan, *by Guido Reni (1575–1642). Michael, the leader or "standard bearer" (Latin* signifer*) of the heavenly host, is frequently portrayed as the head of the forces that threw Satan and his rebel angels from heaven. Satan is also known as the "light bearer" (Latin* lucifer*), a name derived from Isaiah 14.12.*

FAITH, GRACE, AND SALVATION

OPPOSITE The Lamb of God, *a representation of Christ as the paschal (Passover) lamb, sacrificed to atone for human sinfulness. A brooch of glass and gold micro-mosaic set in enameled gold, made by the firm of Castellani, Rome, ca. 1860.*

Every religion witnesses to human sinfulness by pointing out humanity's existential alienation from its origin and by offering paths to salvation—ways to overcome this alienation—through human effort, or some kind of (divine) intervention, or a mixture of both. For Christians the biblical witness, which understands God as fundamentally gracious, places exclusive emphasis on God's unprovoked initiative. Yet God expects a corresponding response in the form of faith (a trusting allegiance to this God alone) and works (exercising a God-pleasing conduct). God forms covenants: with Noah (Gen. 9.11ff.), Abraham (Gen. 17.7), then all of Israel (Ex 25.21). Finally, God "will make a new covenant with the house of Israel and the house of Judah." (Jer. 31.31ff.). God

WHY GOD BECAME HUMAN

In answer to the question why Jesus' sacrificial death has salvific significance, Anselm of Canterbury (1033–1109) advanced a theory of "satisfaction" which, in the Christian view, still bears great merit: human sinfulness, as a deviation from God's ways, has violated God's honor and rule and therefore restitution (satisfaction) is necessary. God destines humanity to be saved; yet because of their alienation from God, from Adam onward, humans must be punished by exclusion from eternal bliss. Even if God simply chose to blot out human iniquities, humans could neither compensate for their former misconduct nor avoid their punishment, death and eternal damnation.

Jesus alone lived in accordance with God's ways, and so his conduct did not necessitate his death: he underwent it voluntarily. Since he was not only human but also the embodiment of God, his sacrificial death had universal significance. It provided atonement for the whole human race, enabling humans to enter eternal bliss.

The Man of Sorrows *by Jan Mostaert (ca. 1475–ca. 1555), showing Christ with instruments of his suffering. Deeply steeped in Latin juridical thinking, Anselm provided a cogent theological theory for why God had to come to humanity as a human being, and how salvation was possible through Christ's death.*

made covenants to offer divine protection, not because God needed a partner. The whole of Old Testament history can be interpreted as God pledging Israel his allegiance, with Israel's actions consistently marred by disloyalty, worshipping other gods while the prophets repeatedly admonish the people. Thus the need arises for a new covenant where God will write his law on the hearts of his people (Jer. 31.33). In the Christian view, the gospel is the final covenant between God and humankind—hence the terms Old and New Testament, which mean old and new covenant.

MEANS OF GRACE

Jesus repeats this new covenant theme at the Last Supper: "This is my blood of the covenant, which is poured out for many" (Mark 14.33). Through his death Jesus establishes a new covenant that goes beyond Israel to comprise all humanity. Paul's version of Christ's words instituting what became the rite of eucharist or Lord's Supper, "this cup is the new covenant in my blood" (1 Cor. 11.25), recalls Exodus 24.8: "Moses took the blood and dashed it on the people and said, 'See the blood of the covenant the LORD has made with you...'" Christ's death is seen here as analogous to the atoning death of the sacrificial animals. The Eucharist was understood as a means by which God offers forgiveness of sins and assurance of eternal life. Likewise, baptism was a means by which one was joined to Christ's death so that "we too might walk in newness of life" (Rom. 6.4). The promise of salvation was obtained through this rite of initiation. Mere performance of the sacraments (eucharist and baptism) is not efficacious; rather, salvation occurs by trusting the words connected with these actions. Augustine called the sacraments "visible words" and reasoned that as soon as the word is joined with the elements (bread, wine, or water), the sacrament is constituted.

Alongside these two basic means of grace, various Christian traditions understood other rites as sacraments. While Roman Catholicism uses the term "sacraments," (see pages 148–149), Orthodoxy prefers "mysteries" (see page 182–183). Baptists avoid speaking of sacraments altogether: they celebrate the Lord's Supper as a strict memorial meal and baptism as a confession of one's own faith. This does not mean a rejection of the means of grace, since for them God's word alone provides assurance of salvation.

In the late Middle Ages, popular piety often understood good works as a possible means of assuring salvation. But the Reformation claimed that human beings can contribute nothing to their own salvation: everything depends on God's initiative. Faith in God can never be without good works, as Luther asserted; but humans always fall short of God's expectations and hence their destiny is ultimately dependent on God's undeserved grace.

A GOD OF GRACE

A key development in Reformation thought was Luther's new understanding of Romans 1.17: "The righteousness of God is revealed through faith for faith." God does not simply *demand* that we be righteous; rather, God *makes* people righteous (grants grace) "through faith" (his faithfulness) in return "for faith" (our trust in God). If we cling to God's promises, as shown in Christ, we need fear nothing from God. Hence "grace alone," "faith/trust [in God] alone," and "Christ alone" became basic watchwords of the Lutheran Reformation.

ART AND ARCHITECTURE

TRANSFIGURED LIGHT: STAINED GLASS

Prisoners of Conscience *(detail) designed in 1980 by the noted French stained glass artist Gabriel Loire (1904–1996) for the Trinity Chapel of Salisbury cathedral, England. As a Christian art form stained glass is associated above all with the spirituality and ethereal qualities of the great medieval European cathedrals. As Loire's work illustrates, these qualities also lend themselves to modern examples of the art.*

Although stained glass is generally thought of as a uniquely Christian art form, fragments found in the excavations of Pompeii and Herculaneum in Italy indicate that colored glass was used in Roman times to decorate the windows of luxurious homes. Evidence for the early use of this fragile material is limited, but stained glass in church architecture is known to have existed at least by the tenth century. In the Gothic period it became an essential component of the tall windows of medieval churches in both nave and aisles, filling the space with the radiant colored light as a metaphor for the divine, bringing "to life" the images of the saints depicted in the glass.

The dedication of a window to a particular saint was often associated with a nearby altar containing their relics; the windows thus formed part of a "constellation of sanctity" which permeated the interior of many medieval churches. Pierre de Roissy, chancellor of Chartres cathedral ca. 1200, wrote that windows symbolize the holy scriptures, which repel evil and illuminate the soul.

The first documented example of widespread use of stained glass in a church was in the abbey church of St. Denis, France, reconstructed by its abbot, Suger, in the 1130s and 1140s. Suger described the window artists as being from many lands, suggesting that large stained glass windows already existed elsewhere. The design of the church suggests that to Abbot Suger the visibility of the glass was of paramount importance.

In the thirteenth century, as cathedrals reached much greater dimensions, new types of designs were evolved that made the tall windows high up near the vaults legible to the faithful below: thus small narrative scenes were replaced by the tall standing single figures of saints. In the last phase of the Gothic period, the height of clerestory windows (for example at Beauvais and Cologne) made a full program of stained glass too expensive, and it was limited to a decorated single band in the center of the window opening.

Stained glass windows were often the gifts of pious donors and thus frequently combine images of saints with smaller representations of the donor in prayer below, or a family coat of arms. As such, they vividly attest to the role of the private (usually noble) patron of large-scale ecclesiastical structures.

RIGHT **Moses and the Burning Bush** *by Master Gerlachus, whose self-portrait appears below. Originally from the cathedral of Münster, Germany, 1150–1160.*

OPPOSITE **Adam and Eve and the Fall**, *part of the Creation window in Chartres cathedral, France. Probably the most intact ensemble of medieval stained glass in existence, the early 13th-century windows of Chartres are among the glories of European art.*

DIVINE JUSTICE

Nothing seems more offensive to the Christian notion of a gracious God than divine judgment. Yet something soiled can only be made clean through a purifying process and not by mere declaration. Moreover, as Augustine asserted, humans have fallen short of God's expectation and deserve nothing but rejection. The Bible indicates that God can do with us whatever God wills (Jer. 18.1–4). This can easily lead to the conception of a capricious God, and the notion that God has predestined some to eternal damnation and others to eternal bliss, as claimed by Calvin (see page 159), goes even further toward a despotic and arbitrary picture. To counter such ideas, Karl Barth (see page 73), himself from the Calvinist tradition, declared that the only one condemned

THE FATE OF THE UNEVANGELIZED

In Mark's gospel, Jesus says: "The one who believes and is baptized will be saved; the one who does not believe will be condemned" (Mark 16.15). In keeping with these words, Evangelicals (conservative Christians) have long consigned to damnation all those not exposed to the gospel, which must therefore be proclaimed to all to assure their salvation. Today, though, some Evangelicals concede that even those who have not heard the gospel may be saved; otherwise the main criterion for salvation is human effectiveness in spreading the gospel.

The church never pronounced who could or could not be saved, but salvation was clearly possible only through Christ's God of grace. The Second Vatican Council (1962–1965) stated that salvation is possible for other believers in this God (such as Muslims) and those who seek God with a sincere heart. Without conceding a universalism, the church leaves those not reached by the gospel to God's loving grace. (See also page 83.)

The Psychostasis, *or weighing of souls, from an altar panel by the Master of Soriguerola. The balance, held by the archangel St. Michael, tips in favor of the righteous soul in prayer while Satan and a demon vainly try to tip it the other way. Catalan, late 13th century.*

(in our place) is Christ, whereas all others are elected to eternal bliss. Does this mean that the traditional notion of an ultimate judgment is obsolete?

Jesus and the New Testament witnesses are convinced of a twofold outcome, expressed in the image of the wide gate to destruction and the narrow gate, found by few, to life (Matt. 7.13–14). On the other hand, the New Testament also contains many indications that God "desires everyone to be saved and to come to the knowledge of the truth" (1 Tim. 2.4).

SALVATION OR PUNISHMENT?

Christians are confronted with the paradox that God's love wants all to be saved, while God's justice requires all the disobedient to be punished. Any attempt to solve this paradox by asserting that God threatens us with eternal punishment in order to save us, fails to consider that divine judgment is not a transition into the universal love of God. It is the disclosure and finalization of our life attitude. Our continuous alienation from God will then become apparent and irreversible. One is measured not by a universal standard but by one's unique possibilities: "For everyone to whom much has been given, much will be required" (Luke 12.48). We are called to measure up to our own potential and not to some ambiguous standard.

In the Christian view, since Christ the Savior is also our judge, even in all its seriousness this judgment has a comforting aspect. Through being accepted as children of God in baptism, Christians are a new creation, and therefore the discrepancy in their lives between what was and what should have been will be overcome by their bond in Christ. Judgment for them will result in eternal life. Therefore the first Christian community could confidently utter "Amen. Come, Lord Jesus!" (Rev. 22.20).

The Last Judgment, *part of a triptych by Rogier van der Weyden (ca. 1399–1464). Christ rises above the Virgin and the Baptist as the dead rise from their graves. An angel leads the saved to paradise, while the damned head in terror for hell.*

THE NEW WORLD: DEATH AND THE AFTERLIFE

In many Christian hymns the idea is expressed that though the body dies and decays, the immortal soul will rise to God. This notion is understandable given the Hellenistic context of early Christianity. Greek philosophers such as Plato and Aristotle regarded the body as inferior to the soul: there was a pre-existent immortal soul that was then embodied into a human being. The body was considered the prison of the soul, liberated by death and eventually united with its source of origin, the divine.

The New Testament also distinguishes between body and soul, and even between body, soul, and spirit. But the Bible makes it clear that both body and soul are created by God and that there is no inborn immortality. As emphasized by the premier Roman Catholic theologian of the twentieth century, Karl Rahner (1904–1984), there is no void after death, but also no continuation through death. Hope beyond death cannot be based on an immortal soul but on God's grace. This is also evident from the Old Testament where God breathes the breath of life into the first human, who "became a living being" (Gen. 2.7). This "breath of life" is God's gift which can be weakened by sickness and is withdrawn again at the end of life.

The Ascent of Elijah. *The prophet Elijah (Elias) is carried to heaven in a chariot of fire (2 Kings 2.9–15); he is shown on the point of dropping his mantle for his successor, Elisha. The Old Testament account became important to Christians as an illustration of the notion of resurrection. A 13th-century fresco in Anagni cathedral, Italy.*

Only a few persons in the Old Testament, such as Enoch (Gen. 5.24) and Elijah (2 Kings 2.11), are immediately transferred from this life into God's presence. All others would go to Sheol (Hebrew for netherworld), which was initially considered a shadowy abode for the dead where they would forever vegetate (Job 7.9–10). After the Babylonian Exile, Sheol came to be viewed as a temporary dwellingplace until the dead were resurrected (Isa. 26.19). In the New Testament we find that either all people will enter Hades (the Greek term for Sheol) upon their death (Luke 16.23) with the righteous enjoying happiness and the rest facing torment, or that the righteous are immediately transferred to heaven or paradise (Luke 23.43), while the rest face the anguish of Hades or Gehenna (as at Mark 9.43–48).

In Jesus' time the conservative Sadducees still denied that there was a resurrection from the dead (Matt. 22.23): they believed that at death there was only a shadowy existence in the netherworld. However, according to the Jewish historian Josephus (37/38–ca. 100), the Pharisees, evidently influenced by Hellenistic thinking, taught that souls are immortal. The incompatibility of the Greek idea of the immortality of the soul and the Christian belief in the resurrection is shown by Paul's missionary activity. When Paul preached for the first time in Athens, laughter erupted when he spoke of the resurrection (Acts 17.32).

THE COMING KINGDOM

Jesus proclaimed: "The time is fulfilled, and the kingdom of God has come near; repent, and believe in the kingdom" (Mark 1.14). In reciting the Lord's Prayer, Christians still pray, "your kingdom come." The realization of this universal rule of God lies in the future, while this future dimension is supposed to determine human activities in the present. The date of the coming of the kingdom cannot be calculated in advance; in the Christian view, therefore, one must always be prepared (see also pages 20–21).

CHRIST'S DESCENT INTO HELL

The Christian confession that Christ "descended into hell," or as it is now more adequately translated, "went to the dead," between his death and resurrection, was first mentioned ca. 370 in a version of the Apostles' Creed. It is nowhere explicitly stated in the New Testament, although several passages presuppose it or at least imply it (such as Matt. 12.40 and Rev. 1.18). In places this descent is understood as a proclamation to some or all who were in the realm of the dead (1 Peter 3.19). Jesus' victorious entry into this realm and liberation of the Old Testament patriarchs from it is vividly expressed by Martin Luther.

While the early church denied that anyone outside the church could be saved, many early theologians understood the descent as a confrontation with the gospel even after death. Such deductions sprang from both the encounter with Jesus' God of grace and from an existential grieving for forebears, including the patriarchs and prophets, who lived before the advent of Christ and the church.

The Descent into Hell. *The account of the descent in the apocryphal* Gospel of Nicodemus, *in which Jesus destroys the gates of Hades, frees the dead from their shackles, and binds Satan, influenced iconography especially in the Orthodox Church. Here, Christ leads Adam by the hand. Russian, Novgorod School, ca. 1275.*

MILLENNIALISM

Revelation 20.1–15 says that the martyrs will undergo a first resurrection and reign with Christ for a thousand years (Latin *millennium*). When Christianity was given official sanction in 313, many theologians thought this would usher in the final millennium; similar hopes emerged ca. 1000. Today the idea of a millennium is important to some Baptist and Pentecostal groups, as is "rapture," the notion that Christians, living and dead, will be taken up to meet Christ when he returns, thereby escaping the trials that precede the ushering in of the kingdom (1 Thess. 4.17). The belief in rapture gained prominence with the Plymouth Brethren of John Nelson Darby (1800–1882) and the Scofield Reference Bible (US, 1909), and is held by many Evangelical Christians.

Even ca. 150 the Christian apologist Justin Martyr mentions people "who say that there is no resurrection of the dead, and that their souls, when they die, are taken to heaven."

RESURRECTION AND REDEMPTION

The Christian notion of resurrection is neither based on the idea of an immortal soul nor on the idea of a resurrection of one's former body. As Paul shows especially in his letters to a Greek congregation in Corinth, this notion is inseparable from the certitude of Christ's resurrection. "If Christ has not been raised, then our proclamation has been in vain, and your faith has been in vain" (1 Cor. 15.14). Paul argues here that since Jesus' self-sacrifice has redemptive qualities, his resurrection to new life has redemptive qualities, too. Resurrection does not mean resuscitation to former existence but passing beyond death to new life. In Christianity there is no Hellenistic disembodied soul or Gnostic eternal divine spark but a new immortal being through a creative act of God. Therefore the Christian creed confesses "the resurrection of the body" not as the reassembling of former body parts but as a resurrection to a new bodily form of life. Therefore the Christian hymnody concerning death and eternal life always portrays an upbeat sentiment.

Nevertheless Martin Luther cautioned: "As little as children know in their mother's womb about their birth, so little do we know about life everlasting." Yet the narratives of the resurrected Christ show him as a person no longer restricted by space and time, or the need for food (compare Luke 24.31–36; John 21.13). Though still being recognizable, he portrayed a totally new form of life. Paul then calls Christ "the first fruits of those who have died" (1 Cor. 15.20). The images in Revelation 21 express the hope for union with God, abolition of anguish and sorrow, and permanent beauty and perfection as the goal of life everlasting. Human yearning for self-transcendence, elimination of death, and progress toward perfection will find its fulfillment.

OPPOSITE The Resurrection, Cookham, *by Stanley Spencer (1891–1959). Painted in 1924–1927, Spencer's view of the day of the general resurrection of the dead transforms the quiet rural churchyard of his hometown in Berkshire, England, into the setting for extraordinary events. Christ is in the church porch, cradling three babies, with God the Father behind. At top left, risen souls embark for heaven in the pleasure steamers that then plied the nearby River Thames.*

THE LAST JUDGMENT

This final destiny is usually connected with the Last Judgment at the end of time when Christ will return in glory to establish his kingdom. "When the Son of Man [Christ] comes in his glory, and all the angels with him, then he will sit on the throne of his glory" (Matt. 25.31) and separate the just from the unjust "as a shepherd separates the sheep from the goats" (Matt. 25.32). While such a judgment and attendant trials is firmly embedded in the Christian tradition, the church also includes in its creed the assurance that Christ descended into hell (see box on page 81), which holds out the offer of salvation. Moreover, the church has prayed throughout the centuries for the salvation of all people.

NEAR-DEATH EXPERIENCES

As the traditional Christian belief in resurrection has been losing credibility in our secular culture, so-called near-death experiences have gained renewed attention as a means of ascertaining whether there is life after death. When persons presumed dead are resuscitated, they often recount strikingly similar experiences: floating out of their physical bodies, coupled with a great sense of peace and wholeness, and looking down on their physical selves from a height. There is often an awareness of another person who helps them to another plane of existence, where they are greeted by loved ones who had died before them or by a significant religious figure in their life. Such near-death experiences were reported in antiquity (Plato) and throughout history. There are also near-death accounts from people who have come very close to being killed (for example, in a car accident) but escaped without injury.

These experiences may be the result of terminal physiological events or extreme shock. It has been suggested that one experience that is commonly reported in near-death experiences—floating upward through a dark tunnel, with a most beautiful, brilliant light at the far end—may in fact simply be the physiological effect of the brain beginning to "shut down" as death approaches.

It is also possible that, in unusual situations of extreme stress, the spirit or psyche could temporarily extend itself beyond the body with which it is usually coextensive. However, they are no proofs that there is something beyond this life.

Tunnel of light. *The experience of moving through a tunnel toward a bright light has often been reported by those who have undergone near-death experiences. Some have described seeing deceased loved ones at the end of the tunnel, apparently beckoning them forward.*

ART AND ARCHITECTURE

THE ART OF MOSAICS

The Kiss of Judas, *a detail of the Byzantine-influenced mosaics in St. Mark's basilica, Venice, 12th century. They are among the finest surviving medieval Byzantine mosaics outside Constantinople (Istanbul).*

Mosaic decoration was widely used in the ancient Greek and Roman world and by the mid-fourth and fifth centuries it had been adopted in a Christian religious context. Mosaics were used in early Christian and Byzantine monuments to decorate nave walls, vaults, and apses, as well as for pavements and tombs, as can still be seen at Aquileia or in the pavement tombs in North Africa, many of which are preserved in the Bardo museum of Tunis.

In more luxurious decorative programs, especially in Christian churches, the individual pieces of mosaic, or *tesserae*, were made of glass set into plaster. The glass often included gold leaf, creating a glistening and flickering wall surface that reflects light, an ideal expression of the dematerialized spirituality fundamental to early Christian decorative schemes. Tomb and pavement mosaics, on the other hand, were usually made of small stones or terracotta, more durable and less expensive materials.

A number of early mosaics survive from the apses of Roman churches, attesting to the popularity of this medium and its importance for the expression of key doctrinal ideas. Early Christian mosaics also witness to the important role of private donors, who are commemorated in pavement mosaics or tomb markers in floors or walls. Catacombs in Naples preserve a few fifth-century arcosolia (arched burial niches) with mosaic portraits.

The art of mosaic decoration reached a high level of refinement in the Byzantine empire during the reign of Justinian (527–565), and in subsequent centuries this highly-developed technique was reintroduced to the West by Byzantine artists in Montecassino, in Norman Sicily, and Venice. It also spread to the south and to the east: there is evidence of Byzantine mosaicists working in the monastery church of St. Catherine in the Sinai in the sixth century and (for Muslim patrons) at the Dome of the Rock in Jerusalem and the Great Mosque of Damascus in the seventh and eighth centuries.

Early medieval churches in Rome also used mosaic, especially those built during the Carolingian renewal, such as Santa Prassede. Another renewal of the technique took place in the late twelfth century with the work of Pietro Cavallini at Santa Maria in Trastevere.

RIGHT **The Transfiguration**, *in the apse of the basilica of Sant' Apollinare in Classe, Ravenna, Italy, built in the reign of the emperor Justinian I (527–565), a high point of Byzantine mosaic art. At the top Moses and Elijah flank the Cross, representing Christ. Below stands the church's dedicatee, St. Apollinaris, among lambs representing the faithful.*

OPPOSITE **The Annunciation**, *from a cycle of mosaics depicting the life of the Virgin Mary by Jacopo Torriti (ca. 1295) in the apse of the papal basilica of Santa Maria Maggiore (St. Mary Major), Rome.*

2 THE CHRISTIAN LIFE

OPPOSITE Almsgiving. *A rich merchant gives drink to beggars, including a friar. Depictions of the "seven corporal works of mercy" (feeding the hungry, giving drink to the thirsty, sheltering the pilgrim, clothing the naked, visiting the sick, visiting the prisoner, burying the dead) were popular in the late Middle Ages as exemplars of Christian behavior (see also page 102). Stained glass panel from Coventry, England, ca. 1430–1440.*

From the beginning of the Christian movement, faith, hope, and love have been extolled as the essential principles of the Christian life. The thirteenth chapter of Paul's first letter to the church at Corinth (written ca. 53–55) addresses the practice of these virtues, and the principal place of love in governing a Christian's actions in the church and in the wider world as an appropriate and necessary response to the paradigm of divine love. The basic triad of faith, hope, and love are also a subtext of the exemplary prayer that Jesus gives to his disciples, known as the Lord's Prayer (see sidebar), which has been central to Christian life and worship in most ecclesiastical traditions worldwide.

The opening phrase of the Lord's Prayer comments on the nature of God and identifies the community of believers ("our") as the recipient of that revelation. The faith finds its source and substance in the revelatory writings of the Old and New Testaments

AUGUSTINE ON FAITH, HOPE, LOVE

When, sometime around the year 421, a certain Laurentius asked Bishop Augustine of Hippo (354–430) for an *enchiridion* (handbook) summarizing the fundamental teachings of Christian belief and life, the theologian-pastor responded with a brief treatise on faith, hope, and love. In it he interpreted the two texts that most persons would have learned prior to their baptism as Christians: the Apostles' Creed (for "faith") and the Lord's Prayer (for "hope"), for through these "faith believes, hope and love pray." Augustine ends the work with an examination of the objects of love, and concludes that the true Christian vocation is one of love since "God is love." Nevertheless, the three virtues are interdependent, says Augustine, for "there is no love without hope, no hope without love, and neither love nor hope without faith."

Saint Augustine of Hippo *by Francesco del Rossi (alias Il Cecchino or Il Salviati, 1510–1563) or Giovanni Battista Zelotti (1526–1578). A fresco in the old library of Santa Maria delle Carcere abbey, near Padua, Italy.*

(and also, for some, the Apocrypha; see page 203). Christian life is nurtured by regular exposure to the scriptures in private and in the corporate assembly by hearing the texts read aloud; by singing them directly or in paraphrase; by reading, studying, and interpreting them; and by praying the texts and meditating upon them.

Summaries of the faith drawn from scripture and theological debates within the church are found in the ecumenical creeds: the Apostles' creed (see page 32), and the theologically denser Nicene Creed (with a slight but significant variation between Western and Eastern Christianity; see pages 186–187). In many churches, one of these two creeds is repeated as part of the Sunday liturgy. These and other affirmations teach the central tenets of the faith and encourage their internalization. Over the centuries, people have drawn upon scripture and the creeds to guide their own perceptions of God's encounters with humanity, which then is attested by their words and actions. These testimonies supply a repository of Christian tradition that shapes and stirs the faith of others.

HOPE AND FORGIVENESS

The several expressions of Christian hope contained in the Lord's Prayer have been applied to Christian life differently across various Christian communities. "Your kingdom come" anticipates the future reign of God, intrinsically connected with an expectation of the resurrection of the faithful dead. At one extreme, communities may separate themselves entirely from worldly engagement; at the other, they fully attend to the world through prayer and social ministries, and may understand themselves to be heralds or even agents of God's reign. Christians trust in God's grace and mercy not only for the future, but also in the present ("Your will be done...but rescue us from evil"). Christian practices vary depending upon how conformity to God's will and reliance upon God's providence are understood.

Christians understand that they are to forgive others in imitation of the forgiving love of God and out of love for God. Acknowledgment of misdeeds and sin, along with penitence, are expected to lead to reconciliation with God and neighbor. The sharing of signs of peace is intended as a concrete indication of reconciliation. The ethic of forgiving, selfless love is borne out by such practices as praying for enemies and strangers as well as friends, and by charitable gestures such as the collecting of alms for the poor and needy.

THE LORD'S PRAYER

The ecumenical version of the Lord's Prayer (Our Father) devised in 1988 is widely used in English-speaking churches:

Our Father in heaven,
hallowed be your name,
your kingdom come,
your will be done,
on earth as in heaven.
Give us today our daily bread.
Forgive us our sins
as we forgive those who sin against us.
Save us from the time of trial
and deliver us from evil.
{To this may be added:
For the kingdom, the power,
and the glory are yours
now and for ever. Amen.**]**

WORSHIP

Whenever Christian communities seek to reform or revitalize themselves and their worship, they turn first to the authoritative scriptures. The Bible does not prescribe any specific form or protocols for worship, though the sequence of events described during Isaiah's vision in the temple (Isa. 6.1–8) and by the post-resurrection encounter between Jesus and two disciples (Luke 24.13–35) have sometimes been viewed as models. However, the scriptures do offer suggestions about what befits the divine recipient of worship and what may edify and sanctify the faithful. The direct dependency upon scriptural sources for organizing worship varies among (and sometimes within) ecclesiastical traditions, with some groups limiting themselves only to things substantiated in the Bible. This priority given to scripture is exhibited within every community's worship by the reading, or reading and singing, of portions of the sacred text.

King David Playing the Harp, *with scribes and musicians, from the Vespasian Psalter of 725–750, perhaps produced in Canterbury, England. Psalters—manuscripts of the Book of Psalms—were second in popularity only to books of the gospels in the Middle Ages. The psalms are traditionally ascribed to David, but many scholars believe them to be by several authors.*

The Psalms declare that human beings are to "worship and bow down" before their Maker and to "make a joyful noise to the rock of their salvation" (Psalm 95). In the Christian community, worship is given to the triune God (see pages 68–69), who was and is revealed to humanity in various ways, but principally through Jesus Christ, the Son and second Person of the Godhead. Christ himself is included in worship, for "at the name of Jesus every knee should bow ... and every tongue confess that Jesus Christ is Lord, to the glory of God the Father" (Phil. 2.10–11). Worship is understood to be animated through the agency of the Holy Spirit, the third Person of the Trinity, who is able to transform feeble human speech into fitting prayers (Rom. 8.26). Christian worship is thus fully trinitarian, for worship is given to and enabled by the Father, Son, and Holy Spirit, in whose name the Christian is created through baptism (Matt. 28.19).

THE PRAISE OF GOD

A consistent refrain throughout the Bible is that God is worthy of praise, so in continuity with the worship of the ancients, praise and adoration is offered for God's mighty deeds known in the past, realized in the present, and anticipated in the future. Praise is rendered by the actions that accompany the reading of the sacred text itself, which may include singing by an individual, the congregation, or a choir. Christians have always glorified God through song, as the New Testament shows (see sidebar on page 91).

Other broad biblical emphases translate into the content of Christian worship. God's people are to "persevere in prayer" (Rom. 12.12), and put all requests before God (Phil. 4.6). Supplication and intercession are to be made for both the mighty and the lowly (1 Tim. 2.1–2), with prayerful care for others to issue forth also in concrete actions (Acts 2.44–47;

WORDS FOR WORSHIP

Several terms used to speak of Christian worship convey its intentions. "Worship" (Old English *weorthscipe*, "dignity, honor"), means to ascribe worth or honor to something. "Service," from Latin *servus* (servant), refers to something done for others, and in the case of worship may mean simultaneously what God does for humans and what humans do for God. An "office" (Latin *officium*), as in "divine office," is a duty or service. In ancient Greece "liturgy" (*leitourgia*) originally meant a beneficial public (*leitos*) work (*ourgia*). Liturgy thus may best be seen as work done by people for the sake of others; liturgy occurs when all worshippers are able to offer their work of worship for the honor of God and benefit of God's world. "Rite" and "ritual" are from Latin *ritus*, meaning a form, pattern or manner of religious worship.

THE PURPOSE OF WORSHIP

A common thread running through the various terms used in reference to Christian worship (see sidebar) is the understanding of worship as both "duty" and "work." Not only has the church taught the necessity of offering God worship, it has also believed that human beings were created for the purpose of such worship. In summing up this longstanding conviction, the first of more than one hundred questions and answers in the *Westminster Shorter Catechism*, which was produced in 1647 by English and Scottish Presbyterians, declares that humanity's chief and highest end is "to glorify God and to enjoy him forever."

This notion of "enjoyment" signals the equally firm belief that God blesses humanity in worship. The fourteenth-century Byzantine theologian Nicholas Cabasilas, author of *A Commentary on the Divine Liturgy*, taught that through worship, the faithful are forgiven their sins and are then made fit to receive and persevere in holiness—a teaching not unlike that found among some Protestant Evangelicals in the twenty-first century. Thus the purpose of worship, as pithily stated in 1903 in *motu proprio Tra le sollecitudini* by Pope Pius X, is both the glorification of God and the sanctification of the faithful.

Heb. 13.16). The perpetual human need for forgiveness from God and from neighbor, and the requisite demonstration of repentance, find voice in prayers of confession that recognize both personal sin and the sin of the community as a whole, and resolution in words of pardon (1 John 1.9). A response to God's mercy and forgiveness is thanksgiving (2 Thess. 5.18), which is expressed in Christian worship through word, song, and prayer, and notably the prayer of thanksgiving (*eucharistia*) that accompanies the celebration of the Lord's Supper (Matt. 26.26–30; Mark 14.22-26; Luke 22.14–23; 1 Cor. 11.23–26).

TRADITIONS OF WORSHIP

There has never been a single approach to or practice of Christian worship, even from the beginning (Acts 11.1–18). Worship enacts or embodies the core scriptural and credal foundations of the Christian faith that are shared across ecclesiastical families, but it also expresses in ritual form the distinctive beliefs and values held by those families. Churches may be grouped by liturgical commonalities, though in some cases these groupings are not mutually exclusive. Among churches originating in the East are the liturgical traditions derived from ancient Alexandria (Coptic and Ethiopian), East Syria (such as Assyrian and Mar Thoma), and West Syria, which has two distinct but related lines (one represented by, for example, the Syrian Orthodox and Armenians; and the other by "Byzantine rite" churches such as the Greek and Russian Orthodox and Ukrainian Catholic). Historically there were also distinct Catholic liturgical groupings

SONGS OF GLORY: CHARLES WESLEY

Charles Wesley (1707–1788), Anglican priest and a leader of the Methodist movement in England, was a prolific writer of hymn texts at a time when hymns were not permitted during the Church of England's liturgies, though they were allowed before and after services. Hymns for worship had been popularized in England by the Baptist preacher Joseph Stennett and by the Congregationalist Isaac Watts, but Anglicans preferred God's "pure" word in metrical psalms and biblical canticles to the scriptural paraphrases or spiritual meditations found in songs of "human" composition. The Methodists used Wesley's hymns during preaching and prayer services, for private devotion, for teaching, and for disseminating their evangelical theology.

Herald Angel. *Wesley often wove together scriptural threads, as in two 1739 hymns,* Christ the Lord is risen today *and* Hark! The herald angels sing. *The original first two lines were "Hark how all the welkin rings, 'Glory to the King of kings'" (welkin being a reference to the vault of heaven), but were altered by George Whitefield to the now familiar 'Hark! the herald angels sing, "Glory to the newborn King." Limewood, Austria, 18th century.*

Harlem Boys Choir *sings during a service at the Convent Avenue Baptist Church, Manhattan, to mark Martin Luther King Day, January 16, 2006. Choral singing has played a role in Christian worship since its beginnings. The use of a specially trained body of singers is said to have arisen around the fourth century, the most noted* schola cantorum *("school of singers") being that traditionally established by Pope Gregory the Great in Rome. This trained the choirs used for most papal functions in the Middle Ages and as an institution was widely imitated throughout the Western church.*

in the West, such as the Roman, Ambrosian (Milanese), Mozarabic, Gallican, and Celtic forms, but today all but the Roman—which itself has gone through a series of reforms—and the Milanese have virtually disappeared from regular use.

Protestant churches are extremely diverse in their worship practices and so quite difficult to group, but it is possible to categorize such families as the Lutheran, Reformed, Anglican, Anabaptist, Methodist, and Pentecostal on the basis of their historic ties and their original theological and liturgical commitments. However, the worship of certain Protestants today—even within some of these families—may depend less upon their historic and identifying patterns of worship and more upon current stylistic preferences, thus creating links across denominations—and in effect new groupings—based on worship styles.

Practices are not always uniform within an ecclesiastical or denominational tradition. Thus among Orthodox churches, while the order and content of the worship used continues to be quite similar, indicators of national and ethnic identity (such as language, ceremonial, clothing) add limited variety. Ongoing expansion of Orthodox Christianity into new areas necessitated certain adaptations, in particular the replacement of the predominant Greek and Slavic languages by native tongues. New conventions might be introduced, such as greater involvement of the people in democratic countries, or certain tribal customs in places such as Africa. Even within a single Protestant denomination there may be significant variety. For example, on a given Sunday, worship in the Church of Sweden (Lutheran) may take the form of a high mass in a grand cathedral; an informal service in a plain room, with singing accompanied by guitars, drums, and synthesizer; and a service held in reindeer-skin tents in the language of the Sami people.

WORSHIP IN SONG

The New Testament identifies "psalms, hymns, and spiritual songs" for liturgical and devotional singing (Eph. 5.18–20; Col. 3.16–17). Embedded within the New Testament are canticles (songs), such as those of Mary (Luke 1.47–55), Zechariah (Luke 1.68–79), and Simeon (Luke 2.29–32), which may have emerged out of apostolic worship (1 Cor. 14.26) and have been in continuous liturgical use since. Other scriptural texts may have begun as liturgical songs or be fragments from a longer song, for example, the "Christ hymn" of Philippians 2.5–11 and the prologue of John's gospel (John 1.1–5).

RITES AND SERVICES

The communion bread and wine. *A service with, as its principal elements, the exposition of scripture and the celebration of the Lord's Supper or Eucharist may be identified as "Word and Sacrament" or "Word and Table" (terms used especially by certain Protestants); "Divine Liturgy" (Orthodox); or "Mass" (Catholics, certain Anglicans, and Lutherans).*

Christians inherited from Judaism the obligation of keeping a principal day of worship in the course of each week (Exod. 20.8-11; Deut. 5.15). Some Christians continued to honor the Jewish Sabbath on the seventh day of the week (Saturday) by attending Jewish services or by holding Christian services either during the day or in the evening. Others preferred Christian worship on the first day of the week (Sunday; Acts 20.7–12), since this day was associated with Jesus' resurrection and appearance to his disciples, and also with the sending of the Holy Spirit. Other terms used for the day of worship connect with these events: the "Lord's Day" (Rev. 1.10), the "day of resurrection," and the "eighth day" (the day after the seventh day) that was a sign of a new creation, a new Sabbath (St. Basil, *On the Holy Spirit*, 66). The virtually universal Christian practice since the early centuries has been Sunday worship, though in modern times a few

denominations (such as Seventh-Day Adventists) consider Saturday worship biblically mandated.

Sunday worship in every place and time has usually contained the basic components found in the practices of the early church. The community assembles in a common location: the action of "coming together" is an important aspect of Christian life. The sacred writings are read and expounded. While preference is given to the "good news" of the New Testament, readings from the Old Testament, and for some also the Apocrypha, often have a place within the course of the week's worship if not on Sunday. The Psalms enjoy frequent use, and may be sung, chanted, or spoken by one or more individuals. Prayers of various kinds are offered.

The Lord's Supper or Eucharist is observed daily, weekly, bi-weekly, monthly, or less frequently. At the conclusion of the service, all are dismissed to ministries of discipleship. Various other components may be added to this common core by particular church traditions.

A Sunday service with the exposition of scripture as the primary element is often called a "Service of the Word" or a "Preaching Service." Other types of typically Protestant services may have a sermon, or a sermon and the Lord's Supper, but today are distinguished by their more informal style and the considerable use of popular music accompanied by an array of musical instruments (for example, "Prayer and Praise," "Praise and Worship," and "Contemporary"). "Emerging worship" is intentionally ecumenical and multicultural, and attentive to both historic traditions and current contexts.

The preaching of scripture *is central to Protestant worship, as shown by this painting of a Huguenot temple (church) in Lyons, France, in which the pulpit dominates the relatively simple interior. French, ca. 1600.*

JUSTIN ON WORSHIP

In his defense of Christianity (ca. 150), Justin Martyr gives an early account of worship in Rome. On Sunday, Christians gathered to hear readings from both testaments. Then the assembly president (bishop) exhorted and admonished the congregation, after which all stood to pray. Bread, wine, and water for the Eucharist were presented to the president, who prayed and offered thanks, to which the people assented with "Amen." All present shared the communion meal, and deacons took it to those unwillingly absent. Finally, a collection of money and goods was taken for the needy.

DAILY SERVICES

Daily worship for a congregation may repeat the Sunday type or use a different form or style. Weekday gatherings are rooted in Jewish Temple sacrifice and synagogue worship and in the Jewish custom of twice- or thrice-daily personal prayer (for example Dan. 6.10). Perhaps as early as the late first century, Christians were engaging in non-eucharistic daily prayer following the scriptural instruction to pray without ceasing (1 Thess. 5.17). By the fourth century, the local church met morning and evening for communal services of praise (from the Psalms) and prayerful intercession. A thanksgiving for light might begin the evening service, which in the East could include the hymn *Phos hilaron* ("Gladdening light").

In addition to the corporate gathering, the devout were expected to pray at other times of the day and night, both privately and in their families. Various models for corporate daily worship developed in the East and West, and today corporate daily prayer may be found in Orthodox, Catholic, and Protestant churches.

RITES OF INITIATION

Ministry is understood as the vocation of all Christians (2 Cor. 5.18, Eph. 4.12), a concept indicated by some communities with the phrase "the priesthood of all believers." Not all carry out that ministry with the same tasks; yet each undertaking is recognized as good for the whole (1 Cor. 12.4–31). Some churches have marked the assignment or choice of certain of these duties with specific rituals. Interpretations of these responsibilities, and of the function of the ritual in appointing or authorizing these roles, vary across the churches.

Christian initiation enters a person into the general ministry of all believers, whether that individual is able to speak for himself or not—and the churches disagree on the appropriate age and intellectual ability of candidates. The process usually begins with some form of preparatory experience, or catechumenate. There may be an organized catechumenate in which a person is informed about, and formed in, the Christian life—the so-called *Apostolic Tradition* (ca. third century?) reports a three-year catechumenal phase—or a more informal period consisting of Bible study alongside discussion about basic Christian beliefs, and regular private and public worship. Training may be expected of parents who intend to initiate their children. Or a person who has already come to believe in Jesus Christ as savior will be brought to the point of professing that faith in the presence of the believing community.

Confirmation, *a relief panel from the bell tower of Florence cathedral, Italy, by Alberto Arnoldi, ca. 1340. Many churches have a rite called confirmation that is sometimes held to be a sacrament (for example, by Catholics, Orthodox, and some Anglicans) and sometimes not (as by most Protestant denominations).*

BAPTISM

When ready, candidates proceed to baptism. There are many variations in practice, but also commonalities in the majority of churches. Persons are asked if they will reject their old way of life in favor of a new life with Christ. In some churches, a candidate turns to the west to renounce evil and the devil, and then turns around to the east to profess faith in the triune God by the use of an ancient and traditional creed or a similar formulation. A prayer calling upon the renewing power of the Holy Spirit may occur at this point. Water baptism follows, in imitation of Jesus and in accordance with Matthew 28.16–20 and the practice recorded in Acts. Different amounts of water are used depending upon the preference for sprinkling, pouring, immersion, or submersion. Washing indicates cleansing of sin and, as dramatized by submersion and reemergence, dying and rising with Christ (Rom. 6.4).

After application of water or plunging, either once or thrice, the newly baptized person is pronounced a son or daughter of God, and may receive a white garment as a sign of being clothed with Christ (Gal. 3.27) or a white candle symbolizing illumination by him (Eph. 5.14; Matt. 5.14), or both. The person may also be declared a member of the church. There are differing views in the churches regarding the relationship between the baptism of infants and church membership, and some communities will expect public profession of faith (in some churches with a rite called "confirmation") when the child comes of age.

The new Christians then typically participate with the rest of the local congregation in the Eucharist. Along with the entire body, they are expected to give praise to God in worship, to witness by their words and actions to the grace of God in Christ, and to engage in ministries of justice and peace. To aid and extend their ministries, other persons are entrusted with specialized gifts and with leadership.

Rites of ordination are given for particular roles of authority and leadership in the Christian community: bishops, presbyters (also called priests, pastors, or ministers), deacons, and in some places and times, subdeacons, lectors, deaconesses, and widows. Not all of these offices are found in every ecclesiastical tradition, nor are they defined in the same way. Thus, ordination rites vary considerably, but in general they invoke divine

BIRTH RITES

Numerous special rites relate to childbearing. Among the oldest is the purification of women after childbirth, a Jewish custom (Lev. 12.2–8) continued by Christian women in imitation of the mother of Jesus (Luke 2.22–39). Called for a time the "churching of women," maternal purification practices existed in the East and West, and continue in parts of the church today. More recent rites or special sets of prayers have addressed infertility, prenatal and neonatal death, survival of childbirth, the viability of the child, and adoption.

MARRIAGE RITES

The earliest evidence indicates that Christian weddings took place in a domestic setting, often the bride's home, and that the priest might attend as an invited guest. The wedding was viewed as a civil affair, but the priest might give the church's blessing to the couple. Eventually the priest took a more prominent role in the proceedings, which in the East moved inside the church ca. the eighth century and in the West to the church porch by ca. 1100. Only at the time of the Reformation did weddings in the West move into the church, though some Protestants rejected this, seeing marriage as purely a civil act.

In addition to ecclesiastical and civil components, Christian marriage rites have always carried considerable local flavor. The oldest Byzantine marriage text, dating to the mid-eighth century, testifies to the practice, which continues today in Orthodox weddings, of placing wreaths or crowns on the heads of the couple.

The Marriage of Tobias and Sarah, *by Giovanni Biliverti (1576–1664), depicts an episode in the Book of Tobit. Parts of the Roman Catholic Wedding Mass derive from this work, such as the blessing in Tobit 7.15 (Vulgate version). Here, unlike in the story, Tobias gives Sarah a ring and the role of celebrant is taken by the archangel Raphael.*

aid for the candidate and (in many cases) the special intervention of the Holy Spirit; reflect in statement and prayer the different levels of authority and the task of the office; provide gestures and actions that set the person apart; and deliver symbols of office.

RITES FOR THE SICK AND THE DEAD

Building upon the biblical paradigm for ministry to the sick (James 5.14–16), healing ministry included prayer, the laying-on of hands, and the use of oil. The complexity of practices in the West becomes clear from the first full ritual texts of the ninth century. Prayers of confession, absolution, petition, intercession, and blessing could be said in the context of the Mass—even a special mass for the sick—or in a liturgy for the sick that could take place in church or home. Penitential psalms were spoken or sung. Exorcistic sprinkling of water or blessed salt might precede the laying-on of hands with or without the use of an aromatic oil. To the accompaniment of special prayers, the oil could be applied to the five senses (eyes, ears, mouth, nostrils, lips), forehead, breast, loins (for men), navel (for women), and to the specific location of pain. By the fifteenth century,

SPECIAL MINISTRIES

Various rites have been used across the churches to set apart persons for distinctive ministries. For example, missionaries may be installed, appointed, commissioned, or consecrated depending upon the ecclesiastical tradition. Prayers for the missionary will certainly be said no matter what the rite, but not all will be given a blessing or the laying-on of hands or be presented with symbols representing their work.

Among the special ministries of liturgical leadership and general organization within a local congregation that have received these types of rites are doorkeepers, readers, acolytes (who light or carry candles and assist in the liturgy), lectors, exorcists, musicians, stewards, church school workers, and moderators of meetings. Some of these rites are also used for persons who live in separate religious communities and engage in focused work of prayer, teaching, and care of the poor: abbesses and nuns, abbots and monks.

The laying-on of hands *may form a part of various Christian rites across the churches. Here, in the first Catholic ordination ceremony in communist Vietnam performed by a Vatican emissary, Cardinal Crescenzio Sepe blesses one of 57 newly ordained priests at Hanoi cathedral, November 29, 2005.*

rites consisting of penance, anointing, and eucharist had become connected more with the dying than with the generally sick. Ritual anointing became the sacrament of extreme ("last") unction, which was followed by the last communion or *viaticum.*

While retaining these practices, Roman Catholics after the council of Trent (1545–1563) began to reclaim anointing other than for the dying, an effort fully achieved in the 1960s with the liturgical revisions of the Second Vatican Council. The council's work also encouraged many Protestants to reconsider the Reformation's rejection of services and oil for healing, although such uses could already be found among the Non-jurors in England (seventeenth–eighteenth centuries), the Church of the Brethren (eighteenth century), and early Pentecostal communities (twentieth century).

Pastoral writers in every age have urged that funerary practices witness to a Christian view of death, howsoever interpreted, in both word and action, while being cautious of popular (and ostentatious) local funerary customs. Sixteenth-century Protestant reformers sought to simplify what had become complex ritual and social processes connected with death and the ongoing commemoration of, and intercession for, the dead. Fearful of perpetuating superstition contrary to God's word, for centuries some Reformed (Calvinist) denominations did away with funerals in church or home and graveside rites, although some found preaching in the cemetery or church after burial to be spiritually beneficial. Today in many Reformed denominations, as in numerous other Protestant bodies, rites and prayers may accompany the dying and their loved ones through the time of death and beyond. These services focus upon new life—achieved by the mourners as they pass from grief to resolution, and anticipated by both living and dead at the final resurrection. (See also pages 148–149 and 182–183.)

Winter sunlight *lights a misty graveyard in Stoke-on-Trent, England. Christians have always cared for their dead, as attested by catacombs, monuments in church buildings, and cemeteries.*

OCCASIONAL RITES

In addition to longstanding rites for occasions such as baptism, marriage and death, services connected with particular people, events, objects, and places, have developed over the centuries as the result of pastoral need. For example, there are rites related to such diverse matters as birth (see sidebar on page 94) and church buildings. The latter have included breaking ground; laying a cornerstone; dedication or consecration; and deconsecration.

FESTIVALS AND FASTS

LENT

New Christians were often baptized at the Easter vigil, so the preceding days were used for preparation by penitence, fasting (or abstinence from certain foods), and prayer. Some communities settled on a forty-day period (excluding Sundays) that began on (Ash) Wednesday, continued through Palm Sunday, and culminated with the *triduum* (see main text) at end of the "Great" (Holy) Week. This period, known in English as Lent (an old word for spring), eventually denoted a general time of public penance accompanied by works of mercy. These disciplines continue, marking Lent as a time to recall human frailty and mortality, to acknowledge human failure and sin, and to express heartfelt repentance—but all look forward to the resurrection joy of Easter. The day before the austerities of Lent (known as Shrove Tuesday, Carnival, Mardi Gras and so on) was often (in the West) a time of merrymaking and even excess.

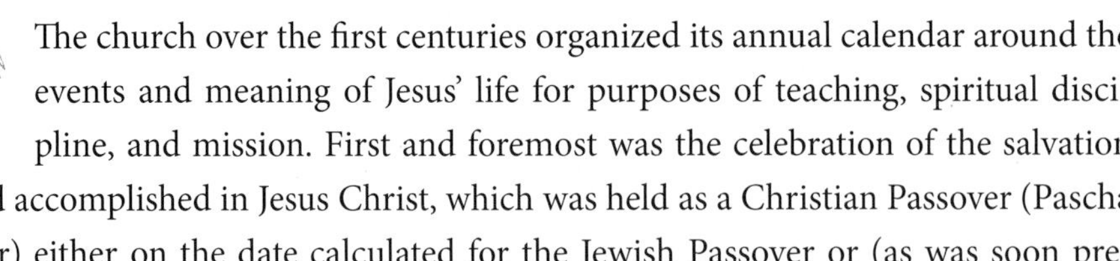

The church over the first centuries organized its annual calendar around the events and meaning of Jesus' life for purposes of teaching, spiritual discipline, and mission. First and foremost was the celebration of the salvation that God accomplished in Jesus Christ, which was held as a Christian Passover (Pascha or Easter) either on the date calculated for the Jewish Passover or (as was soon preferred) on a nearby Sunday. Later the observance was expanded to a period of three days (*triduum*) marked by prayer and fasting followed by feasting.

The *triduum* embraces events in Christ's passion and victory over death: his betrayal (Thursday evening remembrance of the Last Supper, to which, after the seventh century, ritual footwashing was sometimes added [John 13.1–16; 34]); crucifixion (on "Good" Friday, originally "God Friday"); burial and repose in the tomb (Saturday); and resurrection (Saturday evening vigil and Sunday day). Easter rejoicing continues throughout the "Great Fifty Days"—including observance of the Ascension (Mark 16.19) on the fortieth day—until the fiftieth day, the feast of Pentecost, which honors the outpouring of the Holy Spirit (Acts 2.1–4) and hence the birth of the church. Variant calculations used in historic calendars have meant that Christians in the East and the West keep these holy days in different weeks.

The festival of Epiphany or Theophany developed on January 6 in eastern regions, possibly by the late second century, in order to commemorate the manifestation of God

Christ's Entry into Jerusalem *(John 12.12–13) is commemorated on Palm Sunday. From the Pala d'Oro altarpiece (ca. 1000) in Aachen cathedral, Germany.*

to the world through Jesus Christ. Several narratives of Jesus' early life attached to this event, including his birth (and especially the visitation of the Magi, Matt. 2.1–12); his baptism, in which he is identified as the "beloved Son" (as at Mark 1.9–11); and his first miracles, particularly the changing of water into wine (John 2.1–11).

The similar festival of Christmas emerged in the following century in the West—on December 25 because of different local calendars—but Christmas came to focus principally upon the nativity. Both festivals were preceded by weeks of preparation that in the West were marked by penitence (as in Gaul and Spain) or glad anticipation (Rome). The Western church settled on a season beginning on the fourth Sunday before December 25 that both remembers the expectancy of Christ's birth and anticipates his return. Advent (Latin *adventus*, "coming") heralds the start of the church year for many communities.

Minor christological feasts and fasts developed at later dates in both the East and West, and are sometimes shared—for example, the Presentation in the Temple (Luke 2.22–24)—or are specific to one church (such as the Roman Catholic feast of Corpus Christi that originated in the thirteenth century). The relatively new feast of Christ the King instituted by Pope Pius XI in 1925 has also been taken into the calendars of many Protestant denominations.

HOLY PERSONS AND OTHER FEASTS

Devotion to the Virgin Mary, the Mother of God (Theotokós) gave rise from an early date to festivals that honored her directly, connected her with key biblical events (such as the Annunciation, Luke 1.26–38), and responded to expanding traditions about her (such as the Assumption; see page 151). Contemporary with the growth of Marian festivals were days that venerated the martyrs and the saints. Many churches follow, to varying degrees, a complete calendar of days that recognize both universal and local persons of faith, while others observe a single feast of All Saints.

Additional festivals may also be widely shared, such as the feast of the Holy Trinity, while many are peculiar to ecclesiastical traditions. On the feast of Orthodoxy (or the Triumph of Orthodoxy), Eastern Orthodox and Eastern-rite Catholics remember the end of iconoclasm and the restoration of icons. The festival of the Reformation (or Reformation Day) pays tribute to the Protestant reforms of the sixteenth century, and is a favorite of Lutherans.

Ethiopian saints, *part of a fan used in church ceremonies. In addition to individuals revered by the whole church, Christians in many regions commemorate the lives and works of local figures.*

EDUCATORS

Jesus the rabbi ("teacher") directed his chosen disciples to make new disciples by both baptism and instruction (Matt. 28.19–20). Thus each succeeding generation has regarding teaching as the principal means for propagating Christian faith and values. The New Testament places teachers with apostles, prophets, evangelists, and other leaders (1 Cor. 12.28–29; Eph. 4.11); it also speaks of the teaching function of bishops and presbyters (1 Tim. 3.2; 5.17) and warns against false teachers (2 Peter 2.1).

The development of a catechumenate (basic instruction and formation in the faith before and after baptism) by the third century required the services of teachers (see sidebar). This approach declined as infant baptism came to predominate, and from the seventh century onward, the task of teaching children the rudiments of the faith—especially the Apostles' Creed, Lord's Prayer, and Ten Commandments—fell to parents,

SUNDAY SCHOOLS

"Sunday school" is the name given to religious education for all ages given on Sundays, with instruction by clergy, professional Christian educators, and volunteers. It has its origin in the Sunday afternoon instruction and examination of Protestant children in the basics of the Christian faith, for which a catechism might be used. By the 1700s, sessions might also include reading, writing, and account-keeping. Methodists, Congregationalists, Moravians, Baptists, and others in the American colonies and England, organized special schools with similar goals on Sundays for indigent children and children who worked on the other days of the week. Formal organization of Sunday schools, with special attention to children of the poor, is credited to Anglican layman Robert Raikes (1735–1811) of Gloucester, England, whose commitment to social reform through Christian education led to significant changes in English society.

The Ragged School, *a stereoscopic card of the 1860s. Arising from the work of John Pounds (1766–1839), Britain's free "Ragged Schools" provided for the poorest children, whose ragged state often led to other schools barring them.*

All Souls' College, *Oxford, was founded in 1438. With roots in the late 11th century, Oxford is the oldest university in the English-speaking world. The original idea of a university as a community* (universitas) *of scholars is reflected in the 46 self-governing colleges and halls that characterize Oxford's federal structure. The older colleges were religious foundations; until the 19th century all Oxford fellows (faculty) were obliged to be clergy.*

godparents, and local clergy, all of whom may have had minimal education themselves. Manuals helped literate clergy teach basic doctrine. Christian education and formation also occurred indirectly by sermons preached in the vernacular; auricular confession and penitential practices that extolled the learning and enactment of Christian virtues; the church's liturgies; and visual arts and drama both within and outside the church walls.

Formal education was principally available to clergy, monks, and the wealthy, at cathedral and monastic schools and, after the late eleventh century, at schools that taught theology as well as arts, law, and medicine. These became the foundations for the world's great universities, beginning with Paris, Oxford, and Bologna. Theological ferment in universities helped to give birth to the Reformation, whose leaders pressed for more attention to the education of the laity, and to that end produced catechisms, manuals in which Christian doctrine is summarized, often in a dialogue or question-and-answer format.

There was also Protestant-motivated secular education, as in the free "grammar schools" reorganized or founded by England's King Edward VI (1547–1553) to teach Latin and later Greek and other subjects. From the Reformation to the present, Protestant concern for a trained clergy has led to the founding of new colleges and universities that teach the theological distinctiveness of the different denominations. Commitment also to the education of children has seen schools established even for the very young. In England, for example, church-run schools (the majority Anglican) teaching a broad secular curriculum constitute one-third of the public elementary school system.

CATECHESIS

Teachers of catechumens (those receiving instruction pre- or post-baptism) could be clergy or laity, but by ca. 300 in most places they were bishops or their delegated presbyters, who taught by sermon and exhortation. Education was principally at the local level, although regional catechetical schools were established to train clergy, theologians, and teachers. The famous school at Alexandria, Egypt, was underway in the late 100s and encouraged study in science and mathematics along with biblical interpretation and theology. The catechumenate disappeared as infant initiation became usual, but recent decades have seen a renewed interest in this approach to teaching new Christians.

PILGRIMAGE

Pilgrims, *a glazed terracotta relief from the Ospedale del Ceppo, Pistoia, Italy, by Giovanni della Robbia (1469–1529). Medieval pilgrims were distinguished by their staffs, bags (scrips, or "wallets"), broad-brimmed hats, cloaks, and badges, here the scallop shell emblem associated with Santiago de Compostela.*

SACRED DESTINATIONS

Pilgrims generally visited locations where a significant event, vision, or miracle had occurred or where persons or relics had found a resting place. The Italian town of La Verna, where Francis of Assisi reportedly received his stigmata, the hermitage of Guadalupe on the hill of Tepeyac near Mexico City, and the Ethiopian "new Jerusalem" at Lalibela typify the former. Among the latter were Santiago de Compostela, Spain, the reputed burial place of St. James, and where the shell as the symbol of pilgrimage originated; and Canterbury, England, the site of Thomas Becket's martyrdom. Mount Athos (Greece) and Solovetsky (Russia) were among the many monasteries of East and West that attracted pilgrims. Of course, the Holy Land too remained a desirable goal.

There is no scriptural injunction for a Christian to make pilgrimage; in fact, the New Testament rather seems to warn against revering things and places (Matt. 23.27; John 4.20–24). But certainly by ca. 300 Christians were travelling to gaze upon holy objects or relics, visit holy people (both living and dead), and see holy sites, especially those associated with the life of Jesus. The practice of visiting graves of apostles and martyrs is attested by the mid-second century, and on the anniversary of death these visits might include eucharist at the site. The oldest written record of a pilgrimage to the Holy Land is by an anonymous traveller of ca. 333 from Bordeaux in Gaul; another pilgrim, Egeria or Etheria, wrote of her own travels around fifty years later (see box). Despite the growing popularity of pilgrimages, some church leaders were skeptical of their value and appropriateness; but they did appreciate that all Christians were in some sense pilgrims or sojourners migrating toward the heavenly Jerusalem (Heb. 11.13, KJV; 1 Peter 2.11, KJV).

By the Middle Ages, pilgrimage characterized the transient life of every Christian, but also the inward, interior journey of the monastic or ascetic of which the *Revelations of Divine Love* by Julian of Norwich (ca. 1342–ca. 1416) is an example. Pilgrimage comprised travel for the purpose of mission and evangelism, as well as the physical (and spiritual) trek to a holy site (see sidebar). People undertook such sometimes dangerous travel for pleasure, as a sign of piety, as a means of penance, and out of hope of changing some life situation. For example, to increase their fertility, French women went to the abbey of Saint-Germain-des-Prés to have the girdle of St. Margaret draped around their body by a priest.

Luther, Calvin, and other Protestant reformers strongly criticized the visitation pilgrimages, joining their voices to the similar critiques of Thomas à Kempis, Erasmus, and others. The penitential practices (and indulgences) sometimes associated with pilgrimage particularly drew their ire. Among Protestants, pilgrimage as interior spiritual journey found greater acceptance, as expressed in John Bunyan's allegorical *The Pilgrim's Progress* (1678).

PILGRIMAGE TODAY

Pilgrimages continue to long-established holy places and to new locations, some of them connected with modern appearances of the Virgin Mary (see page 150). Intentionally ecumenical centers for worship and study invite pilgrims from across the spectrum of Christian ecclesiastical traditions and from around the world, and particularly young people. The ancient pilgrimage site of Iona, Scotland, has received new interest because of the Iona Community founded there in 1938. The community of Taizé, in Burgundy, France (founded 1940), and the monastery of Bose, near Milan, Italy (founded 1965), both engage visitors in worship, prayer, and commitment to justice and peace.

EGERIA: A FOURTH-CENTURY PILGRIM

An incomplete eleventh-century manuscript is the oldest source for an autobiographical account of a woman's pilgrimage (ca. 381–384) to the Near East. Identified as Egeria (or Etheria), she may have been a nun from western Europe, possibly Gaul or Spain. Her descriptions of places and people fill out other contemporary sources, and her picture of liturgical life in Jerusalem is especially rich and valuable. She reports in detail events of the week before Easter in Jerusalem, and is particularly attentive to the laity, noting their fatigue as they attend lengthy services on the Mount of Olives, at Gethsemane, and in different parts of the "Great Church" (today's Holy Sepulchre).

In recounting why the bishop holds down the "holy wood of the cross" while the faithful kiss it on Good Friday, Egeria gives evidence for souvenir collectors: someone bit off a piece of the wood, requiring the bishop and deacons to be present lest such a theft recur. Down the ages, many churches and monasteries have held what were claimed to be relics of the True Cross.

The True Cross. *An inscription on this reliquary from Sainte-Foy abbey, Conques, France, indicates that it held a relic of Christ's cross. Today, while their authenticity may be doubted, such relics often continue to be revered as symbolic icons. Silver gilt, ca. 1110.*

THE HOUSE OF GOD

A Christian place of worship is both a house of God (*domus Dei*) and a house of the people of God, the church (*domus ecclesiae*), where assuredly God meets believers and seekers. The type of space is not as important as the encounter between God and people, though some communities have come to prefer certain configurations as best satisfying their theological and practical needs. Christians have worshipped in purpose-built edifices—large and small, elaborate and simple, of stone, brick, wood, animal hide, fabric, even glass—and in other buildings co-opted for worship, such as private homes (as in early Christianity; see page 28) or civic buildings (such as Roman basilicas; see pages 34–35). Sometimes worship is held under a tent, in the open, or in a grove of trees. Each of these locations may be delineated permanently or temporarily as "sacred" space. Artworks, such as paintings and sculpture, provide meditative focus and opportunity for instruction.

Settings for worship are intentionally configured to reflect the beliefs of a community and to accommodate the functions that articulate or ritualize those beliefs. The design

CHURCH FURNISHINGS

Virtually all Christian houses of worship contain three significant furnishings, which may vary in size, design and decoration, and location. The reading and exposition of the Bible occur at an ambo or reading desk. There may be two structures: a pulpit for preaching and a lectern for readings.

An altar table for celebrating the Lord's Supper bears the twin meaning of altar for sacrifice and table for eating and fellowship. Which aspect is most stressed depends on how a particular tradition views the nature and purpose of the act. The altar table may be at one end (historically the east) or central, near the congregation.

The size and location of a font (receptacle for baptismal water) or baptistery (baptismal pool) depends on how baptism is understood and on the preferred method. Churches may locate them to one side or directly in line with the ambo and altar table, or may place the font at the entrance to the worship space to signify baptism as the entry into the community of faith.

Eagle lectern *by Giovanni Pisano (ca. 1248–1314). The eagle is the traditional symbol of St. John the evangelist and its popularity down the ages for lecterns is inspired by the opening words of John's gospel. The lectern is often the place in the church where the Bible is kept and is used for scriptural and other liturgical readings. Marble, ca. 1301.*

and decoration of the space shapes and gives meaning to what happens there. A storefront room; a small square building with images of Christ, the Virgin Mary, and saints painted on the interior walls; an ornately decorated Gothic structure with a vaulted ceiling and stained-glass windows (see pages 52–53, 76–77); an auditorium with an overhead screen and the latest in technological equipment—each conveys a different understanding of the divine, the human, and their interaction, and delimits the styles of worship that may occur. Worship that emphasizes the spoken word and preaching, for example, requires particular spatial organization and acoustics. Changing understandings of worship or changed functional needs may require alteration or total renewal of an existing space.

CONGREGATION AND CLERGY

The placing of congregation and clergy in a space identifies in part the roles each is expected to play in worship. A single, open room may locate the leadership at one end or more centrally. A two-room or divided space situates the congregation in one area (the nave) and the clergy, choir, and musicians in another (the choir or sanctuary). They may be separated by a tall screen or wall (such as a rood screen in Gothic and Gothic revival churches; an iconostasis in Orthodox ones) or by a low barrier (such as the altar rail of some Protestant churches). The positioning of choir and musical instruments to assist congregational singing is usually the result of visual and acoustical considerations.

MEETING HOUSES

In the center of many New England towns one will readily find a white-painted Congregational meeting house. Some of these houses of worship date to the early eighteenth century; one seventeenth-century structure survives. The earliest wooden buildings were elongated or square, with the pulpit opposite the main entrance. The congregation sat on benches, sometimes in small enclosures ("box pews") to preserve heat in the winter. Large windows let light into the minimally decorated space. For communion, a small table might be set in front of the pulpit and, for baptism, a basin of water placed on a table.

The Herz-Jesu-Kirche *(church of the Sacred Heart), a Catholic parish church in Munich, Germany, was built 1997–2000 by the firm of Allmann Sattler Wappner. Its striking design consists of an exterior square cuboid of glass enclosing a wooden interior one of vertical slats so constructed that light increases as one approaches the sanctuary (altar end). Conversely, the exterior glass is transparent at the entrance but becomes less so until it is opaque at the sanctuary, shielding the sacramental acts from outside view.*

ART AND ARCHITECTURE
RENAISSANCE AND BAROQUE

Sant' Ivo alla Sapienza, *built as a chapel for Rome's Sapienza university, illustrates the variety and innovation that Baroque architects brought to Renaissance Classicism. Built 1642–1646 by Francesco Borromini, it has a striking corkscrew lantern and a concave facade that blends with the wings of the university.*

RIGHT **The Family Tree of St. Dominic,** *a wooden relief of 1662–1665 in Santo Domingo church, Oaxaca, Mexico. In Spain and its colonies the addition of Moorish and local indigenous elements produced a particularly rich version of Baroque style.*

OPPOSITE *The church of Wies, Westphalia, Germany, by D. and J. B. Zimmermann (1745–1754). Every surface teems with color and activity, typical of the Baroque and Rococo churches of south Germany and Austria.*

From the fifteenth to the seventeenth centuries the Gothic style that had dominated church architecture in most of western Europe largely gave way to designs adapted from or inspired by the Classical world, especially Rome. Beginning in Italy, this development was part of a broader cultural phenomenon later known as the Renaissance, which looked to Classical antiquity for inspiration. Renaissance architects sought to emulate the geometrical precision and balanced proportions of the ancients, as well as adopting their actual forms of columns, arches, pediments, vaults, and domes.

The pioneer of this revived Classicism was Florence's Filippo Brunelleschi (1377–1446), who was influenced by the 1414 republication of the treatise *De Architectura* by Vitruvius (1st century BCE). Leon Battista Alberti's (1404–1472) own 1452 treatise *De re aedificatoria* spread the revival throughout Italy.

High Renaissance Classicism is exemplified by the works of the architect and theorist Andrea Palladio (1508–1580), who gave his name to the influential "Palladian" style. The single greatest example of Renaissance church architecture, however, is St. Peter's in Rome, commissioned in 1506 by Pope Julius II to replace Constantine I's fourth-century basilica. Donato Bramante (1444–1514) headed a series of eminent architects of St. Peter's, most notably Michelangelo (see page 144).

By the time St. Peter's was completed, in the 1630s, Renaissance Classicism had evolved a more adorned and dramatic style referred to as Baroque, which reflected a renewed vigor within the Roman Catholic Church following the shock of the Reformation. This style reached a climax in Rome in the works of Francesco Borromini (1599–1667) and of Gianlorenzo Bernini (1598–1680), who designed St. Peter's Square and many of the basilica's interior features (see pages 66–67). Baroque church interiors can be highly theatrical in their use of space, color, and decoration such as exuberant scrolls, clusters of stucco cherubs, and *trompe-l'oeil* ceilings painted with vertiginous sunlit firmaments. At the same time, Baroque architects remained true to the often highly complex geometry that characterized the Classical style.

In the eighteenth century a lighter but at times even more extrovert decorative style, termed Rococo, became popular in France, from where it spread to Catholic areas of Germany and elsewhere, including Russia.

DANKE
BITTE
DANKE
BITTE

3

THE SOURCES OF CHRISTIAN ETHICS

THE DECALOGUE

The Ten Commandments, or Decalogue, given by God to Moses following the liberation of the Hebrews from slavery in Egypt, appear in two versions (Exod. 20.2–17, Deut. 5.6–21). There are in fact fourteen or fifteen injunctions and different traditions arrange them in various ways; thus Jews regard the opening statement ("I am the Lord your God") as the first commandment, while Roman Catholics and Lutherans combine this with the injunctions against other gods and idols to make the first commandment. Perhaps the most significant issue in translation is whether the commandments forbid killing in general or just murder in particular.

Christian ethics arose from three principal sources: the practices and scriptures of the Jewish world, particularly the Old Testament; the dominant Hellenistic culture of the early Christian era; and reflection on the life, words, deeds, and death of Jesus in the light of the radical transformation brought about by experiences and reports of his resurrection. The first and third of these sources remain, but the second has expanded to include the many cultures with which Christianity has had contact to the present day, as well as the history of philosophical ethics.

Old Testament ethics include the understanding of God as creator and the discovery that the creator God longs to set his people free and live in a covenantal relationship with

Moses Destroying the Tablets of the Law, *by Rembrandt (1659). On Mt. Sinai God gave Moses two tablets bearing the commandments, but Moses smashed them in anger on finding that the Hebrews had erected a golden idol (Exod. 32.19). He later returned to Mt. Sinai and received two new tablets.*

them. The covenant is most explicitly embodied in the Ten Commandments (see sidebar), although it is anticipated in God's covenants with Noah (Gen. 9) and Abraham (Gen. 12, 15, 17). On the other hand are the Old Testament traditions of prophet, priest, and king. The prophet calls the people back to the covenant made with God. The priest seeks to embody that relationship in patterns of holiness and worship. The king epitomizes the aspirations and complexities of Israel's life under God: the definitive king is David.

Early Christians quickly perceived that Jesus fulfilled these Old Testament roles: thus the Temptation (Matt. 3, Luke 4) shows him being tempted into different kinds of prophetic, priestly, and kingly ministry. Those emphasizing Jesus' role as king have tended to seek ways in which the church could be involved in governing the whole of society, drawing on such narratives as those of David and Solomon. Christians who have stressed Jesus' priestly role have often focused on his death on the cross and its unique role in bringing about eternal salvation: the ethical implications have tended to be harder to see. Those who have focused on Jesus' role as prophet have tended to turn to the gospel accounts of his ministry of teaching—especially the Beatitudes (see box)—and healing rather than the cross alone.

THE BEATITUDES

The Beatitudes, recorded rather differently by Matthew (5.3–12) and Luke (6.20–26), are at the heart of Jesus' teaching. The name derives from the Latin for "blessing" (*beatitudo*). Matthew's Beatitudes, at the beginning of the Sermon on the Mount (Matt. 5–7), are a somewhat spiritualized version of the promises recorded by Luke in his Sermon on the Plain (Luke 6.20–49). Where Luke says "poor" and "hungry," Matthew says "poor in spirit" and "hungry for righteousness."

The difference of emphasis today between those who see Christian ethics as primarily about social relations and those who see it as keeping oneself fit for heaven has therefore been there since the very beginning.

The theme that tends to unite these contrasting emphases is the "kingdom [or reign] of God." This is the world that the parables and healings depict, a world anticipated by personal holiness and struggles for right relations, but fundamentally ushered in not in our way at our time but in God's own way and at God's chosen time. (See also pages 20–21.)

Matthew's Beatitudes emphasize future consolation amid present struggle. While all of the verses have inspired movements in the history of the church, perhaps the most influential has been the sixth ("Blessed are the pure in heart, for they will see God"), with its notion of the vision of God as the goal of Christian existence.

The Church of the Beatitudes. *An aerial view of the hill called the Mount of the Beatitudes, where Jesus is said to have preached the Sermon on the Mount, near Tabgha on Lake Galilee. The Franciscan church was built in 1938 close to the remains of a 4th-century chapel.*

CHRISTIAN LOVE: FAMILY AND SOCIETY

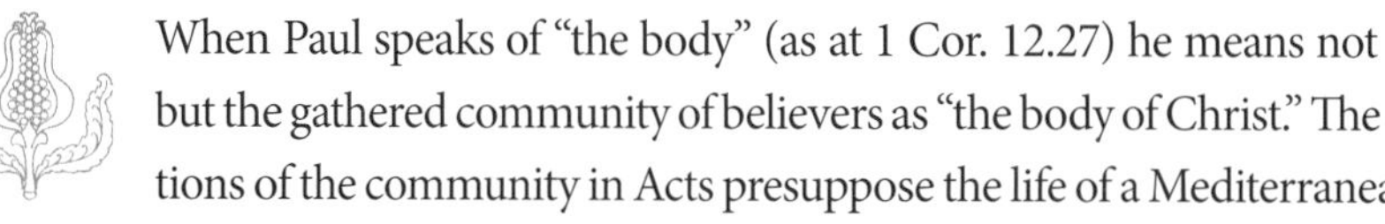

When Paul speaks of "the body" (as at 1 Cor. 12.27) he means not an individual but the gathered community of believers as "the body of Christ." The early descriptions of the community in Acts presuppose the life of a Mediterranean household, a much broader notion than simply family. But the most fundamental unit for the early Christians was church—the assembly (Greek *ekklesia*) of the faithful, where worship, social care, and fellowship were epitomized in the common meal. This meal crystallized the call to radical reappraisal of family relationships, commitments, and property ownership (Acts 2.42–47).

Two references to love stand out in the New Testament for their influence on the history of Christian ethics. Jesus' injunction "Love your enemies" (Luke 6.35) seems a clear indication that Christian love goes way beyond conventional mercy and generosity; and Paul's famous hymn to love in 1 Corinthians, which ends with the words "faith, hope, and love abide, these three; and the greatest of these is love" (1 Cor. 13) has been taken by Aquinas and others as a cue to regard love as the "form of all the virtues." However, it

HOUSEHOLD ETHICS

The New Testament letters include lists of instructions based on contemporary Hellenistic household ethics. In Titus 2.2–6, for example, wives are told to be "self-controlled, chaste, good managers of the household, kind," and "submissive to their husbands." Given the origins of these conventions in Hellenistic cultural norms, Christians have long debated how far such instructions are truly grounded in God, and thus to what extent later generations should be bound by them.

More recent controversy has focused on the role of women as church leaders and ministers (see box). The New Testament passages traditionally read as excluding women from certain roles have now been reevaluated. Slavery was apparently accepted as a fact of contemporary life for many centuries; since the eighteenth century, however, Christians have increasingly seen slavery as abhorrent within a Christian ethic of love.

Waiting for Freedom. *Slaves wait for the proclamation abolishing slavery in the US to take effect at midnight on December 31, 1862. This painting by William T. Carlton (1816–1888) hangs in the White House room where Lincoln signed the proclamation.*

remains unclear how easily the radical kind of love envisaged in Luke sits alongside the love that Paul describes. Meanwhile a contrast runs through the New Testament concerning whether "love" refers to a general sense of well-being and communal care or to a much more radical reordering of conventional commitments in the light of Christ's life, death, and resurrection. The resurrected Jesus thrice asks Peter, "Do you love me?" (John 21.15–23). The translation masks the variation in the Greek between fraternal love (*philos*) and a more genuinely selfless love (*agape*). Some have made a great deal of this distinction, and also referred to a third word (*eros*) as indicating a love centered on desire. Christian traditions have differed widely in viewing desire either as inherently holy (reflecting God's desire for us) or as suspect (because assumed to be selfish or linked to lust).

Christians in the West today commonly assume that the Bible prescribes a nuclear form of family life, but the nuclear family is in fact a very recent cultural development and Christian notions of family have changed with cultural patterns over the centuries. What has remained constant has been the emphasis on the home as a primary place for faith development, nurture, protection of the weak, and practical embodiments of Christian love.

FEMALE LEADERSHIP IN THE CHURCH

One area where the household codes found in the New Testament (see sidebar) have proved controversial is gender and leadership. Some passages forbid female headship, such as "I permit no woman to teach or to have authority over a man; she is to keep silent" (1 Tim. 2.12; compare 1 Cor. 14.34). But other passages seem to assume that women were active in the church in prominent ministerial roles, such as where Paul commends "our sister Phoebe, a deacon [or 'minister'] of the church at Cenchreae" (Rom. 16.1).

Evidence for female leadership is also found in non-Christian sources, such as a letter written ca. 112 to the emperor Trajan by Pliny the Younger, the Roman governor of Bithynia and Pontus in Asia Minor. In the course of a detailed account of his actions against Christians and their "depraved, excessive superstition," Pliny states that he felt it "necessary to find out what the truth was by torturing two female slaves who were called deacons [Latin: *ministrae*]." Some have disputed whether such passages indicate that women were in positions of authority. But the real issue for Christians has been whether or not the injunctions against female leadership are truly grounded in the new life made possible in Christ.

The Rev. Rose Hudson-Wilkin *celebrates the Eucharist at Holy Trinity Anglican church in Hackney, London. Today most Anglican provinces ordain women as deacons and priests, and a number, as in the US and Canada, allow for the ordination of women bishops.*

POLITICS AND THE STATE

Jesus famously said, "Give to the emperor those things that are the emperor's, and to God the things that are God's" (Mark 12.17). Was Jesus making a significant distinction between spiritual and civil authority, or an ironic observation that all things are, in fact, God's? Around this question revolve most issues of Christian political ethics.

Jesus himself was surrounded by various models of interaction with a society under foreign occupation, including conformity (Sadducees and Herodians), political quietism (Pharisees), seclusion (Essenes), and violent militancy (Zealots). Each of these options has had its proponents throughout the history of the church. But Jesus apparently renounced all four. His politics seems to have been focused on his small group of disciples, on

"AN UNJUST LAW IS NO LAW": RESISTING AUTHORITY

With the demise of Christendom (see main text), Christian reflection on politics has focused less on the ethic of rule and more on patterns of resistance. The 1934 *Barmen Declaration* was written by Karl Barth (1886–1968), Dietrich Bonhoeffer (1906–1945), and others in the Confessing Church of Nazi Germany to counter the nationalism and antisemitism of the state-controlled "German Christian" movement, rejecting the idea that the church could be subject to any authority but Christ. Another such statement was the *Kairos Document* (1985) by black South African theologians—a landmark text in liberation theology that advocates "prophetic" theology and criticizes what it calls "state" and "church" theology.

The text that most overshadows political questions for Christians is Romans 13.1–4, where Paul enjoins readers to be subject to civil authority. It is unclear how far Paul's own presumed execution by an oppressive regime (in Rome, ca. 64) qualifies his statement that "rulers are not a terror to good conduct, but to bad," and debate has raged about whether Paul's words apply in situations where a government is tyrannical. For example, Thomas Aquinas' words "an unjust law is no law at all" were famously cited by Dr. Martin Luther King, Jr., during the US civil rights era in the 1960s.

Denouncing injustice. *The Rev. Dr. Martin Luther King, Jr., speaks to a crowd at the March Against Fear rally on the steps of the Mississippi State Capitol in June 1966. King's Southern Christian Leadership Conference (SCLC) was dedicated to nonviolent resistance to racism.*

friendship with the poor, and on critically engaging those in authority: and most of all, on the way of the cross. The latter was a rejection of conformity, quietism, and militancy; but Jesus' movement constituted a sufficient political threat for him to be executed on political grounds (see page 24).

AUGUSTINE'S "CITY OF GOD"

Once Christianity became a formidable public force, it needed a political theology to match. Augustine of Hippo (354–430) provided it. In his *City of God*, he explains that everything in human, secular history, no matter how adverse, is an advance in sacred history. Thus the pagan Roman emperors advanced the sacred story by bringing so many peoples under one rule; even the Visigoths' sack of Rome in 410, which shocked the Roman world, would be seen to have a place in sacred history. This model offered Christians in the ensuing millennium a way to understand their relationship to the civil powers. In the medieval period attention focused on the relationship between the pope and the Holy Roman emperor, most notably in the Investiture Controversy (see page 39).

Building the City of God. *St. Augustine contrasted the Human City, the secular realm, with the City of God, the realm of salvation. Woodblock print, French, 1486.*

Much Christian reflection on politics has assumed that the human person has two dimensions—body and soul—and that it is the latter which lives eternally with God. Thus Martin Luther (1483–1546) described the two realms: the spiritual realm is the freedom and equality of one's eternal life before God, governed through the preaching of the word and sharing the sacraments. The worldly realm is one's fleeting life before humanity, constrained by laws enforced by rulers. The two realms simply have separate spheres. The approach to civil authority of another great reformer, John Calvin (1509–1564), has been profoundly influential in northern Europe and especially in the US (see sidebar).

The early modern period left a variety of arrangements between church and state. In England and Denmark a state church has survived until the present day. In France and northern continental Europe there remained a tension between the principle that the state or monarch had significant authority over the church and the Catholic tendency to see the pope as a major influence on local ecclesial and even political life. Significant concordats were negotiated between the papacy and Napoleon (1801), Mussolini (1929), and Hitler (1933). Perhaps the most important developments were the revolutions in America (1776) and France (1789), which explicitly removed the assumption that the church should inevitably have some tie to the state. This marked the end of the era of Christendom in the West (see pages 131–133).

CALVIN AND THE STATE

John Calvin accepted the distinction between civil and spiritual authority, but had an unusually high view of civil government, which existed to cherish the worship of God, defend piety and the church, form righteous human behavior, and promote peace. This approach underlay Puritan-inspired quests for a godly society in England and New England from the 1640s. But Calvin also recognized that rebellion may in extreme cases be permissible or even required.

CRIME AND PUNISHMENT

CAPITAL PUNISHMENT

Perhaps the best illustration of the different theories of justice (see main text) is capital punishment. Its principle is retributive. The opponents of capital punishment have often argued on distributive grounds—suggesting that mitigating circumstances should incline the justice system to mercy. There have always been misgivings about the impossibility of making amends in the case of wrongful conviction. But perhaps the strongest argument against capital punishment goes back to the restorative intent of monastic incarceration: if the point of discipline and punishment is the eventual restoration of the offender to community and reconciliation with the victim (or their family), capital punishment renders this impossible.

At the heart of the Christian faith lies forgiveness (Matt. 18.22)—the reconciliation between human beings and God made possible in Christ. It is this divine reconciliation that makes it possible for human beings to be reconciled with one another and the whole of creation. Sin is generally seen not as a disaster but as an opportunity to renew discipleship and community. Jesus outlines a specific model in the case of person-to-person sin: attempt to resolve the matter in private or, failing that, within the community of the faithful (Matt. 18.15–21). In a similar vein Paul chastises his readers for taking their disputes to the public courts (1 Cor. 6.1–7).

In contrast to the stress on forgiveness, punishment has also been important in Christian reflections on justice. Here the most telling verse is the "law of retaliation": "eye for eye, tooth for tooth" (Exod. 21.24). Although set in a context of limiting excessive penalties ("*no more than* an eye for an eye"), these words have often been taken to legitimize retribution.

A distinction has usually been made between crime and sin. Some misdemeanors, such as adultery, are generally viewed as sins but not crimes, while the church has at times not viewed a breach of civil law as sinful—as when Christians helped Jews to flee the Nazis.

Christ and the Woman Taken in Adultery *by Lorenzo Lotto (1480–1556). Jesus stopped a crowd from stoning a woman caught in adultery, with the words "Let anyone among you who is without sin be the first to throw a stone at her" (John 8.7).*

Incarceration as part of a pattern leading to reconciliation began with monastic penance. Monks faced solitary confinement less as punishment than as a form of discipline leading to their being restored to community. Indeed, some would trace the origins of Christian ethics to the handbooks produced to help confessors find suitable forms of penance for those who acknowledged their sin. The North American tradition of calling prisons "penitentiaries" begins here: places where prisoners may repent and seek amendment of life. Here the link between punishment and forgiveness is inextricable.

In its first millennium Christianity existed mainly in cultures where justice was retributive—crimes were punished by inflicting an equivalent penalty upon the perpetrator. More recently Christians have sought to introduce the idea of distributive justice, which seeks a fairer distribution of wealth and resources in order to alleviate the causes of crime. A contemporary development that harks back to early church practice is that of restorative justice, in which crime is seen as primarily a matter between two individuals rather than a concern of the state. By bringing perpetrators face to face with victims, and sometimes encouraging some form of restitution, the aim is to promote reconciliation and restoration of relationships.

HOWARD, FRY, AND PRISON REFORM

The pioneer of prison reform was the Englishman John Howard (1726–1790), who was inspired by Jesus' words: "I was hungry and you gave me food, I was thirsty and you gave me something to drink, I was a stranger and you welcomed me, I was naked and you gave me clothing, I was sick and you took care of me, I was in prison and you visited me" (Matt. 25.36).

Howard, a Calvinist, travelled widely in Europe reporting on prison conditions. He worked tirelessly to improve the frequently appalling conditions in British prisons, seeking to improve both the physical and mental health of inmates and the often disorderly and corrupt organization of the prisons themselves.

Among Howard's successors, Quakers were especially prominent, most notably Elizabeth Fry (1780–1845). Born into a wealthy banking family, her concern for prisoners was awakened by the preaching of William Savery, an American Quaker, in 1798. Fry was particularly appalled by the treatment of women prisoners and their children. Her campaigns from 1817 against inhumane conditions and capital punishment helped to bring significant reforms in 1823. Fry was also influential in the creation (1808) of the first asylums where the mentally ill could be cared for separately, rather than in prisons or parish poorhouses, an idea later also promoted in the US by Dorothea Dix (1802–1887).

The Angel of the Prisons *was a name given to Elizabeth Fry by an early biographer. Fry's activities led to improvements in British prisons, particularly for women, and her work was influential in Europe and North America. An opponent of the death penalty, she said that "punishment is not for revenge, but to lessen crime and reform the criminal."*

TRADE AND COMMERCE

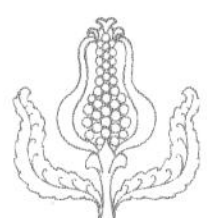

Christian attitudes toward trade and commerce have historically ranged from wholehearted endorsement to deep suspicion. Both views look to Genesis: on the one hand, God the creator is the archetypal worker and artisan, yet in the account of the Fall (Gen. 3), work in general seems to be a form of punishment. The Middle Ages saw the emergence of the tradition of the just price (see sidebar), while the biblical ban on usury, or lending at interest (Exod. 22.24), was maintained. At the time of the crusades and of the growth in international trade fairs, the difficulty of transporting large quantities of money encouraged the rise of banking. This was not in itself regarded as usury, and the papal banks became particularly influential.

GUILDS AND TRADES UNIONS

Christian ethics have influenced workers' associations since the Middle Ages. Inspired by New Testament models of communal self-support, guilds were associations of those engaged in a particular craft or trade. Guilds acquired privileges from governments and facilitated the transition from a commodity to a money economy. They were often regarded with suspicion by church hierarchies as a source of rival loyalties. One aspect of trades unionism represented a continuity with medieval guild tradition: it sought to defend and enhance the rights and conditions of workers by a collective process. On the other hand, it had a more utopian impulse to unite workers across class, gender, religious, race, and national boundaries to aspire to a better world and a transformation in the power-relationships of industry.

Christians have been at the heart of both aspects of trades unionism since its origin. In 1834 a Methodist preacher, George Loveless, formed a "friendly society" of farm workers in Dorset, England, who were subsequently arrested and transported to Australia for illegally swearing an oath. In the outcry that led to their release, they acquired a distinctly Christian nickname: the Tolpuddle Martyrs. Christians were later prominent in founding the British Labour Party: it was said that the party owed "more to Methodism than Marx."

A "guild" window *in Chartres cathedral, France, which was donated by members of a farriers' guild. Guilds controlled the economies of many cities in medieval Europe and developed a threefold training of craftspeople from apprentice to journeyman and master.*

A Busy Marketplace *by Pieter Brueghel the Younger (ca. 1564–1638). The Calvinist Netherlands became a major commerical force in 17th-century Europe.*

THE REFORMATION AND THE "PROTESTANT ETHIC"

The Reformation saw attitudes begin to change. Usury came to be accepted, as long as the interest was not excessive. There was also a new perception that everyday occupations fell within the bounds of God's kingdom. Both Luther and Calvin saw trade and commerce as part of an economy of grace, rather than simply as works of mercy. Luther in particular extended the notion of vocation to secular roles, thus bringing the world of commerce within the language of salvation. The term "Protestant [work] ethic" was coined by the German sociologist Max Weber (1864–1920), who argued that while Catholics were assured salvation by the sacraments and the blessing of the clergy, Protestants had no such assurance and so poured their religious zeal into their labor. With few legitimate ways of spending their gains—for example, purchasing church adornments was excluded and personal luxury frowned upon—surplus capital was invested, and hence Calvinism was one factor in the rise of capitalism and ultimately mass production.

Weber's thesis is highly perceptive. The key figure in economies shaped by Calvinist assumptions (notably in the US) was, and perhaps still is, the entrepreneur who sees his work as one of great moral purpose. Karl Marx saw religion as subject to the dominant force of economics; Weber saw economics as largely subject to the religious spirit.

In recent years the ethical focus has been on three related issues. The first is globalization, whose benefits have brought goods, services, and employment across the world but appears to leave the many at the economic mercy of the few. The second is climate change and its economic implications. The third is debt relief, a movement to counter the tendency of the market to keep heavily indebted countries in a perpetual cycle of poverty.

THE "JUST PRICE"

The medieval notion of the "just price" held that it was unethical to gain financially without actually creating something, and in particular that it was immoral to profiteer from market conditions of scarcity. In the words of Thomas Aquinas: "If someone would be greatly helped by something belonging to someone else, and the seller not similarly harmed by losing it, the seller must not sell for a higher price: because the usefulness that goes to the buyer comes not from the seller, but from the buyer's needy condition: no one ought to sell something that does not belong to him."

POVERTY AND WELFARE

The Hôtel-Dieu *in Beaune, Burgundy, founded in 1443 to care for the poor and sick. The medieval French tradition of calling hospitals and leper homes "Hôtels-Dieu" ("guesthouses of God") shows how care for the sick arose naturally from the tradition of hospitality. Primacy was given to patients' spiritual welfare (see also page 121).*

Christian concern about poverty has roots in Israel's tradition of expressing gratitude for God's deliverance from slavery by caring for those whose neediness echoed Israel's former condition—widows, orphans, and strangers (Deut. 10.18, 14.28–9). It is centrally drawn from the pattern of Jesus' ministry: with no fixed home, he spent time among the poor and outcast and in conflict with the authorities. For Jesus, treatment of the poor is a significant aspect of eternal judgment (Matt. 25.31–46).

For most of church history the Christian duty to the poor has been conducted through education and medicine (see pages 100–101 and 120–121). It is not simply that one needs an education to comprehend the Bible and to participate fully in the liturgy; it is also that education is the surest way for people to help themselves out of poverty.

There has long been a debate between those who see poverty as humiliation, and thus an evil, and those who see it as an aspect of simplicity, and thus a vocation for some.

The history of voluntary poverty goes back at least to St. Anthony in the fourth century; St. Francis is the most famous proponent of this tradition (see pages 42 and 45).

With industrialization, urban poverty in particular, and the political responses to it, became a key ethical issue. Nineteenth-century German liberal theologians began to see the heart of the gospel not so much in Christ's atonement but more in the inauguration of a new society, the kingdom of God, sometimes called the brotherhood of man under the fatherhood of God. In North America the Social Gospel movement of Walter Rauschenbusch in the early twentieth century picked up on this trajectory, which was further explored in Britain by Archbishop William Temple in *Christianity and the Social Order* (1942).

STATE AND PRIVATE WELFARE

In Europe such impulses became a significant part of the growing culture of state welfare provision, beginning in Germany in the 1880s and including the creation of the National Health Service in Britain in 1948. In the US, in contrast, the solution to poverty seemed to lie in private enterprise and personal charity. Dorothy Day and Peter Maurin and their Catholic Worker movement epitomized the way influential people sought to combine voluntary poverty with an expression of compassion in the tradition of the New Testament.

In the twentieth century awareness of global poverty, sickness, and hunger grew with the development of mass communications. The 1960s saw the emergence of "liberation theology" (see sidebar), and movements for debt relief and fair trade, together with questions over feeding an expanding global population, became central to addressing some of the most characteristic issues of the twenty-first century.

LIBERATION THEOLOGY

What is termed "liberation theology" sprang from a conference of Latin American bishops in Medillin, Colombia, in 1968 onwards. Liberation theologians identified the exodus from slavery in Egypt as the central scriptural motif, and spawned a host of contextual theologies that began with reflection on the struggles of oppressed peoples, rather than with abstract theological ideas or traditions. For many Catholics and Protestants a certain style of social scientific diagnosis seemed integral to addressing poverty thereafter—although this reliance by Catholic theologians on economic analysis incurred the disapproval of the Vatican.

CHRISTIAN PHILANTHROPY: DR. BARNARDO

Christian religious and moral education were central to the work of Dr. Thomas Barnardo (1845–1905), a pioneer of children's welfare. At age sixteen, Dublin-born Barnardo had an evangelical conversion experience, influenced by his Plymouth Brethren mother and siblings. In 1866 he began to train as a doctor in London, with plans to become a missionary in China. However, the atrocious living conditions of London's East End moved him to devote his life to helping destitute children.

Barnardo's first home, for boys, opened in London in 1870. While the religious motto of Barnardo's Homes was "Christian, Protestant and Evangelical," he accepted all destitute children regardless of background. His belief that all children deserved a good start in life lay behind one of Barnardo's more controversial policies, from a present-day perpective: emigrating children to Canada, Australia, and other parts of the British empire. Barnardo also established the first fostering scheme when he sent children from the pollution and sickness of urban slums to "good country homes," mainly working-class families who had to agree to raise the child with kindness and moral rectitude: regular prayer and church or chapel attendance formed part of the contract. In an age when many of his contemporaries saw poverty as a shameful result of laziness or vice, Barnardo's greatest legacy was perhaps his refusal to deny care to those who needed it, irrespective of the causes of their destitution.

HEALTH AND MEDICINE

A concern for the sick has always been close to the heart of Christian mission, and the question at the last judgment, "When was it that we saw you sick and visited you?" (Matt. 25.39), has motivated countless deeds of mercy. Three terms stand out in the history of medicine within the Christian tradition. The first is "care." Medicine for most of church history has fundamentally been the practice of care for those whose cure was in doubt. Care and prayer are central to the Christian response to illness (James 5.13–14). In recent times, the expectation of cure has increased for a wide range of conditions, and the primacy of caring over curing has become a key ethical issue, while conditions not previously considered "medical," such as infertility, childbirth, or advanced age, have increasingly been brought within a medical frame of reference.

The second key term is the virtue implied in the word "patient" (from Latin *pati*, "suffer," "endure"). Medicine has remained a moral practice rather than an economic

ABORTION

Abortion is perhaps the most controversial medical issue for Christians today. Broadly four reasons for therapeutic abortion come under ethical and legal scrutiny: to save the woman's life; to preserve her physical or mental health (this can include nonconsensual conception); to prevent the birth of a child with a congenital disorder that would be fatal or associated with significant morbidity; or to reduce the number of fetuses in cases of multiple pregnancy. There are also elective abortions that fall outside these criteria.

The general prohibition on abortion remains largely constant in Christian history. The traditional line is upheld by Catholicism (latterly by Pope John Paul II in 1995), but in Protestant discussions of the issue some or all of the four therapeutic criteria are more often regarded as legitimate. Few Christian traditions have entertained elective abortions outside these therapeutic circumstances. In US public life "pro-life" and "pro-choice" factions have become polarized, and constitute the most visible presence of religious questions in the political sphere.

The image of a fetus *on a tapestry of the Virgin Mary during the "March for Life" at the US Supreme Court on January 22, 2008, an anti-abortion protest on the 35th anniversary of the court's 1973 Roe vs Wade decision that legalized abortion in the US.*

Caring for the Sick, *from an Italian manuscript of ca. 1300. The model for early hospitals was the way in which monks cared for their own sick. Operated by specialist monks or lay brothers, monastic infirmaries generally had beds in long halls, with a chapel at one end or close by. Patients received medical care, a special diet, and other assistance to enable them to return to the monastic community.*

transaction so long as the physician has remembered the duty of care and the patient has remembered to be exactly that—patient or enduring. Patience in this sense rests on a conviction of providence—that life is lived in the palm of God's hand. Some have argued that medicine no longer rests on this kind of faith, and has become a "religion" all of its own.

The third key term, "hospitality," rests on Hebrews 13.2: "Show hospitality to strangers, for thus have some entertained angels unawares." Hospitality relates to the foregoing idea of patience in the sense that the sick were in the care, above all, of divine providence. A "hospital" was once a place where one was, literally, a guest of God (see page 118).

THE LIFE TO COME

When confidence in the resurrection of the body was almost universal, a long and healthy life first time around was not the only or even the most important thing to be wished for: the real life was the one to come. Medicine rose to prominence at about the same time that confidence in the life to come began to falter. Many have now come to see medicine as at risk of being transformed from a practice conducted by those whose faith in the life to come enabled them to cope with the tragedies of this life, into a new "religion" that seeks to extend this present life for as long as possible.

ETHICS AND MODERN MEDICINE

The combination of scientific advance and the transformation of public perception have evoked a host of dilemmas. Some of these concern the distribution of resources—so that what can be done, can be done to more than just a few. Others concern the propriety of medical intervention in areas, particularly concerning the beginning and end of life, which for many centuries had been thought of as simply God's domain. For example, if a couple cannot conceive naturally, is it right for conception to be medically assisted? Is it right for eggs fertilized outside the womb to be frozen and kept indefinitely, or used for other purposes? Such issues are a challenge to pastors and theologians, because they raise questions of why Christians have children; whether every setback in life should look to a medical or technological solution; and whether there are some interventions that come closer to the nature and purpose of life than humans should tread without great fear.

SCIENCE AND TECHNOLOGY

THE CHURCH AND GALILEO

For the Roman Catholic Church, the heliocentric theory of Copernicus and Galileo (see main text) was contrary to scripture (such as Ps. 93.1, 104.5), but it was permissible to discuss such ideas as long as one did not advocate them, which would be heretical. In 1616 Galileo was warned not to "hold or defend" his theory. He endeavored to obey, but his *Dialogue Concerning the Two Chief World Systems* (1632) appeared to ridicule the prevailing Aristotelian geocentric view, and Galileo was tried by the Inquisition for heresy. Forced to recant and banned from publishing further works, Galileo spent the rest of his life under house arrest.

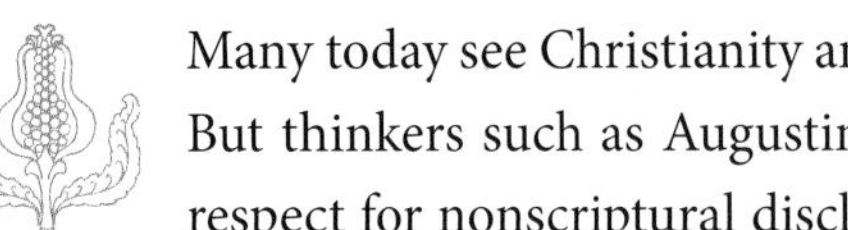

Many today see Christianity and science as constituting rival claims to truth. But thinkers such as Augustine and Thomas Aquinas articulated a healthy respect for nonscriptural disclosures of wisdom and insight. For such theologians the more that could be found out about God's creation, the more that could be learned about God. The birth of the modern university arguably lay in setting aside the view that human weakness is primarily due to sin, and instead asserting that human limitations are largely due to lack of knowledge. By the seventeenth century, one can discern a watershed. Prior to that time, a "discovery" usually meant the unearthing of an ancient manuscript from the Classical era. After that time, discovery meant the finding of something altogether new—a new element, theory, or cure.

One key figure was Francis Bacon (1561–1626), who pioneered a systematic approach to investigating natural phenomena. Bacon's work was a landmark in the rhetorical and theoretical framework for science. Another significant role was played by Blaise Pascal (1623–1662), with his work on fluids and the concepts of vacuum and pressure, together with his major contribution to mathematics. Isaac Newton (1643–1727), most famous for his three laws of motion, was a third towering figure who, like Pascal and Bacon, saw his work as being well within the sphere of Christianity. Indeed for most of the

Viewing the Heavens. *Father Emmanuel Carreira operates the telescope at the Vatican Observatory in Castelgandolfo, south of Rome, June 23, 2005. The Vatican Observatory is one of the world's oldest astronomical institutes. Contrary to popular assumptions, the Roman Catholic Church has long promoted scientific enquiry, with Jesuits at the forefront of Catholic scientific endeavor for 450 years.*

period up until the later nineteenth century, a clash between Christianity and science was avoided by a gradual modification in Christianity's claims concerning the natural world.

CHALLENGES TO TRADITION

Nonetheless the twentieth-century confrontation between conservative Christianity and modern science was not without precedent. For example, the philosophy of David Hume (1711–1776) is based on a rejection of the widely held assumption that human minds were miniature versions of the divine mind. Key moments were the discovery, originally by Nicolaus Copernicus (1473–1543) and confirmed by Galileo (1564–1642; see sidebar), that the Earth went round the sun (heliocentrism); and Darwin's theory that human beings and apes were descended from a common ancestor (see box). Copernicus' discovery meant that humanity was no longer at the center of the universe, Darwin's that humans were no longer inherently different from other animals and therefore by implication superior to them. Both ideas directly challenged biblical sources.

The legacy of such developments tends to be either a Christian ethic that places science and technology in a place of honor, in relation to which ethics must constantly adjust, or an interiorization of Christianity to a private, "spiritual" realm, with relatively little claim on external physical realities.

DARWIN AND DARWINISM

In 1859 Charles Darwin (1809–1882) published *The Origin of Species*. Its argument, that all species have evolved over time through the process of "natural selection," soon became accepted as the foundation of biology, providing as it did a unified theory of the diversity of life. Darwin's work sparked fierce debates. Samuel Wilberforce, bishop of Oxford, asked T.H. Huxley if he was descended from apes on his grandfather's or his grandmother's side; Huxley replied he "would rather be descended from an ape than from a cultivated man who used his gifts of culture and eloquence in the service of prejudice and falsehood."

Darwin's theories were at the heart of a famous trial in 1925, when John Scopes, a high school teacher in Tennessee, was charged with teaching evolution. Scopes lost the case, and the trial has come to epitomize the battle between fundamentalism and science. In recent years similar controversies in the US have centered on a new form of anti-Darwinian creationist theory known as "intelligent design."

Darwin as a monkey, *an English cartoon of 1861 satirizing the theory of evolution. However, Darwin never stated that humans were descended from apes, nor—while he did abandon Christianity—did he ever profess to be an atheist. Many Christians were open to Darwin's theory: thus for Frederick Temple, later Archbishop of Canterbury, it showed God's purpose "in the slow workings of natural causes."*

SEX AND SEXUALITY

OPPOSITE **Solomon and the Queen of Sheba** *in the Song of Songs. Christian tradition regards this work as an allegory of the love of Christ for the church, but ostensibly it presents a love affair between a man and woman. From the Winchester Bible, English, ca.1150–1180.*

The tendency in the Old Testament is to regard marriage and family life as a sign of God's blessing. In the New Testament, however, the time is short and the urgency of mission is great: thus singleness is seen as the norm.

Anxiety about sexual excess surfaces in many places in the New Testament, but what made the Christian ethic unusual was that it regarded unchastity for a man as severely as unchastity for a woman. This made marriage much safer for women than in other contemporary traditions. The early church was not clear whether divorce was ever permissible, since the New Testament is not entirely transparent. For example, when Jesus says "anyone who divorces his wife, except on the ground of unchastity, causes her

CONTRACEPTION AND HOMOSEXUALITY

Contraception and homosexuality remain two of the most potent issues that continue to divide Christians. At the 1930 Lambeth Conference, the Anglican Communion formally recognized the appropriate use of certain forms of contraception. However, the 1968 papal encyclical *Humanae Vitae* ruled out any form of contraception for Roman Catholics other than the rhythm method, and this remains the church's view. Most other Protestant churches permit contraception so long as it does not lead to promiscuity. Many conservative churches would allow it only within marriage, a position similar to the broad consensus within the Orthodox Church.

Homosexuality is even more divisive, as shown by events in 2003. The election that year of Gene Robinson, a man living in an active relationship with a same-sex partner, as Episcopal bishop of New Hampshire, was welcomed by many, but aroused intense opposition in more traditionalist, conservative parts of the Anglican Communion, particularly, but by no means exclusively, in Africa.

The Right Reverend Gene Robinson *is invested as 9th Episcopal bishop of New Hampshire at St. Paul's Episcopal church in Concord, New Hampshire, on March 7, 2004. Robinson's appointment was controversial in the wider Anglican Communion, in which he became the first openly homosexual bishop.*

to commit adultery; and whoever marries a divorced woman commits adultery" (Matt. 5.32), it is not clear whether or not divorce is comprehensively ruled out, or whether or not remarriage is assumed. The goods of marriage, as they emerged through the early centuries, were the bearing and rearing of children, the channeling and enjoyment of physical desire, and the making of a special bond of holy friendship.

The major transformation in the Western church brought about by Pope Gregory VII (1073–1085; see page 39) profoundly affected marriage. It increasingly began to be regarded as a sacrament, and release from its bonds required ecclesiastical consent. Clergy were finally forbidden to marry in 1139. Nonetheless, until relatively recent times most marriages were ones of social convention, entered into without a formal ecclesial ceremony.

SEX AND MARRIAGE

Two themes have shaped the discussion of sex and sexuality throughout church history. The first is the degree to which sexual passion is a holy gift, to be channeled appropriately, or a destructive power, to be harnessed by the disciplines of marriage. The second is the extent to which marriage and embodied love are matters of social custom, adaptable to local cultural expression, or unalterable forms of life revealed in the New Testament. There remains a tension between the latter's affirmation of love and the body (as Eph. 5.28–33) and its identification of singleness as the norm for Christians.

In the modern era a number of factors have tended to dismantle the notion of marriage as an unalterable given. Longer life expectancy and the greater economic independence of women made divorce seem increasingly possible and sometimes necessary. The profound shift from economic unavoidability to romantic urgency as the basis for a relationship, at least in the West, has likewise influenced cultural expectations about sex before marriage and remarriage after divorce. Reliable birth control has made childbearing seem less inherent to the role of wife, while sexual encounters for the unmarried may have come to seem less dangerous or furtive and indeed, in some groups today, almost routine.

In a secular culture where sex had come to be regarded as a natural, even therapeutic, expression of feeling, rather than a dangerous force for the subversion of social and personal stability, it became logical, for many, to affirm sexual expression among those attracted to their own sex. All these developments have caused enormous heartsearching for churches, and remain largely unresolved areas in Christian teaching and practice (see box).

GOD AND SEXUALITY

New Testament texts (such as Mark 10, Eph. 5.28–33) reflect the ambiguity about whether marriage, gender, and sexuality reflect the way God has ordered creation, or, more significantly, the way God has entered history to draw all people to himself, as in the following famous passage: "There is no longer Jew or Greek, there is no longer slave or free, there is no longer male and female; for all of you are one in Christ Jesus." (Gal. 3.28)

WAR AND VIOLENCE

THE REFORMATION AND WAR

While generally a strong opponent of war, Martin Luther was outraged by atrocities committed during the Peasant's Revolt and supported the nobles who suppressed it in 1525. Huldrych Zwingli (1484–1531) died on the battlefield. These and other conflicts that followed the religious division of western Europe, especially the French Wars of Religion (1562–1598) and the Thirty Years War (1618–1648), were as brutal as any hitherto seen in Europe, and in the eyes of later philosophers such as Immanuel Kant significantly discredited claims for the place of Christianity in public life.

The Old Testament includes accounts of wars in which God is sometimes viewed as fighting with and for Israel. By contrast the New Testament appears to have no room for the notion of fighting. Jesus tells his followers to love their enemies and avoid retaliation (Luke 6.27–29.) When Peter cuts off the servant's ear in Gethsemane, Jesus rebukes him and criticizes those who live by the sword (Matt. 26.52).

Marcion (ca. 110–160) tried to resolve the conflict between the two testaments by suggesting that the God of the Old Testament was a vengeful despot and the God of the New was a God of love. But the early church rejected this view as failing to demonstrate the way in which the two were still the same God. Many, probably most, early Christians saw a direct connection between their refusal to worship the Roman emperor and their refusal to fight for him. Christians saw a conflict between Greco-Roman virtue, which presupposed military expression, and Christian virtue, which presupposed peace.

With the coming of the Christian empire in the fourth century, different opportunities and responsibilities began to affect the thinking of theologians. Augustine began to develop a set of criteria—later developed by Thomas Aquinas (1225–1274) and Hugo Grotius (1583–1645)—by which, given their predisposition to pacifism, Christians may

Rows of crosses *in the American Cemetery at Colleville-sur-Mer in Normandy, France, mark the graves of soldiers who died in the Allied invasion of France in 1944. In combating the naked aggression of a violent regime, the conflict against Nazism and Japanese imperialism has been seen by many as a classic example of the Augustinian "just war," at least in its motivation.*

in exceptional circumstances consider a war to be just (see box). The medieval world tended to perceive a division between the religious (such as monks), who followed the ethic of the Sermon on the Mount, with its injunction to love one's enemies, and the worldly, who followed a less binding ethic. The crusades (see pages 48–49) are often seen today as a low watermark in the Christian practice of war: the ultimate end of reclaiming the holy places was taken to justify all sorts of shameful means.

NONRESISTANCE AND RESISTANCE

The nonresistant voice gained a new hearing in Protestant groups that arose in the 1500s and 1600s, through what are now known as the historic peace churches—the Brethren, the Mennonites, and the Quakers. But the great reformers such as Luther and Calvin, while viewing war as evil, were not pacifists (see sidebar). The twentieth century introduced three new dimensions into the question of war. The specter of nuclear war made it seem unlikely that the good that might be achieved could ever outweigh the damage done. The influence of Mohandas K. Gandhi (1869–1948) in the struggle for Indian independence gave attention to nonviolence as a prudential, rather than simply a principled, strategy. And the arms trade emerged as a subject for ethical reflection and an integral part of the imaginative world that made war seem, to many, an inevitable part of human relationships.

AUGUSTINE AND "JUST WAR"

St. Augustine identified three dimensions to war: when to fight (*ius ad bellum*); how to fight (*ius in bello*); and when to stop (*ius post bellum*). A decision when to fight requires a legitimate authority (such as a government or the UN), a right intention (restoration of a suffered harm, such as a territorial invasion), and an overwhelming balance of injustice on one side. In such circumstances, the authority, having exhausted all other avenues, with a strong probability of success and a high expectation that the good to be achieved will outweigh the inevitable damage, may consider the declaration of a war to be just. A just war should be conducted with due discrimination (avoiding harm to noncombatants—a major problem for nuclear and other "weapons of mass destruction"), with due proportionality (avoiding reckless damage), and minimum force.

In recent times criteria for ending wars have been proposed. These seek to avoid revenge, vindictive treatment of those not responsible for the hostilities, and exclusion from the international community. They promote processes such as apology, compensation, and war crimes trials.

Easter at War. *US army chaplain Captain Daniel Bucur leads troops in an Easter service in central Baghdad, Iraq, in April 2003.*

THE EARTH AND ALL THAT IS IN IT

In his *On Christian Doctrine*, Augustine drew an influential distinction between those things humans should "use" and those things humans should "enjoy." The latter were the abundant gifts of God, that never run out, and enjoying them was participating in the worship of God. The former were available to serve the latter. A tension that runs through the history of Christian ethics concerns whether the nonhuman creation is to be "used" or "enjoyed." That tension has become a matter of intense debate in recent times due to the deepening sense of an ecological crisis.

There are broadly four dimensions to the contemporary crisis in the environment. The most publicized issue is the overwhelming evidence of climate change, with a host of ancillary causes (such as the burning of fossil fuels) and effects (such as the reduction in the polar icecaps and rising sea levels).

ST. FRANCIS: PATRON OF THE ENVIRONMENT

One of the most inspirational figures for Christians, and indeed others, with an interest in humankind's relationship to the natural world is Francesco di Bernardone (1182–1286), better known as St. Francis of Assisi. Coming from a privileged background, Francis devoted himself to a life of poverty and to the formation of the order of Friars Minor, or Franciscans (see page 45). Francis is widely commemorated for his love of creation. He famously once preached to the birds, telling them always to praise God. On another occasion he went up into the mountains above Gubbio and persuaded a wolf which had terrorized the townspeople to come down and be reconciled with them. His poem *Canticle of the Sun* refers to "Brother Sun," "Sister Moon," and "Mother Earth." His what in modern terms would be called environmentalist inclinations and his love of peace make Francis a major figure in Christian reflection on ecology.

St. Francis Preaches to the Birds. *The spirituality of St. Francis focused on Jesus' human life and on delight in God in this world. One day he is said to have spoken to the birds flying above him: "My brothers, you ought to praise and love your Creator greatly. He clothed you with feathers and gave you wings to fly and the clear air as your dwelling, and he cares for you though you have neither to sow nor to reap." From a 15th-century manuscript.*

There are at least three other issues besides global warming. One is the rapid depletion of species diversity, currently estimated at tens of thousands annually. This has causes such as deforestation, extensive deep-sea fishing, and the widespread use of pesticides and herbicides. Another is soil erosion and desertification, related to poor farming methods, overgrazing, and the use of inappropriate land for crop production. And finally there is the damage caused by chemical pollutants to global ecosystems.

A vegetable garden *in downtown Seattle, Washington, part of the city's community garden program, which promotes the use of urban land for communal cultivation by organic methods. Christian concern for the environment is inspired by Genesis: "The Lord God took the man and put him in the Garden of Eden to till it and keep it." (Gen. 2.15)*

CHRISTIANS AND CREATION

Christian ethics responds to this crisis first by drawing on the theological theme of creation. Within the Genesis account (see pages 70–71) there are two dimensions, sometimes seen in tension with one another. One is that humanity is called to dominate and subdue the nonhuman creation, as Genesis 1.28 might suggest. The other dimension suggests that humanity is called to live in harmony with the nonhuman creation, with mutually beneficial results, as in Genesis 2.15.

A second key theological theme in relation to issues of ecology is that of resurrection. A foundational article by the historian Lynn White, "The Historic Roots of Our Ecologic Crisis" (1967), put the blame for the alienation of the Christian imagination from the created world on early modern mechanistic views of the universe. But blame has also been directed at views of salvation that seem to save humanity from the physical world, rather than for a renewed world. The resurrection, by which God in Christ is restored to a world made new, affirms the creation by showing how the Earth is permanently a part of God's destiny for humanity and all creation.

One particularly problematic area for Christian ethics is the question of whether humanity is genuinely in the center of God's purposes, or whether the nonhuman (or even inanimate) creation has its own value independent of its usefulness to human flourishing. Perhaps the most controversial area in this regard is the status of animals. The areas in question include the hunting of wild animals, notably foxes, the intensification of breeding and slaughter systems, and the use of animals for scientific or cosmetic experimentation. While many Christians would be comfortable with the premature ending of the life of an animal to achieve a direct human benefit, so long as the animal was well cared for in its lifetime and suffered minimal distress, others would regard animals as moral subjects in much the same way as humans, and would rule out all killing or maltreatment of animals.

4 COMMUNITY AND CHRISTENDOM

There has never been one Christian community. All the evidence suggests that in its early years Christianity consisted of numerous scattered enclaves, planted and nurtured by charismatic and often itinerant figures like the apostles Peter and Paul, in cities in Palestine, Asia Minor, Egypt, the Mediterranean coast of Africa, Greece, and Italy. One divide of which scholars are certain is that between Jewish and Gentile Christians. This was foreseeable, for the earliest Christian communities were Jewish messianic sects. There had been such sects before (the community at Qumran, for example) and there would be many others later. From Acts of the Apostles it is plain that Paul undertook a mission to work among the Gentiles that was eventually recognized by the church in Jerusalem: from this time Christianity was no longer a purely Jewish sect.

To describe communities of the faithful Paul continually used the Greek *ekklesia*, a word that came to mean "church" in the senses of an individual community; the community of all Christians; and the place where Christians meet for worship. Up to Paul's day, however, *ekklesia* had two meanings. First, it was a Greek political term, meaning a meeting place for discussion. Second, it identified those who had been "called out" (from *ek-* meaning "out from" and *kaleo* meaning "to call"). There is nothing self-conscious about Paul's use of the term, and he nowhere defines it. All that can be inferred

The village church of Oia, *on the island of Santorini, Greece, stands out from the jumble of neighboring buildings. With the end of persecution in the fourth century, a distinctive architecture signaled the places where Christ was worshipped. With certain exceptions (such as remote sites associated with particular holy persons or events), churches have always been marked by their proximity to the community which they serve.*

St. Paul Writing an Epistle, *by Claude Vignon (1593–1670). The idea of "the body" as a distinct political unit pre-dated Paul, but the apostle gave this notion a theological slant when he used it to emphasize the unity in Christ of the scattered Christian community of his day.*

is that it was the name used for where Christians gathered to have *koinonia* or fellowship (Greek *koine,* "in common," and *koinon* "communion").

In the mid-first century, as far as can be gathered from Paul's letters concerning the contributions of the Jewish diaspora toward famine relief in Palestine, there was a loose network of associated communities that made certain levels of collaboration possible. What they held in common is clearly articulated in the letter to the church at Ephesus, written by Paul or one of his followers: "One Lord, one faith, one baptism, one God" (Eph. 4.5). Paul employed a unique image to speak of this oneness: "the body." Wherever Christians were, whatever variations there might be in their teaching and practice, they constituted one body, with Christ as its head.

ROME AND "CHRISTENDOM"

In 313, when the Edict of Milan ended all official Roman hostility toward Christianity, the Christian population was perhaps ten percent of the empire's total population, which scholars have estimated at around fifty million. Christians spoke a variety of languages, lived in a variety of landscapes, and were still not organized centrally. Schisms and sects still arose to challenge mainstream teaching; Christian orthodoxy was slow to emerge, but under Constantine I (ruled 306–337) the impetus toward centralization and doctrinal clarity began. Under the patronage of the Roman state the nature of the Christian community changed dramatically, and the reverberations of Constantine's acts were felt down the centuries. Christian apologists like Eusebius of Caesarea were quick to

CHURCH AND EMPIRE

In his *History of the Christian Church,* Eusebius of Caesarea (ca. 263–ca.339) relates a story about the eve of the battle of the Milvian Bridge in 312, when the emperor saw a vision of the cross and the Greek words *en touto nika* ("by this conquer"). He ordered his troops to carry the banner of the cross the next day, and they won the battle.

Whatever the truth of this account, Eusebius's *History* shows the extent to which Christendom was becoming synonymous with Roman imperial power. It is structured around the central figures of the emperors Augustus, who ushered in the universal peace into which Jesus was born, and Constantine, whose reign announced the universalism, or catholicity, of the church.

recognize in what direction the winds of favor were blowing (see sidebar on page 131). Certainly, it was Constantine who sponsored the first ecumenical council at Nicea in 325, which began to distinguish Christian orthodoxy from heresy. Legend also has it that Constantine helped Pope Sylvester to erect the first basilica of St. Peter at Rome over the tomb of the apostle, and if this is correct then with Constantine the centrality of the Roman papacy was establishing itself and "Christendom" emerged. A further landmark came in 392, when the emperor Theodosius declared Christianity the sole state religion.

Christendom, literally the domain of Christ, has been defined as an ideal of universal, theocratic government, with the one universal ("catholic and apostolic," in the words of the Nicene Creed) church guiding the hand of the Christian emperor, who in turn protected the church. Christendom in this ideal sense of a unified religious, geographical, and political entity was shortlived, for barely half a century after 392 the western empire had collapsed, leaving the church, led by the papal see, as the single unifying institution of the Christian community in the West, whose provinces were now ruled by an array of German dynasties. The church itself was divided between a fragmented West and a Byzantine East where vestiges of Constantine's imperial church persisted for a thousand years, with emperor and Orthodox church as mutually dependent institutions.

Golden bust of Charlemagne. *Commissioned by Holy Roman emperor Charles IV in 1349 for the cathedral of Aachen, once Charlemagne's imperial chapel, the reliquary holds part of Charlemagne's skull and was carried in procession during imperial coronations.*

CHARLEMAGNE AND ISLAM

However, the ideal of Christendom did not perish. In the West the strategy of invasion, subjugation and conversion came to a remarkable peak in the late ninth century with a man who quickly became a legend as a champion for Christ: Charlemagne, the first ruler in the West to be titled "Roman emperor" since the fifth century. Charlemagne's conquests were important in reviving the idea of Christendom because of a new factor in international politics at that time. Hitherto, Christianity's enemies had been either internal heretics or external pagans such as the Saxons or the Norse. However, the internal enemies were often amorphous local communities rather than institutionalized bodies organized over extensive terrain, while the paganism of the external enemies was not one which sought converts in the name of an absolute truth.

But from the early seventh century, Christianity's own expansionist vision was countered by another missionizing religion: Islam. In 722, Charlemagne's grandfather, Charles Martel, defeated a Muslim army near Tours, France. This dramatically halted further Islamic advances into

Europe, although in Charlemagne's day Christianity had already been sidelined in former Roman territories from Syria to Spain. The conquest of these erstwhile imperial provinces shrank the land over which either the papacy or the Byzantine empire had effective jurisdiction. Martel's achievements had laid the foundations of a powerful Frankish state which became, under his grandson, the Carolingian empire. It was this geographical area that now embodied the idea of a church under imperial protection (see box).

Christendom after the Middle Ages tended to be understood as a religious-geographical term, meaning the Christian world, or the lands where the population was overwhelmingly Christian. From the Reformation, as the scholar Ernst Troeltsch (1856–1923) perceived, the notion of "church" gave way to that of "sect," with individual Christians identifying themselves not so much as members of catholic (universal) Christendom in the sense of one church and the society of which it was an integral part, as members of a particular Christian group that chose to delineate itself from other religious groups.

In modern times, secularism and the constitutional separation of church and state in most Western states have further reduced the notion of Christendom. Its usage today is in some respects similar to Paul's idea of "the body"—the community of the faithful living within a wider society that, in some places, may be largely indifferent to its presence.

THE PILGRIM CHURCH

As the Roman empire declined, some theologians began to distinguish between the earthly church and the true church, the church as an imperial institution and the church as the mystical Bride of Christ. Augustine of Hippo called the latter the "pilgrim church," the true Christian community, the true kingdom and perfect society whose members would be revealed only at the end of time. Theologically, this was one way in which the church as the spiritual community in Christ was distinguished from Christendom, which was at the same time a religious, political and geographical entity.

THE HOLY ROMAN EMPIRE

Charlemagne (ruled 771–814) conquered most of western Europe, re-establishing a politically unified Western (Latin Christian) civilization. In recognition of this achievement, Pope Leo III invested him, in St. Peter's in Rome on Christmas Day 800, as the first western "emperor of the Romans" since the fifth century. The title died with Charlemagne, because Frankish succession laws meant that his empire was divided among his three heirs. It was not until 962 that Pope John XII, in return for Frankish military aid, revived the imperial ideal by crowning Otto I as "Holy Roman emperor."

For much of its existence the Holy Roman empire comprised Germany and surrounding lands, including much of Italy (but not Rome itself). However, only for relatively brief periods was the emperor ever able to wield effective authority over such a large and diverse area, comprised of more than a hundred separate states; and far from the harmonious collaboration between church and empire that characterized the ideal of Christendom in late antiquity (see main text), the pope and emperor were often rivals (see pages 37–39). The Reformation and, later, the Thirty Years' War (1618–1648) further undermined the empire as a political entity, with Protestant rulers only nominally loyal to Catholic emperors of the Austrian Habsburg dynasty. By 1700 the empire had become, in the Voltaire's famous words, "neither holy, nor Roman, nor an empire."

The imperial ideal did not end when Napoleon finally abolished the empire in 1806. He saw his own empire as its successor, naming his crown "the Crown of Charlemagne." The last Holy Roman emperor, Francis II (ruled 1792–1835), retained his imperial title by creating the Austrian empire. In 1871, the king of Prussia was proclaimed emperor of a second German empire (*Reich*); the "Third Empire" was Hitler's Nazi state. Finally, as a pan-European entity with a geographical, political, and ethical dimension, it could be argued that today's European Union is also not too distant in spirit from the ancient imperial ideal.

SAINTS AND MARTYRS

The Christian cult of saints, or holy persons (Latin *sanctus*, male, or *sancta*, female) living a life dedicated to Christ, arose against a background of both Jewish and Gentile practices. In the Hebrew Bible, two men are taken up into heaven: Enoch (Gen. 5.23) and the prophet Elijah (2 Kings 2.11). Enoch and Elijah were much revered by Jews of Jesus' day. The tombs of the patriarchs Abraham, Isaac, and Jacob in Hebron were also sites for pilgrimage and places of special reverence. Greeks and Romans venerated great human beings (predominantly male): there was a cult of hero worship among the Greeks, while the Romans deified and worshipped certain mortals, such as the emperor.

For Christians, the resurrection of Jesus announced an eternal life in which death no longer had dominion. The dead remained living, but with God. Unlike Jesus and later Mary, who were believed to have been assumed bodily into heaven, a saint's body remained on earth, and these relics and the graves and tombs in which they lay became the

THE FIRST CHRISTIAN MARTYR

The Acts of the Apostles, which dates from before the First Jewish War of 66–70CE, narrates what Christian tradition holds to be both the first martyrdom and the making of the first Christian saint. Stephen, a follower of Jesus, is brought before the Jerusalem council for publicly preaching "that Jesus of Nazareth ... will change the customs which Moses delivered to us." Stephen's impassioned discourse before the council (Acts 7.2–7.53) causes such outrage that he is effectively lynched—he is seized, taken outside the city, and stoned to death.

The stoning is witnessed and approved by "a young man named Saul"—the apostle Paul (Acts 8.1)—and precipitates a "great persecution" against the Jerusalem church. Saul plays a leading role in the persecution before his dramatic conversion experience on the Damascus road. In a sense, the death of Stephen serves as a prelude to this event, and is thus the first exemplar of the power of sainthood and martyrdom.

The Martyrdom of Saint Stephen, *part of a predella (panels below the altarpiece) by Pietro di Miniato (1366–1450). Stephen's stoning was the first Christian martyrdom and the first recorded act of persecution against Christians following Jesus' crucifixion.*

material objects of a veneration that arose from the third century CE. It was not simply that that the holy one now in heaven would listen to prayers said in these places and intercede with God on their behalf; people believed that the saints were still on earth, as spiritual presences and dispensers of divine grace. In his *Confessions*, St. Augustine chides his mother Monica for visiting graves with offerings of food and drink, and there was a growing recognition that such popular veneration was dangerously mixed with paganism.

Ten twentieth-century martyrs *at Westminster Abbey, London, were unveiled in an ecumenical service in 1998. They include (fourth in, from left to right) the Grand Duchess Elizabeth of Russia, Dr. Martin Luther King, Jr., Archbishop Oscar Romero and Dietrich Bonhoeffer.*

The inscription on the tomb of St. Martin of Tours (died ca. 397) reads: "Here lies Martin … he is fully here, present and made plain in miracles of every kind." Still today, the declaration of someone as a saint, known as canonization, requires proof that the person has wrought miracles for those who have prayed for their intercession (see sidebar).

MARTYRS AND MARTYRDOM

From Stephen onward the cult of the saints was closely associated with martyrdom. The word martyr literally means "witness," and describes anyone who willingly dies for witnessing to, and refusing to renounce, their faith. Martyrs were understood to go straight to the bosom of Christ; approaching the body of a martyr, or any object associated with them, therefore brought one into direct contact with the divine. Veneration arose around such relics; the tombs of martyrs, which were often found outside the city walls following the general burial custom of antiquity, were opened and the saints' relics moved into the city itself, often housed within elaborate shrines within dedicated churches. Some churches, such as the basilica of St. Peter in Rome, were founded directly over the tomb sites.

Protestants who died for their faith during and after the Reformation were held in great esteem by their co-religionists but they were never venerated or canonized, and most Protestants rejected the cult of saints. However, Protestants continued to honor many of the old saints as exemplars of holy lives that witnessed to Christ.

CANONIZATION

In the Catholic Church, the formal process that leads to canonization is fairly recent and is conducted by a special office of the Vatican. A lengthy examination includes biographical investigations and volumes of documented evidence. In the past, however, a saint was made by popular acclaim. Long Christian tradition records that the first saint was Stephen (see box), but his sainthood was formally confirmed by Pope Gregory VII only in 1083. Similarly, many local saints in Celtic areas such as Wales, Cornwall, and Brittany were never officially canonized by the church.

SERVANTS OF GOD

The Ecumenical Patriarch of Constantinople, *Archbishop Bartholomew I, visits a monastery on Mount Athos, northeastern Greece, in 2006. "First among equals" of the bishops of the Orthodox churches, the Ecumenical Patriarch is the spiritual leader of an estimated 250 million Christians worldwide.*

In Acts, those in the Jerusalem "council" who endorse Paul's mission to the Gentiles are referred to as apostles and elders (Acts 15.22). This suggests that, even at this early date, the Christian community had an authoritative structure, centered on the Jerusalem church led first by Peter and then by James, the brother of Jesus. Paul's own, earlier, account of the council hints at a looser organization, speaking only of James, Cephas (Peter), and John as "acknowledged pillars" (Gal. 2.9)—but whether of the whole church or just that of Jerusalem is unclear. Communities outside Jerusalem appear to have maintained a high degree of autonomy. Paul's letters mention holders of certain offices (teachers, prophets, healers, and so on) and a hierarchical structure (apostles, bishops, elders, and deacons). It remains uncertain how these offices and structures worked in practice, or how persons were selected and installed. Second-century writers mention itinerant ministers ("apostles" and "prophets") and local structures of bishop, priests, and deacons (see box).

There seems to have been little attempt to centralize the wider Christian community before Constantine I's legalization of Christianity in 313 and the development of the papal office in the fifth and sixth centuries. As the Roman empire declined, the power of the papacy grew in part because the church increasingly gained a monopoly on education.

PATRIARCHS

To begin with, each bishopric was independent and bishops met at synods to decide common doctrinal matters. Wider regions were supervised by senior bishops known as patriarchs, the great five patriarchates being those of Rome, Constantinople, Alexandria, Jerusalem and Antioch. The patriarch of Rome—the pope—was acknowledged as "first among equals," owing to the city's historical importance, but not as head of the church. Papal claims to supremacy over the entire church was a main cause of the split between the Roman and Orthodox churches (see page 186). Orthodoxy retains the patriarchal structure, with the Ecumenical Patriarch of Constantinople (Istanbul) being the "first among equals" today.

By ca. 600 it provided educated administrators and an organizational structure that allowed new lands such as England to be converted effectively through the creation of parishes under a priest and deacon, dioceses under a bishop, and archdioceses under an archbishop (senior bishop). A curia, or papal administration, developed to assist the Roman church in administering such a large area, and the papal office of cardinal arose (see page 147).

With the Reformation forms of church governance multiplied. Some Protestant bodies retained an episcopal structure, particularly where they were the official state church, with the monarch replacing the pope as head of the church on earth. Many churches, on the other hand, witnessed a new democratization, encouraged by the reformers' teaching on the priesthood of all believers. Calvin's community at Geneva replaced bishops with "elders" (or "presbyters," reviving the Greek New Testament term, hence the word "Presbyterian" in the names of some Calvinist bodies). No formal ordination was required: elders were appointed by the community by public acclamation, a practice that continues among many Calvinist churches today. Among the most dramatic of recent changes, a number of Protestant churches now accept women as church leaders (see pages 236–237).

OFFICES IN THE EARLY CHURCH

By the middle of the second century, leadership in the Christian church was organized around three key offices. The bishop (Greek *episkopos*, overseer) was the main leader of the Christians in a particular city or territory. He had primary responsibility for public teaching and was often a focal point for the unity of the church. In his liturgical duties, he was assisted by presbyters ("priests," from Greek *presbuteroi*, literally "elders"). If there were enough Christians for multiple congregations, the presbyters were often the worship leader. Deacons (Greek *diakonoi*, servants) assisted the bishop in his administrative responsibilities, with special attention to care for the poor.

There were also designated readers, exorcists, doorkeepers, acolytes, widows, and virgins. It is increasingly recognized that women participated in church leadership as presbyters and deacons from the early centuries. In the New Testament, women appear as evangelists, prophets, and teachers (Rom. 16.3; 1 Cor. 11.5; Acts 18.26), as deacons (1 Tim. 3.11), as widows with special responsibility for prayer (1 Tim. 3.5). Catacomb images show women presiding at the altar in a posture of prayer. Abbesses continued to be ordained into the order of deacons into the eleventh century.

Britain's Queen Elizabeth II *is welcomed by a cardinal, Archbishop James Harvey, on a visit to the Vatican in 2000. Usually bishops or archbishops, cardinals are papal adminstrators and counsellors in addition to their own pastoral duties. They exclusively elect the pope.*

SCHOLARS AND MYSTICS

OPPOSITE Monetary Regulation, *from the compilation* Decretum Gratiani *by the Benedictine monk Gratian; the book became the basic canon law text. From a 13th-century French manuscript.*

Early Christian scholars, such as Justin Martyr (100–165CE), Irenaeus (died ca. 200), and Tertullian (160–235), engaged in apologetics (defending and explaining the faith to outsiders) and in collecting and editing the texts of what became the New Testament. From the first council of Nicea (325), major theologians like Eusebius of Caesarea (263–339), Athanasius of Alexandria (296–373), and other "Church Fathers" (see page 30) worked systematically to distinguish orthodoxy from heresy; indeed much theological scholarship down the ages has sprung from doctrinal disputes within the church.

TERESA OF AVILA

Teresa of Avila (1515–1582) is one of the most colorful of mystics. Her *Autobiography* tells of a young, pretty woman with romantic yearnings for chivalrous knights, who was nursed into piety at convent school. Having run away from home to join the Carmelites, her life was characterized by both struggle and determination. The first struggles were with her father (who refused to allow her to become a nun), but later she was challenged by a number of male friends, including one confessor who thought her mystical experiences were from the Devil. Her final struggles concerned the Carmelite order and the reform that she sought for the organization of monastic life by emphasizing the solitary vocation. Her raptures and visions were described in three books, the *Autobiography*, *The Way of Perfection*, and *The Interior Castle*. They center on the humanity of Christ and, in particular, the Passion.

Our Lady of Mount Carmel *with St. Teresa of Avila and St. John of the Cross, by Giambattista Tiepolo (1692–1770). The two Spanish mystics (kneeling) collaborated on reforms to the Carmelite order that led to the creation of the mendicant Discalced (Barefoot) Carmelites in 1593.*

From the eleventh century, theological scholarship began to leave bishops' palaces and monastic cloisters for the lecture halls of the new universities. The oldest, at Bologna, was established in the eleventh century for the study of law, particularly canon (church) law. Theology as an academic discipline has produced eminent professional theologians over the centuries. From the late eighteenth century it also evolved specialisms such as biblical criticism, dogmatics, philosophical theology, and ethics.

CHRISTIAN MYSTICISM

Christian mystical literature has its origins in the Platonic understanding of contemplation as a means of ascending to a greater state of enlightenment. St. Augustine recorded being lifted up toward "the eternal being," but the first to describe such spiritual ascent as "mystical" was Pseudo-Dionysius (sixth century), who profoundly influenced both Western and Eastern mystical traditions. In Orthodoxy there is no theology that is not understood as mystical. The line of Orthodox mysticism runs from the Desert Fathers (early hermits and ascetics of the Egyptian desert) to St. Seraphim of Sarov (1759–1833) and Mount Athos (see page 191).

The great medieval flowering of Western mysticism included figures such as the visionary abbess Hildegard of Bingen (1098–1179) and the Dominican Meister Eckhart (1260–1328) and continued into the Renaissance with mystics such as St. John of the Cross (1542–1591) and St. Teresa of Avila (see box; also considered a Doctor). Their writings are often characterized by *via negativa*, an approach to understanding God that is beyond all words and images. This appeal to an ineffable mystical union with the divine can be found in Eckhart's descriptions of the abyss or John of the Cross's "dark night of the soul."

In the seventeenth century, partly because of the Reformation and the Catholic reform that followed it, mysticism became more formalized, even routine, with the mystical increasingly understood as available to all. Even so, certain individuals have stood out, such as the Catholics Blaise Pascal (1623–1662), Madame Guyon (1648–1717), and more recently Teilhard de Chardin (1881–1955) and Thomas Merton (1915–1968); there have been notable Protestant mystics also (see sidebar). Today contemplative prayer is regarded as a common Christian practice and there are numerous sites, many of them ecumenical, to which individuals may go for meditative retreats and spiritual guidance.

PROTESTANT MYSTICS

Noted Protestant mystics have included Jakob Boehme (1575–1624), Jean de Labadie (1610–1674), and George Fox (1624–1691), the founder of the Quakers. From Fox's visions and his emphasis upon the leading of the Spirit developed the Quaker values of peace, the inner light, and silence. Lutheranism also developed a contemplative tradition, known as Pietism (see page 169).

THE SHARED LIFE

The first Christian religious communities may have had their origins in Jewish groups such as the Essenes and the Therapeutae. From early on, individual men and women chose to separate themselves from worldly activities and devote themselves to the solitary life. When John Cassian and his friend Gennadius, often regarded as fathers of the monastic tradition, travelled to Egypt, they were struck by the number of Christian solitaries (Greek *monachos*, hence "monk") or hermits living in the desert there. At Marseilles in the early fifth century John Cassian established two monasteries, one for men and one for women, that he called "cenobitic," from the Greek for "a life in common."

Such religious communities shared, then and now, a liturgical life of prayer and study, a common table, and a rule or constitutional order, such as those of St. Basil of St. Benedict (see sidebar and page 42). Alone in the desert or elsewhere, the hermit fought

THE BENEDICTINE DAY
The Benedictine Rule was more moderate than many of its predecessors, recognizing human frailty and allowing for adequate food and rest. It encouraged a life that balanced worship, study, physical labor, and rest, taking into account the agricultural rhythms of the year. Daily life was structured around the divine office, in which prayers, especially Psalms, were recited throughout the day. Each office has a name derived from the time of day: for example, matins is morning prayer and terce is prayer at the third hour of the day. This model of daily life punctuated by prayer remains influential today. Not only monks and nuns, but devout laypeople will pray a modified version of "the hours."

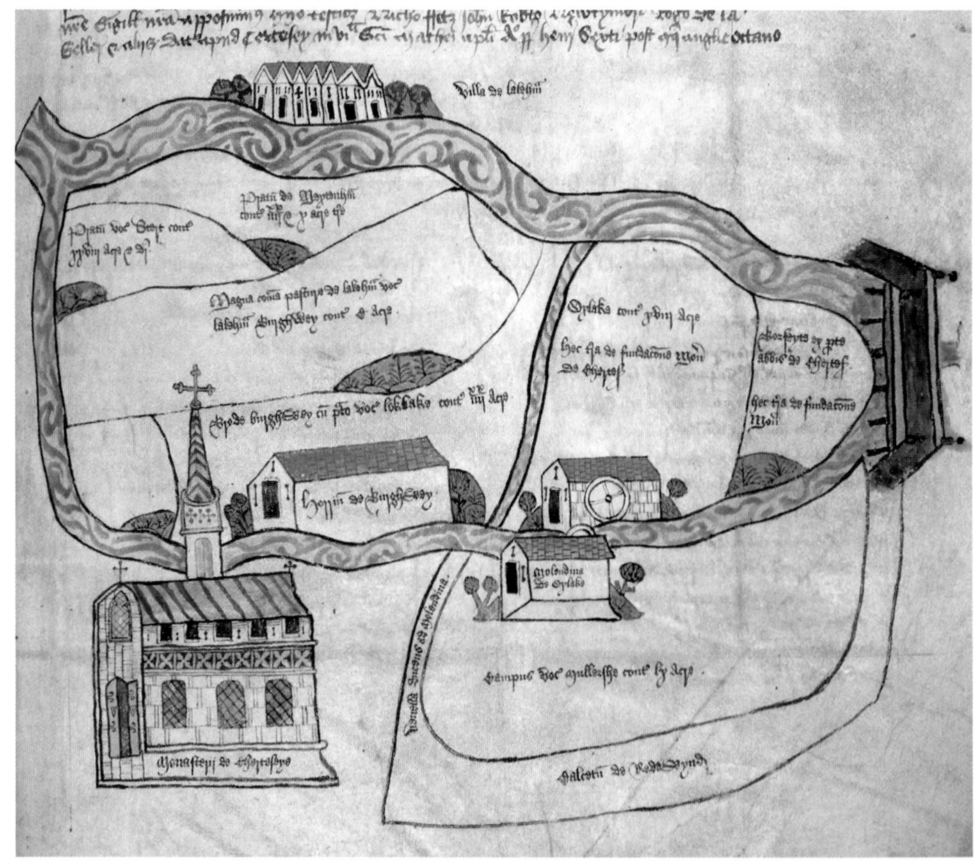

A map of Chertsey abbey *in Surrey, England, ca. 1432, with the abbey church at bottom left. A Benedictine foundation, Chertsey was typical of many wealthy medieval abbeys in being a major economic enterprise. The map shows that it formed the heart of the local community and possessed its own barns, mills, fishponds, and fields.*

the battles within himself or herself and that which had to be disciplined and brought to utter abandonment before God was the individual person. But Benedict left his hermit's cave to head a monastery, and the monastic life was a rejection of solitary individualism and an affirmation of humans as social animals.

The head of the community is the abbot (from Greek *abbas*, "father," in turn from Aramaic *abba*), the feminine equivalent being an abbess. One model for these communities, then, was a family, in which a father ruled over a number of brothers, or a mother ruled over a number of sisters. A second model was the heavenly city, the perfect society. The very architecture of monasteries made them into little cities, with hospitals, libraries, breweries, kitchens and guest rooms. The community was set apart from the world of business and politics, sometimes being established in mountains or secluded valleys.

The monastic life developed as life in western Europe changed. The Dominicans, Franciscans, and later the Jesuits all sought to establish religious communities in urban environments, rejecting the notion of the isolated perfect society in favor of a missionary vision to conquer heresy in the city and serve the poor.

PROTESTANT COMMUNITIES

Martin Luther's personal rejection of the monastic life, and the abolition of Catholic monastic orders in some Protestant regions at the time of the Reformation, does not mean that Protestantism has been resistant to religious communities. The notion of the perfect society of disciplined and organized Christians living a life in common was given expression in new ways. For example, in Geneva, from the 1540s, John Calvin sought to govern every detail of civic living, including private life, from the perspective of his evangelical theology.

If the experiment at Geneva ultimately failed, other Protestant Christian communities arose and even flourished. Pietist communities spread across northern Europe, some springing out of older reform movements within the Catholic Church, like the Moravian Brethren, who go back to the Bohemian reformer Jan Hus (ca. 1372–1415). Transplanted into Germany in the eighteenth century, the Moravians established a community at Herrnhut, Saxony, that is still active today. The Anabaptist movement provided fertile ground for new religious communities, such as those of the Hutterites, Mennonites, and Amish. Many of these are to be found today in the US and Canada. Anglicanism revived its own forms of religious orders from the mid-nineteenth century.

Barn-raising. *Amish men rebuild a barn destroyed by fire at Milroy, Pennsylvania, 1992. The Amish tradition of "barn-raising"—coming together to erect a barn in the space of a single day—is a remarkable example of community collaboration.*

THE LAITY

The words lay and laity, from the Greek *laos* meaning "the people," arose to distinguish those ordained as priests or ministers from the communities to which they ministered. Those who held offices in the early church (see pages 136–137) differed from their congregations principally in function, but as Christianity developed, the difference between clergy and laity became much more one of rank and status. In part this is understandable, if Celsus, a second-century critic of Christianity based in Alexandria, was accurate in his assertion that the majority of Christians were of humble origin, while the clergy were educated (able to read, write, and preach).

The development of ordination, and the theology of ordination as a sacrament or mystery, increased the sense of the clergy as a class of people set apart from others. This

OPUS DEI

The Prelature of the Holy Cross and Opus Dei, popularly called Opus Dei ("God's Work") is a Catholic lay society that was swept to notoriety by Dan Brown's *The Da Vinci Code* and the film that was made of it in 2005. Established in Spain in 1928 by St. Josemaría Escrivá de Balaguer (1902–1975), the society became a personal prelature in 1982 under Pope John Paul II and today operates in sixty-four different countries. Its aim is to integrate spiritual formation with the working life of laypeople, with a particular emphasis on the values of family life. Toward that end, Opus Dei provides opportunities for retreats, lectures and spiritual guidance, often at houses purchased particularly for the society's mission.

Although mainly composed of laypeople, it is governed at a senior level by a Prelate—appointed by the pope—with two main representatives called Vicars. These assign pastoral responsibilities to priests who serve the society. The Prelate and Vicars work through appointed councils in which there is a lay majority.

A statue of St. Josemaria Escriva de Balaguer, *recently erected in an alcove on the outside wall of St. Peter's basilica in the Vatican, is blessed by Pope Benedict XVI on September 14, 2005. The founder of Opus Dei was canonized by Pope John Paul II in 2002.*

An Alternative Worship Service *at St. Peter's church, Vauxhall, London, held in November 2005 to celebrate the second birthday of Vaux, a community founded by those who wished to explore the Christian faith through unstructutred forms and their own preferred types of media.*

setting apart was a consequence of vocation, being "called" by Christ, and was therefore understood as a special commission. The laying on of hands at ordination was viewed as directly passing on the spiritual charism that Jesus gave to the apostles, and to Peter in particular. The laity lacked this charism, associated with vocation and ordination, and therefore were obliged to submit to ecclesiastical authority.

In Protestantism, the teaching on the priesthood of all believers led to a leveling of the hierarchical difference between clergy and laity. Increasingly, laypeople became much more involved in ecclesial matters. For example, a House of Laity with voting rights forms part of the General Synod, the legislating body of the Church of England, and lay bodies exist in the equivalent legislatures of other Anglican and Episcopal churches. In fact, the day-to-day running of most churches, including much of their pastoral work, would be impossible without lay participation.

LAY DUTIES

Specific duties of the laity were elaborated on in canon (church) law and in various catechisms (later articles of faith and confessions): for example, they are to live moral lives and show their commitment to the church. Neither Cassian nor Gennadius, two of the founders of monasticism (see page 140), was ordained when they visited the Egyptian desert, nor were the solitaries they encountered—until the founding of the Dominicans in 1216 most men and women living in communities belonged to the laity. Today, Roman Catholic laypeople can become "third order" members of religious orders such as the Dominicans and Jesuits (see page 43). There are certain circumstances where laypeople are given dispensation to administer sacraments (baptism and confession).

LAY EDUCATION

In the twelfth century, nearly all university students embarked on careers in the clergy. However, by the fifteenth century nearly half of graduates were destined for secular positions. During the same time, the availability of lay education in basic literacy in both Latin and the vernacular increased greatly. In cities, cathedral schools were established; in more rural locations, monasteries continued to provide basic education. The profusion of works in the vernacular in the fourteenth and fifteenth centuries, including prayer books, poetry, instructions for hearing mass, histories, and so on, reveal the growing demands of lay readers, both male and female. The printing press, invented in 1450, capitalized on this growing demand.

5 THE POPE AND THE CATHOLIC HIERARCHY

Among the most hierarchical religions in the world, Catholicism is governed by the pope—the bishop of Rome—and some five thousand bishops. Together they oversee more than one billion Catholics, making it the largest Christian denomination. Today, the pope (from Latin *papa*, "father") rules the world's smallest independent state yet is a powerful figure globally in religion, politics, and social policy. Since it was founded, the Roman Catholic Church has played a significant role not only in the spiritual lives of its adherents but also in the development of Western culture and its bodies politic. Popes have owned principalities, advised monarchies, established moral codes, governed educational institutions, served as patrons of music

St. Peter's basilica, *the Vatican, Rome. As implied in its title, Roman Catholicism has a geographic center, now the 109 acres (44 ha) of the Vatican City within Rome. But from 754 until 1871 popes ruled a substantial area, the Papal States, that included part of Italy.*

and art, and fought wars—all in the name of the church. Their decisions have helped to shape the religious, social, cultural, and political landscape (see page 155). However, the church's long history also includes scandal, corruption, and abuse of power. Nevertheless, the number of the church's adherents has steadily grown, its basic structures have remained in place, and its role in history, while often debated, has remained influential. The Holy See, the political dimension of the Vatican, maintains diplomatic relations with most countries.

THE ROLE OF THE POPE

Catholics believe that the office of the papacy follows what is known as the Apostolic Succession, an unbroken line from the apostle Peter, who was appointed by Jesus as the rock upon which he would build his church (Matt. 16.16–19—although some Protestant scripture scholars dispute the interpretation and significance of this passage).

In addition to being a spiritual leader for Catholics, the pope has the responsibility for the teachings and the functions of the Roman Catholic Church. In this role he is

PAPAL INFALLIBILITY

The dogma of papal infallibility is relatively recent, having been officially proclaimed only at the First Vatican Council (Vatican I) in 1870. The teaching does not mean that anything the pope proclaims must be taken as true. On the contrary, infallibility pertains only to papal statements that are explicitly noted as being *ex cathedra*, meaning "from the chair" (of Peter). In fact it has been invoked only twice in the history of the church, both times to honor the Virgin Mary. The first (by Pope Pius IX in 1854, before the infallibility doctrine was official) proclaimed Mary's immaculate conception (see page 151) and the second (by Pope Pius XII in 1950) her bodily assumption into heaven.

At Vatican I some Catholics opposed the idea of making the doctrine official and some left the church over the issue. Most Protestant theologians continue to view the doctrine as a barrier to the unity of the Christian churches.

St. Peter with the Keys to Heaven, *by the Austrian Friedrich Pacher (ca. 1435–after 1508). Catholics believe that the office of the papacy follows an unbroken line from Peter, appointed by Jesus as the rock upon which he would build his church (Matt. 16.16–19). Here, the apostle also wears the papal triple tiara, or crown, rarely worn by modern popes.*

guided by three sources from which the church derives its teachings and practices: scripture, tradition, and the Magisterium (the teaching authority of the church). The revelation contained in the Bible serves as a primary source of the church's teachings, but not the only one. Catholicism holds that the third person of the Trinity, the Holy Spirit, continues to guide the church, authorizing it to interpret revelation and to declare teachings that are implied in scripture or revealed to the church through the work of the Holy Spirit itself. The church also attempts to maintain consistency from generation to generation, upholding tradition.

The pope, the supreme pontiff (from the Latin *pontifex*, literally "bridge-builder") of the church, has broad authority to govern and is assisted in his duties by the bishops, who oversee regions (dioceses) where Catholics practice. Together the pope and the bishops (including archbishops, as senior bishops are called) form a governing body.

One very prominent group of bishops is the cardinals. Originally *cardinalis*, the adjective from Latin *cardo* ("a reinforcing beam"), described those priests who presided over the four major basilicas of Rome (St. Peter, St. Paul, St. Mary Major, and St.

EASTERN CATHOLIC "PARTICULAR" CHURCHES

About two percent of Catholics worldwide belong to those Eastern or "Particular" churches that maintained positions of theology held by Rome and remained in full communion with the papacy after the split of 1054 (see page 39). They are also described as "autonomous ritual churches," because although they recognize the authority of the pope, they follow rites similar to those of the Orthodox churches.

Divided into five main traditions (Alexandrean, Antiochean, Armenian, Chaldean, and Byzantine) and twenty-two separate churches, each Particular Church has its own elected local hierarchy that is approved by Rome. The liturgical rites, canon law, and spiritual practices all differ from those of the Latin church. Rome's relationship with the Eastern churches is overseen by the Vatican Congregation for the Oriental Churches, which includes patriarchs (chief bishops who govern federations of dioceses) and archbishops from these churches.

Ghara Kelisa (Black Church) *is a 10th-century Armenian church near Maku, in the modern-day Islamic Republic of Iran. It was erected in honour of St. Thaddeus, an apostle martyred in the area while spreading the gospels in the 1st century.*

Scarlet-clad cardinals *gathered for the funeral mass of Pope John Paul II in April 2005. The blood-red choir dress, seen here, signfies the clerics' willingness to die for their faith. Ordinary dress is a black cassock with red piping and a red sash.*

Lawrence). Noteworthy for their titles and distinctive garb, their number has varied from as few as a dozen in the early centuries of the church to as many as around two hundred in 2008. The cardinals, sometimes referred to as the "Princes of the Church," have grown to have a prominent role in church governance because they generally head important archdioceses and Vatican offices. In early modern Europe, in a number of countries individual cardinals assumed great secular power by achieving influential positions in government—for example, cardinals Richelieu and Mazarin in pre-Revolutionary France, and Cardinal Wolsey in England under King Henry VIII. Within the church, however, since 1059 the cardinals' most important task has been as the exclusive electors of the pope (in modern times himself always a cardinal). Today the papal electorate is limited to cardinals under the age of eighty.

GUIDANCE FOR THE FAITHFUL

Formal pastoral letters from the pope are known as encyclicals. They are addressed to the bishops and, since Pope John XXIII (1958–1963), to "all persons of good will" (*quam homines universi cupidissime*). The subjects of these letters vary widely, from social justice, to the church's relation with other religions, to pastoral practices. Intended to guide and instruct, these are not infallible although their teachings are supposed to be followed by the faithful. Most of the fundamental doctrines that the church articulates come from councils in which, since the eleventh century, the pope convenes the bishops of the church to discuss and proclaim church teaching. The Second Vatican Council (Vatican II, 1962–1965) was the last such gathering.

"GOD IS LOVE"

The first encyclical issued by Pope Benedict XVI in December 2005 was *Deus Caritas*, about the subject of faith through Christian love, addressing issues of the nature of giving and receiving love. The pope also made it clear that social justice is the responsibility of politics and the laity, but that the church should inform such debates with reason guided by faith; the church's social activism should be devoted to charity with a religiously motivated character.

THE SEVEN SACRAMENTS

TRANSUBSTANTIATION

Vatican II described the sacrament of the Eucharist as "the fount and apex of the whole Christian life." The focal point is the moment of "transubstantiation," when, Catholics believe, the bread and wine actually turn into the body and blood of Christ. This transformation occurs when the presiding priest says the words "This is my body" and "This is my blood" over the bread and wine. The doctrine holds that at the Eucharist the "substance" of the bread and wine becomes the body and blood of Christ while the "accidents" (appearances) remain the same. How the bread and wine become the body and blood of Christ cannot be explained scientifically and is regarded, along with the Trinity, as one of the central mysteries of the faith.

The central ritual in Roman Catholic worship is the Mass, which is celebrated daily and attended by the faithful in large numbers on Saturday evening and Sunday (see page 94–95). The climax of the Mass is the Eucharist, one of the seven sacraments celebrated by Roman Catholics that are considered to confer God's grace. Three—baptism, Eucharist, and confirmation—are known as sacraments of initiation because they are the gateway to the Catholic community. In the ancient church these were conferred at the same time, as they still are today for adults at Easter, but ordinarily are conferred today at various chronological intervals of a Catholic's life.

INITIATION

The act of baptism initiates one into the church, during which the use of water offers an outward symbol of cleansing from sin and of the Holy Spirit entering the person. Infant baptism is the norm in Catholicism, though a person may be baptized at any stage of life. The church recognizes the universality of Christian baptism so that Protestants who wish to become Catholic need not be rebaptized.

The Eucharist, ordinarily received during the ritual of the Mass (see pages 94–95), is thought to sustain the church community. Protestant Christians have their own form of Eucharist but do not agree with the Catholic doctrine of "transubstantiation" (see sidebar, left). The sacrament of confirmation affirms a person's commitment to being a Catholic, completing the sacraments of initiation. Normally the church confers this sacrament on adolescents from the ages of about thirteen to seventeen.

VOCATION AND HEALING

Marriage is the only sacrament that is not conferred by a bishop, priest or deacon; the latter witnesses the marriage but the bride and groom complete the sacrament together. The Catholic Church does not recognize divorce, since sacraments cannot be cancelled, but marriages can be annulled (signifying that a sacrament was never conferred), and the children from an annulled marriage are legitimate.

The one sacrament conferred only by a bishop is holy orders—that is, becoming a deacon or priest who will confer the sacraments. Catholicism still reserves this role for men only, a policy sometimes questioned in the modern world (see page 154–155).

Reconciliation, commonly called confession, is a distinctive feature of Catholic Christianity (and also Anglicanism). In the ritual, the penitent privately confesses his or her sins to the priest, who forgives the sins in the name of God. In the ancient church, penance, like baptism, was received only once because penitents were sometimes excluded from the church for up to a year. Before Vatican II, many Catholics went to confession weekly but today in some countries many do not go even annually.

The roots for the anointing of the sick, or unction, are found in the New Testament Letter of James, during which he states: "The prayer of faith will save the sick, and the Lord will raise them up; and anyone who has committed sins will be forgiven." (James 5.14–15.) There were times in the church's history when the sacrament was administered only when death was imminent, giving rise to the term "extreme unction" (Latin *unctio extrema*, "final anointing"), which some Catholics still use. However, the sacrament is intended for all who are ill, not only for those who are close to death.

The Altar of the Seven Sacraments *by Rogier van der Weyden (1400–1464), ca. 1445–1450, is a triptych composed as three naves. The central panel is dominated by the crucifixion scene, which explains why the work also represents the Eucharist. The side naves contain depictions of baptism, confirmation and confession (left) and ordination, marriage and extreme unction (right).*

THE MOTHER OF GOD

If there is one figure besides the pope who separates Protestants and Catholics, it is Mary, the mother of Jesus. Both communities acknowledge her role in scripture, but Catholics have a special devotion to Mary as the mother of God—a phrase not found in the New Testament but used in the church from about the fourth century—and believe that Mary was a perpetual virgin, bestowing on her the title "Blessed Virgin." She is the most popular Catholic saint and in many respects her position is similar in Eastern Orthodoxy, which likewise celebrates four annual feasts centered on the Theotokós, or "God-Bearer." Mary, who appears in the Qu'ran, is also revered by Muslims, who believe that she was Jesus' virgin mother, while denying his divinity.

APPEARANCES OF MARY

Many Catholics are fascinated with miraculous apparitions, or appearances, of Mary at such places as Guadalupe in Mexico, Fátima in Portugal, Lourdes in France, and numerous less celebrated locations worldwide. Many believe that Mary appeared to children in these places, offering messages of hope and resulting in pilgrimage sites to which millions of Catholics have journeyed in search of Mary's intercession. Such sites have a long history; for example Walsingham in Norfolk, England, was a popular pilgrim destination for five centuries following the claim by a local widow in 1061 that Mary had appeared to her in person.

Today, however, the church is extremely cautious about endorsing such claims without evidence and thorough investigation. For example, neither the local church nor the Vatican has officially endorsed reported apparitions since 1981 at Medjugorje in Bosnia-Herzegovina, although it has not forbidden private pilgrimages to the popular site.

Our Lady of Fátima*: On 13 May 2007 a statue of Mary was carried to a mass in Fátima, 80 miles (130km) north of Lisbon, Portugal, to mark the 90th anniversary of the Virgin's supposed apparition to three shepherd children. Tens of thousands of pilgrims attended the event.*

The Coronation of the Virgin with Saints, *attributed to Benedetto Buglioni (1459–1521). The image relates to the Catholic belief that after her death, Mary was assumed body and soul into heaven, where Christ crowned her Queen of Heaven. From the portal of the church of Ognissanti (All Saints), Florence. Mary's presence in Catholic art (see pages 152–153) rivals that of Jesus.*

For many Catholics, Marian piety is as important as their sacramental life, and they pray to her that she might intercede with her son Jesus on their behalf. She is a model disciple of Jesus and an important figure in his life, as chronicled especially in the gospel of Luke and testified to by events such as her role in Jesus' first miracle, the transformation of water into wine (John 2.1–10); and in his passion, death, and resurrection. *The Catechism of the Catholic Church* (1992) states: "The Virgin Mary most perfectly embodies the obedience of faith." During times when the church emphasized the divinity of Jesus rather than his humanity, Mary offered Catholics a human side, and she has endured as a key figure in Catholic art, theology, devotion, and piety.

FEASTS OF MARY

All Catholics celebrate four Marian feasts annually: the Purification (February 2); the Annunciation (March 25); the Assumption (August 15); and the Immaculate Conception (December 8, previously the feast of Mary's birth). Only the first two mark events recorded in the New Testament (Luke). The dogma of the Immaculate Conception, the belief that Mary was conceived without stain of original sin, has its roots in the belief in her perpetual virginity, found as early as the second century. The dogma of the Assumption, the belief that Mary was assumed bodily into heaven at her death, was held from the fourth century.

HONORING THE VIRGIN

The church has bestowed more titles on Mary than on Jesus, including Our Lady of Sorrows, Our Lady of Victory, Queen of Peace, Queen of Heaven, Mother of God, and Mother of the Church. Countless churches, schools, and shrines have been named in her honor and hymns in admiration of her are sung throughout the world. The church devotes the month of May to Mary. She is the focus of the most popular Catholic recitation, the rosary, whose main prayer is the Hail Mary (*Ave Maria*). Some non-Catholics object that Catholics have raised Mary to divine status. But the church honors her key role in salvation history as the human mother of the savior, and holds that she should not be treated as an end in herself. Her importance is in relation to Jesus, who saved her as well as others.

Concerned that Marian piety might decline after Vatican II, Pope Paul VI issued the encyclical *Marialis Cultus* (Devotion to Mary) in 1974 as an attempt to renew devotion to the mother of Jesus. To further encourage a continued esteem for Mary, John Paul II issued *Redemptoris Mater* (Mother of the Redeemer) in 1987, which declared 1988 a Marian Year.

ART AND ARCHITECTURE

THE VIRGIN IN WESTERN ART

The Black Virgin of Montseratt *in Spain is one of a number of dark-skinned madonnas in Europe. It dates from the late 12th century.*

RIGHT *A roundel of stained glass from Germany, titled* The Virgin as Queen of Heaven, *ca. 1530, produced by a glassmaker from a print by Dürer.*

OPPOSITE The Assumption of the Virgin, *1516–1518, by Titian (ca. 1488–1576; detail), is from the Venetian basilica of Santa Maria Gloriosa dei Frari. Mary flies between the apostles, at the bottom, and God, above. The belief that Mary was assumed bodily into heaven at her death is without scriptural reference but was affirmed in the sixth century by Gregory of Tours (died 594), although not solemnly declared until Pope Pius XII's announcement in 1950.*

The earliest representations of the Virgin Mary in Christian art exist in the form of frescoes, such as those at the catacomb of Priscilla in Rome, and tend to emphasize either her role as the mother of Christ, or as an intercessor. One third-century fresco depicts the Virgin bent over the child in her lap, while a beardless figure to her right holding a scroll and pointing to a star probably represents Isaiah prophesying the immaculate conception.

New modes of representing the Virgin were developed during the papacy of Leo III (440–461) and were based on the concept of Mary as Theotokós, as established at the ecumenical council of Ephesus (431). In Rome, the fifth-century doors of the church of Sta. Sabina contain two panels; in one, Mary stands as an orant between Peter and Paul, representing the church, and in the other she is elevated on an imperial throne receiving the homage of the magi.

The Virgin dominated medieval paintings and sculpture as an intercessor, and representations of her seem to have received a special stimulus from the reforms of Pope Gregory VII in the second half of the eleventh century. She came to represent both historical tradition as well as the sovereign authority of the church and during this period images of Mary begin to proliferate in the Papal States and the domains of Matilda of Canossa, who was Gregory's biggest supporter in Italy during the Investiture Controversy (see page 39). At Cremona and Modena, the throne on which the Virgin sits becomes the Throne of Divine Wisdom, a metaphor legitimizing episcopal jurisdiction and legal authority. This motif was adopted in a series of portals at the French cathedrals of Chartres and Notre Dame, Paris, and became a symbol of the authority of the church over secular matters. For example, in one of the west portals of Notre Dame the Virgin is enthroned between a standing bishop and a kneeling king.

Increased devotion to the Virgin Mary is attested in the dedications to her of numerous cathedrals and churches in the twelfth and thirteenth centuries, a process no doubt stimulated by the sermons of Bernard of Clairvaux. From about this time, in tympanum adornments she is depicted with a crown, seated to Christ's right on an equally adorned throne. She also appears in scenes of the Last Judgement, as an intercessor for humankind.

MODERN CHALLENGES

Catholicism seeks to preserve its traditions without radical discontinuity, while recognizing that the church must also live in the present. Historically, most of the church's popes have been European, and the majority of its cardinals still are: fifty-eight of the 115 electors of Pope Benedict XVI in 2005. Yet this bias now has to contend with the fact that most of the world's Catholics live in the southern hemisphere and the church is increasingly becoming inculturated all over the globe.

Catedral Metropolitana *is Oscar Niemeyer's modernist creation in Brasília, Brazil, consecrated in 1970. The concrete-framed "crown of thorns" structure is draped in walls of clear glass—painted in the 1990s—and is glass-roofed, seemingly open to heaven. In the white marble interior, three large angels hang in the nave suspended from steel cables.*

DECLINING VOCATIONS

The church relies upon vocations—a belief that one is called by God—to religious life to provide sacraments and a committed workforce. However, in recent decades while the world's Catholic population increased from 653 million to 1.11 billion, the number of vocations declined modestly to 405,000 in 2004. In some areas (for example, Latin America and Africa) the number of men training for the priesthood has increased, but less than the rate of population growth. The situation for religious orders is worse, with brothers down from 79,000 in 1970 to 54,000 in 2004, and sisters down from more than one

million in 1970 to 776,000 in 2004. Some orders envisage a future with trained laypersons. In contrast, during the same period the number of permanent deacons has risen from 300 to 31,000. Deacons are an order of ordained men who may be married but cannot celebrate Mass or hear confessions. Some have suggested that ordaining women would both ease the shortage and give equal standing to women in the church. However, the prohibition against women priests was formally upheld by the late Pope John Paul II.

The reputation of the priesthood and of bishops was also damaged in recent years by the church's admission that a small but significant number of priests had sexually abused minors. The Vatican responded by requiring bishops to craft policies to ensure that such tragedies would not be repeated.

The church also faces challenges from secularism in which organized religion is marginalized, from globalization that can negatively affect the poor whom the church is committed to protect, and from public policies that conflict with Catholic teaching on issues such as abortion, same-sex marriage, and religious freedom. Despite these, the church continues to grow, the pope continues to be an influential voice in global affairs, and most Catholics remain loyal to the traditions of their church.

CLERICAL CELIBACY

St. Paul commended celibacy (1 Cor. 32–24) although he recognized the value of marriage. The first pope was married and during the church's first three centuries so were many bishops and priests. The tradition of celibacy was upheld unevenly until the Lateran Councils of 1123 and 1139 formally required it, in part to resolve issues of ownership of church property. Celibacy has been maintained since then to the present day.

THE CHURCH IN AFRICA

In the past 30 years, the Roman Catholic Church has grown from 55 million members to 144 million in Africa, where it faces many challenges and some contradictions. The church's moral teachings are often willingly embraced by African Catholics and championed by the hierarchy. Pope Benedict XVI has encouraged the African clergy to resist the socially permissive ways of Europe that have led to wide acceptance of birth control, same-sex relationships, consumerism, and individualism. In many places, Africa faces extreme poverty, AIDS, genocide, and civil war. The church speaks out against poverty and unfair elections, and supports human rights and education. Yet, it is also true that Catholics have been among those responsible for atrocities. The church encourages maintaining faith amidst suffering and stresses fidelity and abstinence while providing direct care for AIDS victims. It actively recruits new members from indigenous traditions and competes with other world religions, in particular Islam, for converts. While numbers of seminarians in Africa preparing for priesthood has grown steadily, the ratio of priests (1 per 28,000) to Catholics remains far behind Europe (1 per 3,500).

The Basilica of Our Lady of Peace of Yamoussoukro *in officially secular Côte d'Ivoire is the second largest church in the world. Built in the then president's birthplace, the cost of the building when it was consecrated in 1990 was about 300 million US dollars—a particularly significant sum in a poverty-stricken land.*

LUTHERANS

Around the world about sixty-five million Christians identify themselves as Lutheran. Often thought of as the first Protestants, they take their name from the reformer Martin Luther (1483–1546), a German monk and theologian, who disliked having a church named after him. He preferred terms such as "evangelical" for his movement and beliefs, because it signaled devotion to the Christian gospel, which was his focus. From 1517—which many regard as the start of the Protestant Reformation (see page 54)—until the nineteenth century, Lutherans were to be found chiefly in northern Europe (Scandinavia and many territories of Germany) and North America. Lutherans were late to begin sending missionaries to Asia, Africa, and the Middle East. Today

A LUTHERAN COLONY: NEW SWEDEN

Protestants early on extended their reach beyond Europe. Most familiar are the English ventures in North America, but other Protestant states were also active colonists, notably the Calvinist Dutch. Lutheran powers also established settlements and governments in North America, among them Sweden, which in the mid-seventeenth century had become a major European power. From 1638 the New Sweden Company founded a narrow strip of settlements along the Delaware River in territory that was later to become part of Delaware, New Jersey, and Pennsylvania. The chief settlement of New Sweden, or Nya Sverige, was Fort Christina, named for Queen Christina of Sweden (ruled 1632–1654), at the confluence of the Christina and Delaware rivers.

Fort Christina was captured during a dispute with the neighboring Dutch colony of New Netherland in 1655 and effectively absorbed. However, the Swedes and Finns who made up the majority of New Sweden's population enjoyed a degree of autonomy even after New Netherland itself was annexed by the English in 1664. The last Swedish territory was incorporated into the new colony of Pennsylvania in 1682. Fort Christina was eventually absorbed in the city of Wilmington, Delaware, which to this day incorporates the Swedish flag in its city arms.

The Old Swedes Church, *now Holy Trinity Episcopal church, in Wilmington, Delaware, was built in 1698–1699 as a Swedish Lutheran church serving Fort Christina, the first Swedish colony. It claims to the oldest church in the US still standing as originally built.*

Lutheranism remains numerically significant in Europe, but many churches are empty, and the vitality, including dramatic growth, is in sub-Saharan Africa. The growth came after the churches there, accepting the mission by Europeans and Americans, took off on their own under native leadership.

Despite cultural differences, Lutherans are quite united in seeing themselves as drawing their teachings from the Bible and stressing as their main theme God's gracious act in the self-sacrifice of Jesus Christ on the cross. Luther and the Lutherans rejected any notion that humans could please God and find salvation through their own efforts, their "good works." The code words are that humans are "justified," which means "made just" and "reconciled to God" by grace through faith. The Lutheran ethic or systematic approach to engaging in works of justice or mercy is that "faith is active in love." Lutherans have been inventive at meeting human needs through voluntary agencies. They strongly support "vocation," which sees all laypeople "called," as are clergy, to find and serve in roles in life under God and for human good.

Lutheranism was and is a fairly conservative reform movement. It kept what they could from the Catholicism it inherited and criticized. Instead of seven sacraments, Lutherans celebrate two. Baptism is administered also to children, by connecting water and the Word of God. Like baptism, holy communion, also called the Lord's Supper or Eucharist, is a "means of grace," through which believers receive forgiveness of sins, when in faith receiving the consecrated bread and wine which is, for them, the real presence of Christ.

A 1630 edition *of Luther's German Bible, a work that had a profound impact on German language and culture and influenced other translations, including the King James Bible.*

LUTHERANS AND THE STATE

Lutherans in Europe were identified, perhaps over-identified, with the state where they were "established" and official, as in many parts of Germany and Scandinavia; only vestiges of establishment, in the form of tax support or other privileges, remain there. In most places Lutheran churches are completely independent of government, but call upon their members to be responsible citizens and to participate in culture through the arts, business, or acts of citizenship. They take doctrine or theology seriously. Having their roots in a university (Wittenberg), Lutherans put a premium upon education at all levels.

In Nazi Germany the Lutheran church was a "state church," and only a heroic minority of Lutherans resisted the Nazi takeover and regime, while others remained passive (see page 112). After 1945 the communist regime of East Germany also controlled religion, but some Lutheran churches assisted in ending the regime in 1991.

CALVINISTS

JOHN KNOX

Calvin's sometime disciple, John Knox (ca. 1510–1572), had a greater direct impact in Britain, particularly as leader of the Scottish Reformation and founder of the Kirk, the Presbyterian Church in Scotland. Knox was perhaps the most courageous and outspoken of the major reformers, in his opposition to Catholicism and especially to the Catholic monarchs Mary Tudor of England and Mary, Queen of Scots. As well as his misogynistic tract against the "monstrous regiment" (rule) of female monarchs, Knox is remembered for his prime role in providing confessions (or "creeds") for the Church of Scotland; his scholarship; and his expressive preaching.

No Calvinist churches bear the name of their founder in the way that Lutherans bear that of Luther; instead they appear under names such as "Reformed," "Presbyterian," "Congregationalist," and "United Church of Christ." These churches nevertheless all trace their heritage to the Frenchman John Calvin (1509–1564). A less stormy character than Luther, Calvin was a staid and systematic type of leader whose 1536 book of doctrine, *The Institutes of the Christian Religion* (see pages 56–57) set forth his understanding of the Bible and the Christian doctrinal tradition with such clarity and force that it had a shaping impact on Protestantism not only in Geneva, where he lived after fleeing Paris in 1535, but in the Netherlands, the British Isles, and North America. Many impulses called "Puritan" were Calvinist and his accents, though modified, still give life to preaching in Presbyterian churches everywhere.

Calvin and Calvinists criticized Catholicism for its demand of loyalty to the pope and hierarchy alongside attempts to see humans made right with God ("justified") largely

"Tipping Up the Great Pot," *a satirical Huguenot (French Calvinist) engraving of 1562 predicting the downfall of the Catholic Church. The efforts of bishops, priests, and monks are in vain as Truth armed with the sword of the gospel tips up a cracked and spilling pot in which a broth full of mitres, croziers, and cardinals hats, cooks over a fire fueled by the bodies of three Protestant martyrs. At top left, the pope topples from his throne.*

owing to their own efforts to please God through their works. Instead, this Reformed tradition stressed God's generous and spontaneous love through a "covenant of grace" associated with Christ. That said, it is often noted that Calvinism, stressing well-ordered Christian life, readily resorted to church law and adherence to the commands of God.

PREDESTINATION

Observing baptism and the Lord's Supper as the sacraments, Calvinists resist any notion that anything mysterious goes on with water, wine, and bread. These are offered as divine ordinances, memorials, and symbols. However, one of the defining features of Calvinism was its emphasis on divine predestination, foreknowledge, and election. This taught that God determined before a human was conceived whether he or she would be saved or condemned. The idea that one could be predestined to be damned as well as saved bred fear among many and invoked disdain from others. In practice, though, Calvinists have never sat passively in joy, sadness or uncertainty because they see human action as foreknown and controlled by God; on the contrary they are strongly activist. Among Protestants they were the most at home with government and lawmaking, and became established by law in Geneva, Scotland (see sidebar), Holland, and much of New England, insisting on a monopoly in church life, exacting taxes, and suppressing dissent. In the past two centuries, however, Calvinists have often led in supporting independent, voluntary, and free churches.

FLIGHT OF THE HUGUENOTS

In France, Calvinist Protestantism grew in significance after the mid-sixteenth century, its adherents being known as Huguenots, a word of uncertain origin. Before long French religious and political tensions erupted into large-scale conflict, the Wars of Religion (1562–1598), marked by nationwide violence including tragedies such as the 1572 St. Bartholomew's Day massacre (see page 56). The leader of the Protestant party, King Henry of Navarre, succeeded to the French throne, as Henry IV, in 1589. He was able to secure his crown only by converting to Catholicism, but in 1598 his Edict of Nantes granted the Huguenots a measure of civil rights and liberty of worship. When Henry's grandson Louis XIV revoked the edict in 1685 there was a great emigration of Huguenots to England, Holland, Prussia, Switzerland, America, the Cape of Good Hope, and elsewhere. Their departure was a significant economic loss to France, and a gain to the lands where Huguenots settled.

The Miracle of St. Cande. *This painted and enameled glass panel depicts an event during the Huguenot sack of Rouen in 1562. According to Catholic reports, when Protestant troops tried to burn the relics of St. Cande in front of the chapel of St. Victor, the relics rose miraculously above the flames.*

BRITISH REFORMERS

In assessing Protestant beginnings in England, focusing on the divorce of King Henry VIII (ruled 1509–1547; see page 57) as the motive for reform can mean paying too little attention to the religious character of the first English reformers. Far more went on than the dissolution of monasteries and sequestration of their lands and wealth, and, in some cases, the smashing of images in churches. Most significantly, Henry VIII was named head of the English church by Parliament. While some "Protestant-minded" scholars went to Wittenberg and Geneva to pick up Lutheran and Calvinist ideas, the king tried to hold to existing doctrinal positions, though he did make provision for the reading of the Bible in churches. Such reading, also by laity, brought about many reformist ideas.

Creativity in the Church of England was evident less in theology than in liturgy. Archbishop Thomas Cranmer, in the reign of Henry's son Edward VI (ruled 1547–1553),

"ESTABLISHMENT" IN NEW ENGLAND

It seems ironic that dissenters against establishment in the form of Anglicanism in England should form a new colony and establish Congregationalism in Massachusetts Bay and Connecticut. The colony provided for the support of ministers and the building of meeting-houses, while Congregationalist ministers presided over public ceremonies. As in England, those who held the spiritual monopoly were tempted to exclude and suppress Baptists, Quakers, and others. So firm was the religious establishment that it effectively lasted for decades after the First Amendment to the US Constitution forbade Congress from passing laws "respecting an establishment of religion."

In 1636, the sixth year of the Massachusetts Bay colony, the founders set up a "New College" in Cambridge. In 1639 it was renamed Harvard College after a minister, John Harvard (1607–1638), bequeathed it his library and half his moderate wealth. Its students were expected to conform to Congregationalist ideals and prescriptions.

The Harvard seal. *Harvard College aimed to educate Congregationalist ministers, but from the first it stressed the liberal arts and helped prepare professionals such as lawyers and business leaders for New England. This seal adorns the Harvard Business School, Boston, founded 1908.*

Queen Elizabeth I *by Marcus Geeraerts the Younger (1561–1635). Following the attempt by her half-sister, Mary I, to restore Catholicism, Elizabeth's 1559 Act of Supremacy reestablished the Church of England, with herself as its "Supreme Governor." Her father Henry VIII had declared himself "Supreme Head," a title that drew criticism on the grounds that Christ alone was the head of the church. This portrait was painted to commemorate the defeat of the Spanish Armada in 1588, an attempt to invade England and restore Catholic rule.*

oversaw and published *The Book of Common Prayer* (1549 and 1552; see sidebar). These moves meant an embrace of Protestantism, a trend which Edward's Catholic half-sister, Mary I (ruled 1553–1558) aborted in her efforts to return the church to papal control. Elizabeth I (ruled 1558–1603), the third child of Henry VIII to succeed, turned once more against the papacy, and encouraged what came to be the Church of England, or Anglican church, in forms that survive to the present day.

THE PURITAN CHALLENGE

The conservative reforms in the Anglican church left some English Protestants dissatisfied. Some challenged Elizabeth's settlement as perpetuating "papal abuses"—for example, the use of vestments by the clergy or kneeling at communion—and were dubbed "Puritans," from their supposed desire for a more "pure" form of Christianity. Tensions developed among these contending factions, and by the 1570s the more radical Puritans had begun to attack the Church of England's episcopal form of government. Some favored a Presbyterian polity, which meant ruling by "elders" (presbyters), and others turned Congregationalist, a pattern in which each local congregation was sufficient to itself. The culmination of these tensions was the English Civil War (1642–1649), between Royalist conservatives and a Puritan Parliament. However, this "Puritan Revolution" led to only temporary and partial victories for these more extreme Puritans in the years of

THE BOOK OF COMMON PRAYER

Cranmer's *Book of Common Prayer* of 1549 was revised a number of times before it attained its final form in 1662. Renowned for the beauty of its language—it is the origin of phrases such as "speak now or forever hold your peace" and "ashes to ashes, dust to dust"—the book is a prime source of Anglican doctrine, traditions of prayer, and liturgy. *The Book of Common Prayer* also refers to modern revisions used in different branches of the Anglican Communion that, like *Common Worship* (2000) in England, have largely replaced the 1662 prayerbook in weekly use; but the 1662 version remains normative and authoritative.

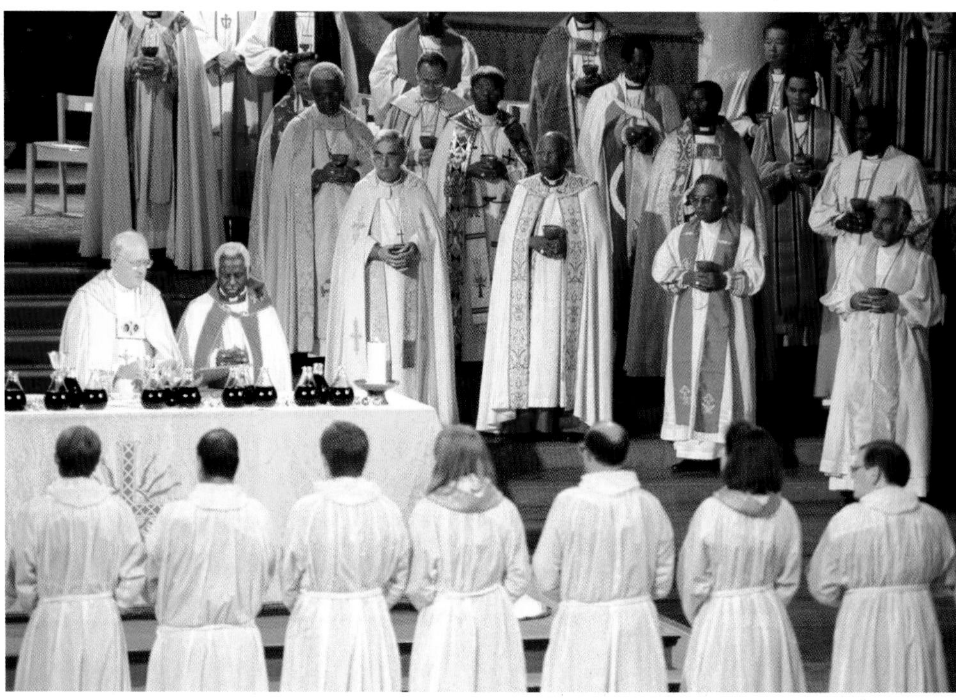

The Archbishop of Canterbury, *George Carey (center left) with Anglican primates during the opening service of the 1998 Lambeth Conference. Held every ten years or so, the conference is one of global Anglicanism's "Instruments of Communion." All Anglican archbishops and bishops are invited to meet for worship, study, and conversation, along with bishops from other churches "in communion" with Anglicanism, bishops from United Churches, and guests from other denominations and faiths.*

the Commonwealth, or republic (1649–1660). By then some Puritans were choosing exile and the freedom to form their own churches in New England.

Centuries of English and Scottish commercial and military endeavors mean that the Anglican Communion (the Church of England and its regional varieties, such as Episcopalians) is now the largest Protestant body in the world—though some elements in the Communion stress their "Catholic" side and resent being included as Protestants.

Anglicans today can trace their main outlines to the times of the Elizabethan settlement of the sixteenth century. Less committed to doctrine than were continental Protestants, they did develop and respond to the Thirty-Nine Articles, the fundamental statement of Anglican belief that was approved after much controversy in 1571. It might be better to refer to the Articles as a summary of teachings rather than creeds or doctrinal statements. From Elizabethan times the stress has been more on "comprehension" (the "broad church"), which allows for a certain tolerance or doctrinal vagueness, though there have been numerous occasions for doctrinal dispute and even heresy trials.

The Book of Common Prayer is another agency that holds the Anglican Communion together. It is used throughout the world, and has been the marker of Anglican loyalty for centuries. Finally, more than any other Protestant group, Anglicans are devoted to the historic episcopate. This refers to the belief that church order proceeds through the succession, since the apostles themselves, of one generation of bishops after another through the practice of prayer and "the laying on of hands" by bishops already in the succession. "Apostolic Succession," as this is called, is not well-defined, but to Anglicans, however it is conceived, it is integral to church life.

DIVERSITY OF FAITH

The many Protestant movements in England and Scotland after the separation from Rome were so diverse that they resist synthesis. Some elements do stand out. Most kept a strong interest in the dissemination and reading of the Bible in the language of the people. The Calvinist idea of "the covenant" was strong, especially in Puritanism. A third theme, freedom, led to imaginative radical reformist groups, especially at the time of the Commonwealth. With colorful names like "Levellers" (or "Diggers") and "Fifth Monarchy Men," some of these sects were so antiestablishment they were viewed as subversive. More sedate radicals moved into Unitarianism, a form of Christianity which denied the Trinity (see page 69).

As modern forms of biblical criticism and theological movements developed in the nineteenth century, Anglicanism incorporated many elements, some of them conservative and some radically liberal, but acceptance of Apostolic Succession and the use of *The Book of Common Prayer* has helped it weather many storms associated with modernity into the twenty-first century. Homosexuality is one of the issues that remain potentially divisive at the start of the twenty-first century (see page 124).

WESLEYANISM

English church reform did not end in the sixteenth and seventeenth century. In the eighteenth a new movement arose out of Anglicanism under the influence most notably of John Wesley (1703–1791), hence its name, Wesleyanism or, more often, Methodism (see pages 62–63). The Wesleyans were gifted organizers and mobilized laypeople and "circuit-riding" preachers to travel to chapels all around the English countryside, and soon after to the new United States, where Wesleyanism became the fastest growing form of Protestantism in the nineteenth century. From the US they sent missionaries into many nations, as they set out to "spread scriptural holiness," an impulse that later became central in movements of "social Christianity," with its impact on public life (see pages 234–235).

ITINERANT METHODISM IN AMERICA

After the American Revolution, Methodists became highly active in the new nation. Theirs was a three-part program: to inspire the "warmed heart" for God, to organize to spread the divine Word, and "to spread scriptural holiness across the land." To that end they developed an itinerant ministry, which was tightly controlled from various headquarters and advanced by "circuit riders" on horseback. They were regularly moved from post to post, so that they would not get too attached to one place.

Among the leaders was Bishop Francis Asbury (1745–1816), who crossed the Appalachian mountains about three hundred times, sharing with his ministers the dangers of life on pioneer roads and in the backwoods, putting up for the night wherever people would be hospitable, and then preaching and praying. Within decades Methodist churches were providing for the spiritual needs of frontier people in communities of almost any size—including the smallest.

Spreading the word. *Goddard United Methodist Church, Fleming County, Kentucky, seen through Goddard covered bridge (built ca. 1825). Vigorous mission efforts in rural areas made Methodism the fastest growing Protestant denomination in the 19th century.*

RADICAL REFORMERS

While most Protestant movements quickly came to be established, which meant set up and protected by law and privileged by governments, some groups wanted to be entirely independent of such civil ties, and to exist on their own as voluntary movements. Also, while most Protestants kept many elements of Catholic culture and some of its practices—including the baptism of infants and the celebration of the Lord's Supper or Eucharist with a sense that the bread and wine had more than memorial significance—substantial minorities were suspicious of anything that to them looked "magical." They would observe sacred ordinances, but without attaching the meanings which they thought other Protestants were stressing superstitiously.

These minority "other Protestants" were, and are, so diverse that it is hard to find a word which might cover them all. There are no neat borders around their informal boundaries, and they bear many different names. They include Quakers, Mennonites, Amish,

FREEDOM ON THE AMERICAN FRONTIER: ROGER WILLIAMS

Roger Williams (ca. 1603–1683), one of the most revered contributors to traditions of religious freedom in the US, arrived in Massachusetts in 1631 as an ordained Anglican minister from England, where he consistently opposed official church establishment but also most Puritan church life. He saw the church as impure, too compromised, too much tied to the state and civil authority. Such radical ideas were ill received in Salem, which exiled Williams to the wilds, where he worked among the Narragansett Indians. In 1636 Williams and his followers founded a new settlement named Providence in Narragansett Bay, later part of the colony of Rhode Island. Following its founder's principles, Providence was the first English settlement in America to offer complete religious freedom. In 1639, to identify himself completely as a dissenter, Williams was rebaptized by immersion and then rebaptized others, founding a Baptist church that still exists today. But he found that too confining as well, and spent decades promoting a Christianity independent of state or formal church.

The First Baptist Church in America, *which claims to be the oldest Baptist church in the US, was founded by Roger Williams in Providence in 1639. He resigned as minister within months, rejecting all formal churches. The church's Meeting House (right) dates from 1774–1775.*

A Quaker meeting, 1790. *Quakerism is characterized by worship in "meetings" where any individual may speak as moved to do so by the spirit.*

and Church of the Brethren, and have tended to adopt forms of church government that resist hierarchical patterns and instead accent the local, the zone in which ordinary laypeople can make a difference. Independent of the state and strong advocates of freedom, these radical reformers and their heirs strongly support the separation of church and state, and are critical of all official (that is, civic) expressions of religion. These churches are sometimes known as "Peace Churches," because their search for peace has often followed radical directions. Taking the Bible literally, as most members of these churches do, has called them to follow teachings of Jesus in the Sermon on the Mount not to resist violent attacks. At the extreme among the peace movements are the Society of Friends or the Quakers, who see peacemaking as a central activity. Most of them also stress ethics and human service, though always on a voluntary, nongovernmental basis.

THE QUAKERS

Among the religious sects that proliferated in England during the Civil War and Commonwealth (1642–1660) were groups founded on the belief that direct experience of God was available, unmediated, to all. The best known of these was the Religious Society of Friends, or Quakers, founded by George Fox (1624–1691), the most remarkable of a number of individuals who had similar ideas at around the same time. Fox believed that an "inward light" resided within every individual, and described this light as the "spirit of

ADULT BAPTISM

The groups known as "Peace Churches" have also from the beginning practiced adult baptism. In cultures where virtually everyone had already been baptized as a child, their spiritual forebears were referred to derisively as Anabaptists ("re-baptizers") for undergoing a second baptism. Their approach has sometimes been called "believer's baptism," because they connect baptism with one's personal decision to come to faith; baptism is a symbol of that decision and of being a member of the people of God. Because their teaching on subjects such as this differed so much from Catholicism and official forms of Protestantism, the Anabaptists suffered persecution in Europe, with many meeting death as martyrs or being driven into exile. Some groups, such as the Mennonites and Amish, eventually settled in America (see also page 57 and 141).

Christ." Because all possessed this light equally, there was no justification for the office of priest or pastor. Any Christian could lead worship, and in any place—Fox dismissed churches as mere "steeple-houses." Moreover, believers needed no special rites to bring them closer to the spirit. In insisting that one's own experience of the inner light revealed the meaning of scripture, Fox denied the Puritan insistence on a literal reading of the Bible. From these beliefs grew the Quaker practice of "silent meetings," with no set structure, people sitting in silence until the spirit moves any individual to speak.

The Quaker insistence of the essential equality of every human being—one product of which was a principled opposition to slavery, notably exemplified by John Woolman (1720–1772) of New Jersey—was to have far-reaching implications, particularly after the foundation in 1681 of the New England Quaker colony of Pennsylvania (see sidebar).

WILLIAM PENN AND PENNSYLVANIA

A son of wealth in England, William Penn (1644–1718) had all the advantages of education and elite status, but chose to become a Quaker, a fact that led him into difficulties. When King Charles II paid off a debt to the Penn family, William took it in American land that became Pennsylvania, a kind of utopian colony where Quaker values were prominent, notably freedom of conscience. Penn was an idealist who in the course of time found that not all colonists lived up to his ideal, and he eventually returned to England. But his record of fair dealing with the Native Americans, his peaceful ways, and his promotion of religious tolerance—which attracted persecuted religious and political groups from many parts of Europe and elsewhere in America—assured his reputation as among the foremost religious leaders in the colonies.

A giant bronze statue *of William Penn—37 feet (11.3m) tall and weighing 27 tons—stands atop City Hall in downtown Philadelphia, the "City of Brotherly Love" that Penn founded in 1682 as the capital of his new province of Pennsylvania ("Penn's Woods"), named for his father, Admiral Sir William Penn. It is sometimes referred to as the "Quaker State."*

BAPTISTS

Another strand of Protestantism in which churches baptize only adults are those "mainstream" Baptists, many of whom trace their ancestry back to dissenters against the established church in New England, mainly in the eighteenth century. They are rarely called "Anabaptist." From New England, through the American south and west, they have been missionary-minded and have spread their teachings and churches around the world. Thus the Southern Baptist Convention, formed in the mid-nineteenth century, is today the largest Protestant denomination in the US. Long devoted to a radical separation of church and state, as it gained power in the latter decades of the twentieth century this Convention began to take a somewhat different attitude, for example supporting government-sponsored or -sanctioned prayer in public places, such as schools.

ETHICS AND TRADE: QUAKERS IN BUSINESS

In his journal, George Fox stated that he had earned and invested enough as an apprentice to support himself in his ministry. Fox's business acumen set a precedent, because from the late seventeenth century Quaker businesspeople gained a degree of success and commercial influence that was out of proportion to their small numbers.

Immediately after the restoration of the monarchy in England in 1660, new laws (collectively "the Clarendon Code") effectively prohibited entry to public office, the universities, and the professions to all but members of the established Anglican church. Many Quakers consequently turned to trade, soon gaining a reputation for probity and fair dealing. For instance, they eschewed the then common practice of bargaining and always sold goods at a fair, fixed price. Always considering business as a means of doing God's work, they also insisted on what might nowadays be termed "corporate" responsibility and on dealing fairly with their employees. They invested some of their profits in decent housing for workers and gave support to trades unions, provided for the education of employees, and set up pension funds for retired workers.

Many Quaker entrepreneurs, such as the Wedgwood and Darby families, were at the forefront of the Industrial Revolution in Britain, not least because they had few other outlets for their energies and abilities. Although some of the confectioners, rail companies, and banks they founded may have long since passed into non-Quaker hands, Quaker names such as Cadbury, Barclay, and Lloyd remain familiar in the international world of commerce.

The Iron Bridge at Coalbrookdale, *Shropshire, England, dating from the late 1770s, was cast by Abraham Darby III, the third generation of a family of Quaker iron smelters. The bridge was the first in the world to be made out of cast-iron.*

SCHOLASTICISM AND PIETISM

Scholasticism is the name given to an approach to philosophy and theology in medieval Catholicism (see page 51). Great thinkers like Thomas Aquinas (1225–1274) used the philosophy of Aristotle to provide a framework for approaching and outlining the faith. During the Reformation, Martin Luther scorned Aristotle's reason as a framework for faith, and most Protestant leaders also stressed faith over reason when speaking of human contact with God. However, not all of Scholasticism was left behind when Luther's closest colleague Philip Melanchthon (1497–1560) wrote his system, the *Loci Communes* (1521) or when John Calvin wrote his monumental *Institutes* (1539; see page 158). The reformers found that if they were to continue to influence university life and thought they needed to resort to some version of philosophy, and many gravitated toward Aristotle's mode of reasoning. This led German Lutherans of the

A BENEVOLENT GOD: ARMINIANISM

Calvinism stressed the sovereignty of God and divine decrees that "predestined" everyone for salvation or damnation. This offended the Dutch scholar Jacobus (James) Arminius (1560–1609), who denied that predestination was crucial to salvation. One was saved by one's faith, in accordance with the decree that they who believe, shall be saved (as Mark 16.16, Rom. 10.9). God predestined who would be saved because he foresaw who would have faith. In 1610, after Arminius' death, his followers issued a Remonstrance, or statement of belief, which led to a split in the Calvinist Dutch church. The Dutch Republic commissioned the jurist Hugo Grotius (1583–1645) to formulate an official policy of toleration toward the disputants, and his 1613 edict declared that the state should leave finer details and differences of religious doctrine to the private conscience.

Arminianism took many different forms. Along with Pietism, it heavily influenced John Wesley, since it motivated evangelists to convert people to a benevolent God. Arminianism's benign deity also influenced more liberal Protestants, and became a factor in the formation of Unitarianism in Europe and North America. Arminianism played down doctrines of divine punishment and stressed ethics and endeavors to promote the common good.

A bronze statue of Hugo Grotius *(Huig de Groot) in his birthplace of Delft, Holland. Inspired by the debate over Arminianism within the Dutch church, the great jurist and lawyer drafted an edict that was an important monument in the history of church-state separation.*

seventeenth century to seek reasoned affirmations that the Bible contained no error and was completely reliable, also in matters of science, geography, and history.

The Fleet of the Dutch East India Company *(1675) by Ludolf Backhuysen (1631–1708). The Calvinist Netherlands built up a powerful merchant fleet and navy during the Twelve Years' Truce (1609–1621) in its war of independence from Catholic Spain. In the same period, Dutch Calvinism split between Arminians and orthodox Calvinists. The latter eventually prevailed, but the Dutch republic became a haven for religious dissenters, including Huguenots and many of the "Pilgrims" who sailed to America in 1620.*

PIETISM

The academic theology of Protestant Scholasticism seemed almost predestined to grow stale and sterile, since it addressed the head more than the heart. In the very universities where Protestant Scholasticism ruled at the turn of the eighteenth century, especially in Germany, a new generation arose that did begin to speak the language of the heart. Known as Pietists and inspired by the writings of Philip Jakob Spener (1635–1705; see page 62), some formed what were called "little churches inside the big church," "conventicles," and prayer-circles, where laity and clergy gathered to study the Bible, sing hymns, pray, and prepare themselves to go forth into the larger community with their acts of charity.

In England, Wesleyans and others also made what one philosopher called a direct, intuitive appeal to the minds and hearts of the Bible, much as mystics and spiritual leaders had done throughout the Middle Ages (see pages 138–139). Protestant Pietist movements had a vision that meant carrying a message of the love of Jesus and the inspiration of the Holy Spirit to unconverted peoples. Thus in New England, where Puritan preaching had often been quite formal, the Pietists—critics called them as "Enthusiasts" or, more moderately, "Awakeners" or "Revivalists" (see pages 172–173)—began to use emotional language as stimulants to piety and expressions of the love of God .

PROTESTANTISM AND THE ENLIGHTENMENT

The Enlightenment (see page 60) is usually characterized as a movement that would replace "revelation" with "reason." It is possible, and profitable, to speak of the Protestant or post-Protestant Enlightenment, since most of its leaders, among them Thomas Jefferson, Thomas Paine, and George Washington, were brought up as Protestants, and many, especially in America, remained members of Protestant churches even as they were developing new religious ideas. Many Enlightenment thinkers developed philosophically-grounded views of the sacred. Thus when they spoke of God, they avoided biblical language. God was not the Lord, or Jehovah, or Yahweh, or the God of Abraham, Isaac, and Jacob, or the Father of Jesus Christ, but more likely the Supreme Being, Grand Architect, Providence, or Heaven.

God, who could be reached by reason, worked through nature and natural law and was seen as an impersonal (or, if personal, a benign) Providence who set the universe on course and did not intervene in natural law. The play *Nathan the Wise* (1779) by German

The Jefferson Memorial *in Washington, DC, was founded in 1939 in honor of Thomas Jefferson (1743–1826), Enlightenment polymath and a Founding Father of the US, of which he was the third president (1801–1809). It was largely Jefferson who drafted the Declaration of Independence. Raised an Anglican, he is often described as a Christian Deist; he was devoted to the teachings of Jesus but his edition of the gospels removes the virgin birth, miracles, and all other supernatural events.*

philosopher Gotthold Ephraim Lessing (1729–1781) typically dramatized the essential and effective unity of the religions. Lessing and others, such as Hermann Reimarus (1694–1768), stimulated what was called "the higher criticism of the Bible," assembling intellectual tools for interpreting sacred texts exactly as one would approach secular ones.

While many Enlightenment figures remained friendly to religion if it promoted morality, others such as the Scottish philosopher David Hume (1711–1776) saw the religions of the churches as "superstitions" that inhibited human progress. Most of the Enlightenment thinkers believed in progress, beginning as they did with a vision of the human not as corrupted, with original sin, but as correctable, on the path to perfection.

The chasm between the churches and Enlightenment figures in salons and universities was not always wide, nor were the borders between them impermeable. Leaders in both could work, as did the American "Founding Fathers" and Protestant church leaders, to promote morality and virtue; they could also promote religious freedom over against religious elements which opposed it. Some Protestants used Enlightenment-style biblical criticism to draw out of the Bible teachings they admired but which they thought had been corrupted by Pietists. Enlightenment understandings of developing sciences were welcome, but when its leaders attacked the churches they were set back. By the early nineteenth century, religious revivalism and a "Second Great Awakening" demonstrated that revelation and experience were firmly back on the agenda.

VOLTAIRE

François-Marie Arouet (1694–1778), alias Voltaire, symbolizes the more radically anti-Christian Enlightenment. Since his base was in Catholic France and his critical writings were devoted to attacks on the Catholic church and priesthood, he is a less prominent figure in Protestantism than in Catholicism. So passionate and effective were his attacks, however, that other Christians felt his sting and shaped some of their defenses of the faith with him in mind.

At the same time, Voltaire would not be classified as an atheist, and put his energies into the topic of theodicy (God's justice), pondering the ways of God toward humans, since God, believed to be a divine creator, often appeared to be destructive. Voltaire advocated belief in immortality and God, not because he personally believed them but because he thought that such beliefs would inspire people to lead more ethical lives.

Voltaire *aged around 25, by Nicolas de Largillière (1656–1746). Voltaire exerted influence in Prussia, Holland, and England, often when he defended mavericks persecuted by official churches. "If God did not exist," he famously wrote in 1768, "it would be necessary to invent him."*

REVIVALISM

In the second third of the eighteenth century, new stirrings roused the Protestant churches and help lead them to growth in revivalist movements. Revivalists, or "wakeners," believed that sin had come between God and his creatures. Among these sins was spiritual lethargy, demonstrated by a decline in church attendance. This situation the revivalists set out to remedy by reviving the faith. Sometimes revivalists would criticize the local preacher and congregation, and then seek to introduce more vigorous speech, song, and action into worship. In Protestant Germany, the impact of revivalism was less obvious, while in England many Wesleyan leaders could be seen as revivalists. However, it was North America that furnished most evidence of revival.

VOLUNTARY SOCIETIES

In Europe, Protestant works of justice and mercy mainly continued patterns inherited from late medieval Catholicism. That is, they were closely linked to civil authorities, who were supposed to care for the poor and ill, along with clergy who devoted themselves to such needs. However, in the decades around 1800 revivalists saw a need for new forms to deal with misery in the new industrial cities of Britain and also on the North American frontier, where civic agencies were nonexistent.

The result was the establishment of voluntary societies, bodies of individuals who associated for a common purpose; thus the American Temperance Society (1826) campaigned against liquor. Usually lay-led and often inter-denominational, such voluntary groups gathered funds, spread information, trained leaders, and confronted all manner of human ills, such as hunger, poverty, liquor, prostitution, and, eventually, slavery. Other societies existed to spread the faith itself, such as the American Bible Society (1816) and American Sunday School Union (1817).

The Ladder of Fortune, *an American lithograph of 1875 illustrating the ladder of virtue leading, among other benefits, to "the favor of God." In the background social ills are depicted such as gambling and financial speculation.*

Foot Washing Ceremony, *by Howard Cook (1901–1980). This watercolor depicts a ceremony in a church near Tuscaloosa on September 4, 1934. Revivalism, particularly the Second Great Awakening, led to the foundation of many African-American churches, where worship was often characterized by joyful expressions of physical rapture.*

THE "GREAT AWAKENINGS"

From the 1730s the Calvinist George Whitefield (1714–1770) travelled in England and the colonies preaching eloquent, stirring sermons that led many to be converted or "revived," with their faith expressed more emotionally than before. Revivalists like Whitefield gathered enormous crowds in Philadelphia or Boston. Meanwhile, Jonathan Edwards (see sidebar) and many others preached the wrath of God on sinners, and invited hearers to come forward, repent, accept the work of the Holy Spirit, and live energetic and focused lives. Edwards and his kind came to be seen as leaders in America's "First Great Awakening."

At the turn of the nineteenth century Wesleyans in England and Awakeners in America helped generate new revival movements. In England they prospered especially in industrial cities, where established churches could not change their styles or democratize quickly enough. The preachers of this "Second Great Awakening," typified by the educator and social reformer Charles Grandison Finney (1791–1875), went with settlers from the US East Coast to the frontiers, there gathering congregations and preaching "scriptural holiness." Many revivalists, like Finney, also highlighted social issues such as slavery or urban poverty. Their focus remained that of their eighteenth-century predecessors: God's sovereignty, human sin, the power of the cross of Christ who died for sinners, and the call of the Holy Spirit.

Earlier seen as rustic folk, revivalists adjusted to urban life and leaders such as Dwight Moody (1832–1899) in America evolved urban-style revivals, erecting tabernacles or tents that held large crowds, ensuring that conversions would be spectacles. This urban tradition lived on through the twentieth century under leaders such as Billy Graham (born 1918).

JONATHAN EDWARDS

The Puritan preacher Jonathan Edwards (1703–1758) has been the most studied and influential theologian in North American history. In the observation of many, he was a genius in philosophy, theology, preaching, and evangelizing. He spent most of his ministry in one congregation, in Northampton, Massachusetts, where he preached learned sermons that somehow struck the minds and hearts of members and newcomers who were converted. He is always described as a key agent of the First Great Awakening in America, which set patterns for revivals ever since. His image seems contradictory: he could preach a "damnation" sermon like "Sinners in the Hand of an Angry God" (1741), but be optimistic about the advance of Christ's church and the glory being manifested by God in the New World. In 1750 Edwards was edged out of his pulpit and ministered to Native Americans. Appointed president of the College of New Jersey at Princeton, he died within weeks of taking up his appointment.

MODERN MOVEMENTS

Some expressive movements that emerged out of Protestantism in the seventeenth and eighteenth centuries were foretastes of some striking new developments in the nineteenth and twentieth centuries, particularly in America. Thus Mother Ann Lee (1736–1784) migrated in 1774 from England to America, and developed her United Society of Believers in Christ's Second Appearing, or "Shakerism," a form of faith that promoted communalism, pacifism, simplicity, and gender equality. It took its shorter name from the ecstatic dancing, or "shaking," that sometimes accompanied worship.

In the 1830s Joseph Smith laid the foundations of the remarkable phenomenon of Mormonism (see box). William Miller (1782–1849) and then Ellen Gould White (1827–1915) led Seventh-Day Adventism, a healing movement which foresaw an immi-

Sabbathday Lake Shaker Village, *New Gloucester, Maine, is the last active Shaker community. The number of Shakers peaked in the mid-1800s at ca. 5,000 in communities across the eastern US. The simple elegance of Shaker crafts, seen here in the furnishings of the Sabbathday Lake meeting house, has found wide appeal in modern times.*

nent end of the world. Mary Baker Eddy also concentrated on healing, and founded the Church of Christ, Scientist (Christian Science) in 1879 (see page 177).

New movements also emerged from mainline Protestantism, among them the "Social Gospel" that developed, alongside Christian Socialism in England, at the beginning of the twentieth century. Its leaders, such as Walter Rauschenbusch (1861–1919), took biblical language of the kingdom of God and envisioned ways in which it could be a blueprint for a better society in which poverty and inequality could be addressed.

Many of the leaders of the Social Gospel movement were liberal Protestants, as were those who participated in the formation of the modern Christian ecumenical movement. In the course of time it drew on the energies of Eastern Orthodoxy and, after the Second Vatican Council (1962–1965) included Roman Catholics, but most of the time it was headed by Protestants such as missionary Bishop Charles Brent (1862–1929) and the American lay Methodist John R. Mott (1865–1955) who grieved over the difficulties faced by Christian missionaries when they competed more than they evangelized—offenses that divided Christianity, and were most manifestly created by Protestantism. They led international meetings after 1910 and formed local, national,

MORMONISM

In 1830 Joseph Smith, Jr. (1805–1844), claimed visions of a restored New World Christianity, a revelation that accepted the Bible but added a newly-found scripture, *The Book of Mormon*, which tell of God's dealings in ancient America, which was visited by the risen Jesus. Smith attracted many followers but also great hostility, and the first "Mormons," as they came to be called, were driven from place to place. Smith himself was murdered by a mob in 1844 in Carthage, Illinois. Led by Brigham Young, the Mormons trekked west to what was to become the state of Utah and founded Salt Lake City in 1847. Utah remains the center of Mormonism's main denomination, the Church of Jesus Christ of Latter-Day Saints (also referred to as the Church of Jesus Christ or LDS Church), which has around thirteen million members and is one of the world's fastest growing churches.

The church has numerous distinctive teachings—such as the belief that humans can become exalted, though never equal to God, in the afterlife—but has always centered on the work and teachings of Jesus. Contrary to one popular misconception, Mormons do not practice polygamy, which the church banned as long ago as 1890.

The Mormon Tabernacle, *Salt Lake City, Utah, was built in 1864–1867 for gatherings of the Church of Jesus Christ of Latter-Day Saints. Its pioneering elliptical roof created near-perfect acoustics for preachers and musicians alike; it is the home of the Mormon Tabernacle Choir.*

and world federations such as the World Council of Churches to give expression to unity already attained and to work for more. (See also pages 228–229.)

PENTECOSTALISM

North America from 1607 to the present day has attracted immigrants who brought their faiths and churches with them, which they transformed and adapted in a new environment. At the same time, America has played host to inventive prophets, mystics, and organizers who filled niches that existed between denominations, and allowed for an innovative spirit to have its sway. The most prominent of these fresh versions of Protestant Christianity are the Pentecostal movements, many of which grew out of Wesleyan "holiness" impulses.

Pentecostalists would not see themselves as new movements so much as recoverers of themes connected with events related in the second chapter of Acts. On the Jewish feast of Pentecost, fifty days after the resurrection of Jesus, Acts reports that his followers experienced an outpouring of the Holy Spirit that inspired new converts to "speak in tongues," unrepressed syllables seen as witness to God's presence and to engage in healing. The Pentecostalists, led notably by the pioneering African-American layman William Joseph Seymour (1870–1922), claimed that the gifts of the Holy Spirit in the early church were still available and were to be exercised. Thus Pentecostalists "spoke in tongues," Spirit-language that sounded unintelligible, and endeavored to bring about miraculous

AFRICAN-AMERICAN CHURCHES

The vast majority of African-American and other black Christians are Protestant. This was the case because Protestantism was dominant in the slave states and the religion of slaves was influenced by the Baptist and Methodist faiths of their owners. When emancipation came, most African-American churches were segregated counterparts of white denominations. They were orthodox, but stressed themes of liberation which spoke to the circumstances of oppressed and stigmatized people.

The word "Baptist" or "Methodist" is in the name of several of these denominations; an exception is the Church of God in Christ, one of the fastest growing religious bodies in the US. Its characteristic feature is in its Pentecostal or charismatic character, that is, in its welcoming and displaying "the gifts of the Spirit," healing, "speaking in tongues" and the like (see also main text).

Hip-Hop Church. *Lamar Hayney raps at a service of the Hip-Hop Church, New York City. Like many African-American churches, it has a serious goal of "outreach to the disenfranchised, the brokenhearted, the oppressed, and those considered 'disposable' by the larger society."*

The world from within. *The Mapparium in the Mary Baker Eddy Library at Christian Science Plaza in Boston, Massachusetts, headquarters of the Church of Christ, Scientist. Commissioned by the church in 1935, it is a huge stained-glass globe which, being viewed from within, allows the countries of the world to be seen in their proper perspective.*

spiritual healing. Pentecostalists see themselves as orthodox, and the rest of the church as too passive in accepting and putting to work divine gifts.

Emerging in Kansas in 1900 and California in 1906, Pentecostalism prospered among African-American churches and was long seen as a rural sectional movement. However, it was not long to be confined to the US. While it never gained much of a place in European Protestantism, Pentecostalism is by far the fastest growing form of Christianity in sub-Saharan Africa, Latin America, and parts of Asia. In this respect Protestantism, which at times seems to be a spent force in its European homelands, has found fertile new soil where it is flourishing with great vitality.

"NEW THOUGHT"

Not all innovations were new versions of Protestant Christian faith. Some were critical of biblical religion and argued that existing churches failed to do justice to truth and to human needs. Among these were so-called "New Thought" organizations, some of which have taken on fresh life in what has come to be called "New Age" religions. Many of these are influenced by Asian-based traditions such as Buddhism and Hinduism, and others draw upon other ancient and esoteric wisdom or a complex of philosophies.

They share the idea that the universe makes sense and that humans can discern enough of it to improve their own existence. They speak of connecting humans and divine forces, nature, and the cosmos, without any need for a Bible. Often these groups are led by charismatic leaders and sometimes they fade when the leaders ages or dies. Yet New Thought appeals to serious seekers who feel confined by the Bible and other classic religious texts and want to reach out for new revelations or new ways of making sense.

CHRISTIAN SCIENCE

In *Science and Health with Key to the Scriptures* (1875), Mary Baker Eddy (1821–1920) proclaimed a new metaphysic that saw the world's evils as illusory, on the grounds that God was wholly good and perfect and could not have created them. The Church of Christ, Scientist that she subsequently founded in 1879 holds, for example, that illness is unreal and can be healed by spiritual means when, like Christ, one has attained a true understanding of God's perfection. For this reason, Christian Scientists often eschew conventional medicine in favor of "prayerful treatment" (one's own prayer and that of others). However, there is no compulsion on church members to avoid medical treatment.

CONTEMPORARY TRENDS

Protestantism has been a cultural force of great power during the last half millennium. For example, scholars in many disciplines have followed the German sociologist Max Weber (1864–1920) in speaking of "the Protestant ethic." This Weber noticed among Calvinists and Puritans especially, who had to certify their election to the covenant not only with reference to rewards after death but through conscientious involvement in earthly life. They were to be industrious, frugal, filled with an understanding of their vocation whether in the fields of economics, diplomacy, or labor (see also page 117).

Protestants, whose early leaders took slavery for granted, also helped work toward its abolition in the eighteenth and nineteenth centuries. Similarly, while churches followed and bolstered European colonial endeavors, many of them also later supported anticolonial movements. Protestants, who had once acted as if they were the only true Christians, came to promote not only Christian ecumenism (see page 228) but also interfaith relations with non-Christians, beginning with the 1893 "World's Parliament of Religions" in Chicago, first suggested by chiefly Protestant lay leaders (see also pages 230–231).

Protestant intellectual elites were stimulated by any number of modern movements in theology. After the Enlightenment, not exclusively but most radically in Germany, what was termed "higher criticism of the Bible" developed (see page 171). Again in Germany more than elsewhere, theologians such as Hermann Reimarus appropriated radical philosophical ideas and came to interpretations of the faith that were troubling to most Protestants. Sometimes these philosophies or theologies were progressive, setting forth teachings which competed with older Protestant ideas about human limits and sin. The pioneer in this respect was Friedrich Schleiermacher (1768–1834), a German theologian who, although he was always attentive to scripture, located classic theological ideas in human experience more than in scriptural revelation. Other times Protestant theologians were more radical and tended to views of social class that formed a background to the writings and work of Karl Marx (1813–1883). Yet other Protestants, in their appreciation of other religions, began to turn syncretist, and to suggest that Christian faith was not necessarily truer or more salutary than others.

Some Protestants in the US, and later throughout much of the world, reacted with what one might call a hardline resistance or "fundamentalism" to "modern" trends as they defined them: moral or theological corruptions of a presumed once pure faith. From the 1920s to the 1970s this kind of fundamentalism was chiefly an instrument of church controversy over evolution, biblical criticism, and the millennium.

EVANGELICAL PROTESTANTISM

Fundamentalist movements led to the formation of new church bodies, seminaries, publications, and so on. In the 1970s, however, fundamentalists began to produce conservative political movements that attracted millions. Among these fundamentalist groups—now called "evangelicals"—the more militant stressed literal readings of the Bible and supported moral issues such as opposition to abortion or homosexual expression. Aggressively evangelistic and passionately devoted to their cause, these movements—which in the US took names like "The Moral Majority" or "The Christian Coalition"—became more politically involved and more effective than the older "Social Gospel" type of liberal Protestants (see page 175). While there are great varieties within these movements, overall they created a new image and agenda for American Protestants (see also pages 226–227).

Despite such challenges to the older style of Protestants, many stripes of Protestantism, from fundamentalist to liberal, in the poor world and the rich, continue their witness. In its many forms, the movement continues to nurture the heritage of the sixteenth century reformers, stressing devotion to the Bible, to Jesus Christ, to the formation of community, and to personal expressions of faith.

The Crystal Cathedral, *Garden Grove, California, was completed in 1980 as the home of a Protestant Evangelical ministry founded in 1950. The name alludes to the building's design and size—it contains over 10,000 panes of glass and holds more than 3,000 worshippers. Like many contemporary US Evangelical "megachurches," the Cathedral broadcasts its services globally on television and the Internet. The weekly broadcast, called* The Hour of Power, *draws some 20 million viewers and is the world's most popular Christian television program.*

7 THE FAITH

The Orthodox Church today is a family of self-governing churches united by a common faith and common sacraments. The churches are located principally in the Near East, Russia, and eastern Europe, with some significant communities in North America and other parts of the West. The autocephalous (self-governing) churches include the four ancient patriarchates of Constantinople, Alexandria, Antioch, and Jerusalem and others in Russia, Serbia, Romania, Bulgaria, Georgia, Cyprus, Greece, Poland, and Albania. There are over 200 million baptized Orthodox Christians in the world today, most of them (more than half) in Russia.

As with the Catholic and Protestant West, Eastern Orthodoxy's roots grow out of

THE NON-CHALCEDONIAN CHURCHES

The Council of Chalcedon (451) described the relation between Christ's divine and human natures in terms that prompted Orthodoxy's first major, and most lasting, schism (see page 33). Large sections of the church, called the "Non-Chalcedonian" or "Oriental Orthodox" churches, seceded from the council out of fear of Nestorianism, so named after Nestorius, a fifth-century bishop of Constantinople. The Non-Chalcedonians—which include today's Armenians, Copts, Ethiopians, Malabar, and Syro-Jacobite communities—believed that Nestorius separated the two natures of Christ into two distinct persons, one human, the other divine. These churches are sometimes called "monophysites" ("one-nature-ites") but this is inaccurate. True monophysites believed that the human nature of Christ was mingled with the divine so that one new nature, a mixture of human and divine, remains. However, the Non-Chalcedonians affirmed the integrity of both natures within one person. Although they are not in communion with the Chalcedonian churches, theologically they appear no less Orthodox. Negotiations on a reunion of the churches have been underway for several decades, with varying degrees of success. Most theologians now agree that their original differences occurred over terminology, not substance.

The Church of St. George *is one of a number of distinctive rock-hewn churches in Lalibela, Ethiopia. It belongs to the Ethiopian Orthodox Tewahedo Church;* tewahedo *means "being made one", a reference to its belief in the single, unified person of Christ.*

the common history of the early church. Orthodoxy is notable for having maintained its traditions over the intervening 1,600-plus years without Scholastic, Renaissance, Reformation, or Enlightenment periods of ecclesiastical history. In the wake of the Council of Nicea (see page 33), from the fourth century CE onward, the Eastern churches acquired an identity shaped by the beliefs and practices of the church in the Byzantine empire. There were two major schisms in its history: the first occurred within the Eastern church itself over how to express the relationship between the divine and human natures of Christ (see box); the second occurred between East and West from the tenth to thirteenth centuries centering on the pope's claims of universal jurisdiction over the Eastern churches, and on the eternal relations between the three persons of the Trinity.

Christ the Merciful *is a 12th-century Byzantine icon, from Constantinople, made of glass and stone tesserae with strips of gold leaf on the edges.*

CHARACTERISTICS OF ORTHODOXY

An Orthodox church often exudes a profound sense of mystery and antiquity. As in the primitive church, the Orthodox still baptize by threefold immersion; they still bring babies to receive holy communion; and they still recite the original form of the Nicene Creed.

A community consciousness forms the basis of Orthodoxy's reverence for the early Church Fathers. Saints Irenaeus, Athanasius, Basil the Great, Gregory Nazianzus, John Chrysostom, Maximus the Confessor, Gregory Palamas, and many others are considered as contemporary witnesses to the faith. Through a *consensus patrum* (consensus of the Fathers), they serve as reliable teachers of the faith. A special position is given to Mary because of her unique relation to Christ as the "God-Bearer" (Theotokós), but Orthodoxy does not believe in her "sinlessness" or "immaculate conception" (see page 151).

Another characteristic of the Orthodox faith is the centrality of the gospel in doctrine, liturgy, and sacraments (see pages 182–183). The gospel (*euaggelion*) is the "good news" of salvation received through faith in Jesus Christ and baptism into his body, the church. Since sin brought death to humanity, "God became humanized so that humans might become divinized," according to St. Athanasius (fourth century). This is known as *theosis* or deification, the transformation of the human person into the divine likeness through Christ in the sacramental life of the church. Monastic practices (see pages 188–189), which cultivated deification, have played a crucial role in the spirituality and mystical theology (see pages 190–191) of the Eastern church.

"ORTHODOXY"

The term "Orthodoxy" comes from the Greek for "correct" (*orthos*) and "worship" (*doxa*). It refers to the belief that the Eastern Church preserves, as the bishops of the second council of Nicea II (787) put it: "... without diminution all that pertains to the catholic [universal] church ... without change or innovation."

A LIFE OF WORSHIP

Orthodox worship is best summarized by the dictum: "The rule of prayer is the rule of faith" (*lex orandi lex est credendi*). The Orthodox Church's main Sunday service (see sidebar) consists of two parts: the preaching of the Word of God, and the partaking of the Eucharist. This service, as well as an entire annual cycle of twelve feasts and fasts, centers on Pascha (Easter; see box). Together, they ground the church's identity in Christ and the sacramental life. These sacraments, also called "mysteries," call the faithful to strive to become what they are in Christ.

JOHN CHRYSOSTOM

The main worship service celebrated on most Sundays in the Orthodox Church is named the Divine Liturgy of St. John Chrysostom. John Chrysostom (349–407) was the patriarch of Constantinople and the most famous bishop in the history of the Orthodox Church. "Chrysostom" means "golden-mouthed," a name given to him after his death because of the power and eloquence of his preaching. More than 600 of his biblical homilies and treatises have survived, more than those of any other Church Father.

THE SPIRITUALLY HEALING MYSTERIES

The sacraments of the Orthodox Church are not limited to seven, as they are in Roman Catholicism (see pages 148–149); instead, everything in and of the church is seen as sacramental in one way or another. There are, however, special moments when the Holy Spirit applies the mystery of salvation to the believing community.

Through baptism, infants undergo triple immersion in the name of the Trinity. St. Gregory of Nyssa (335–ca. 395) speaks of baptism as a "womb and tomb." As "womb" it is the sacrament of new birth in Christ; as "tomb" it is death to sin. Immediately after baptism the baptized undergoes chrismation, or confirmation, anointing with holy oil (chrism) to indicate the endowed presence and power of the Holy Spirit. (This differs from confirmation's development in the West, where it became, in effect, a rite of passage marking the age of discretion or early adolescence.) Directly after baptism and chrismation, the Orthodox Church administers the Eucharist to nourish the newborn life.

St. John Chrysostom, *in an 11th-century mosaic from the cupola of the choir in Hosios Loukas monastery, Boeotia, Greece. Credited with the Divine Liturgy, it was not entirely written by him, although the eucharistic prayers are largely his. Its present form was finalized by the ninth century and consists of two parts: the Liturgy of the Word, which focuses on the preaching of the gospel, and the Liturgy of the Eucharist, which focuses on the partaking of communion.*

The sacrament of repentance has three forms: confession to a priest, or to a lay monk or layperson, and the excommunication rites of re-entrance into the church. St. Simeon the New Theologian (949–1022) suggests that any baptized layperson with the gift of discernment may give absolution after confession. Through the sacrament of ordination, bishops, priests, and deacons govern the church and manifest the action of Christ among his people.

Marriage is a sacred mystery, reflecting the union between Christ and his church. Byzantine canon law does not allow a clergyman to marry twice, or to marry a widow or divorcee. As a concession to human weakness, laypeople, however, may marry up to three times, with a period of abstention from the Eucharist.

Holy unction is reserved not only for the dying, as in "extreme unction," but is offered whenever there are times of physical, mental, and spiritual need. Fasting also plays a central role in Orthodox piety, so a series of annual and weekly fasting periods are prescribed by the church. Alongside communal feasts and fasts, there is personal prayer before icons in the home. The prayers come from manuals whose words are taken from service books used in public worship. In this way, personal devotions are connected to community life, but parishioners may still pray spontaneously as they wish.

"CHRIST IS RISEN": ORTHODOX EASTER

The feast of the Resurrection of Christ during Easter, often referred to as Pascha (a term derived from the Hebrew *Pesah*, for Passover), is at the heart of Orthodox worship, preaching, and spiritual life. Pascha is the liturgical focal point in the Orthodox calendar. The weekly celebration of the Sunday liturgy is devoted to Christ's Resurrection, rather than to his sufferings, and celebrates his victory over sin, death, and the demonic. During Easter, Orthodox Christians sing: "Christ is risen from the dead, trampling down death by death, and upon those in the tombs bestowing life!" For fifty days, from Easter to Pentecost, the Orthodox greet one another with the words "Christ is risen!" to which the response is: "Indeed, He is risen!"

The Orthodox Church believes in Christ's actual bodily resurrection—not in the sense of a resuscitated corpse that will one day die again, but the emergence in time and space of a new beginning of life, here and now. It is from this Paschal mystery that Orthodox baptism takes its meaning: a new life given a new humanity characterized by resurrection ethics. For this reason, icons of the Resurrection often show Christ creating this new humanity by trampling down death and Hades, with Adam in one hand and Eve in the other.

Easter Saturday *in a Greek Orthodox Church, Thessaloniki, Greece, and a traditional leaf-throwing ritual, announcing the new life given through the resurrection.*

ART AND ARCHITECTURE

EASTERN ORTHODOX CHURCHES

Praskvica Serbian Orthodox *monastery is near Sveti Stefan, Montenegro. Its ornate icon screen or* iconostatis *is a typical element of Orthodox church interiors, along with vaulted ceilings and painted or mosaic-covered interior walls. Theology united with beauty to glorify God and facilitate human deification.*

After Christianity became tolerated under the emperor Constantine in 313 the design of church buildings was adapted from secular Roman civic ones (see pages 34–35); most were basilicas, although layouts varied across the empire.

Following the collapse of the western Roman empire, church architecture in the eastern (Byzantine) empire began to evolve its own distinct styles. However, the model for Orthodox architecture to this day is the great church of Hagia Sophia (Greek for "Holy Wisdom") in Constantinople (modern Istanbul, Turkey). Commissioned by Emperor Justinian I, it was completed in 537 then rebuilt just two decades later after its original dome collapsed. It was the world's largest cathedral for nearly a thousand years, and the seat of the patriarch of Constantinople until 1453.

The Hagia Sophia is in the form of a squared cross crowned by a dome. The interior is divided into three parts: the entrance, or vestibule, symbolizes a point of departure from this world; the middle nave is the assembly place of the people of God who live between this age (vestibule) and the age to come (sanctuary); and the sanctuary, where the priest stands offering the Eucharist. From its all-embracing ceiling Christ looks down as the "Ruler of All" (Greek *Pantokrator*). Icons (see pages 192–193) adorn the sanctuary and rest on an icon screen (*iconostasis*). All Orthodox churches throughout the world are patterned in one way or another after the architecture of the Hagia Sophia, although there are distinctive regional variations.

RIGHT *Voronet monastery in Bucovina, Romania, founded in the 15th century by Stephen the Great is famous for its painted exterior and abundance of blue-chromatic frescoes illustrating biblical scenes, angels, martyrs, and much more.*

OPPOSITE *St. Basil's cathedral, Moscow, is characteristically Russian with its onion dome and a tent roof.*

By the thirteenth century, Russia had developed its characteristic "onion" domes. Their distinctive shape was originally designed to prevent a heavy build up of snow in the long winters, but they took on symbolic meanings, such as the shape of the flames given by the Holy Spirit at Pentecost (Acts 2). Wooden "tent" churches, with a tall conical or polygonal steeple, were also made to prevent the accumulation of snow. Developed in rural Russia, they were widely modeled in masonry from the sixteenth century.

In Lebanon and Romania, Orthodox churches in monasteries are sometimes long and narrow with a single apse traversing the full width of the church. In Bulgaria, a long barrel-typed domed church is popular. In North America, church architecture is becoming more consciously patterned after "Old World" styles (Russian, Greek, and others), though with no cultural uniformity.

PATRIARCHS AND PRIESTS

HOLY FOOLS

Russia was home to a phenomenon known as "Holy Fools." It was the special vocation of these devout charismatics to live the "hard sayings" of Jesus—poor, destitute, and at times naked. While never harming anyone, they were eccentric prophets who raised their voices against those who lied, cheated, and did violence to others. One of the best known was St. Basil the Blessed, after whom the Kremlin cathedral takes its name. Basil once dared to warn Tsar Ivan the Terrible (1530–1584) that his violent deeds would doom him to hell. During Lent, Basil took a slab of beef and presented it to Ivan saying, "Why abstain from meat when you murder people?" But Ivan lived in dread of Basil and refused to harm him.

By the fifth century, a pentarchy of five sees (bishoprics) had been established in the church of the late Roman empire: Rome, Constantinople, Alexandria, Antioch and Jerusalem. Within the pentarchy, Rome was given a primacy of honor as the "first among equals." In the Orthodox view, the Roman see's position was given neither by divine nor apostolic right, but because of its historical role as a "big brother" in settling religious disputes, its size, and its location in the traditional capital of the empire. At the ecumenical council of Constantinople (381), that city was given second place after Rome itself. Each of the five patriarchs, as these bishops were known, was sovereign within his own sphere of jurisdiction with no bishop able to claim supremacy over the others. However, after Rome and Constantinople split by the thirteenth century, the Orthodox churches regarded the Ecumenical (imperial) Patriarch of Constantinople as first among equals, but not as a "pope" in the modern sense of the term. Orthodoxy has no such figure. The position of the Ecumenical Patriarch resembles that of the archbishop of Canterbury in the worldwide Anglican communities; the churches look to him for global leadership while remaining decentralized and self-governing, yet united in faith and sacraments.

THE COMMUNITY OF THE CHURCH

Following the church's structure during the early centuries, Orthodox theologians today often speak of the church in terms of "communion ecclesiology." By that they mean the very nature of the church is relational, not individual. It is above all a community comprised of those in heaven and on earth whose worship is attended by the angelic host. A key aspect of communion ecclesiology focuses on the ministry of the bishop. Each bishop exists in an interdependent relationship within his community, not above or apart from it. For this reason "apostolic succession" is not simply a succession of individuals going back to the apostles, but is more fully viewed as a succession of communities to which the individual bishops belong, safeguarding the faith by their communion with one another. At the heart of each community stands the Eucharist, which expresses their unity in faith.

This community consciousness formed the basis of Orthodoxy's rupture with Rome. Theologically, Rome thought of the church in terms of the supremacy and universal jurisdiction of the pope, but the Eastern churches thought in terms of collegiality and equality of all bishops. Also, by the sixth century Rome and the Latin (Western) church taught that the Holy Spirit proceeds eternally from the Father "and the Son" (*filioque*) while the Greek (Eastern) church adhered to the original wording of the Nicene

Creed, which confessed that the Spirit proceeds from the Father alone. The East rejected the *filioque* because it was believed to disrupt the internal balance of the Trinity and because it was never ecumenically agreed upon. Although 1054 is traditionally cited as the date of the split between Eastern and Western Christianity (see page 39), most scholars now recognize that the climax of schism was definitively reached in 1204 with the sack of Constantinople by Western crusaders.

Unlike the sharp division which arose between clergy and laity in the medieval West, Orthodoxy embraces a time-honored tradition of "lay theologians" as teachers. The role of women as saints, martyrs, and monastics has also played a vital role in Orthodox history. Female deacons were utilized in antiquity, but only recently has the Church of Greece reactivated the practice in principle. The ordination of women to the priesthood remains limited to males, though the question has only begun to be vigorously explored.

CHARISMATICS

Alongside the ordained ministries stand those with "charismatic" gifts. "Elders," such as St. Anthony of Egypt (fourth century), have had the particular gift of discernment to administer personal counsel. Elders can be a priest but often are male or female lay monks or simply lay people. Some, such as St. Simeon the New Theologian (tenth century), strongly cautioned the clergy against substituting barren ritualism for a "conscious experience of God in the heart."

Some charismatics were of a more extreme nature, such as St. Simeon Stylites (fifth century) who lived atop a pillar in Antioch, where thousands heard him preach and several Bedouin tribes converted as a result. Other charismatics included Russia's "Holy Fools" (see sidebar). Today these spiritual gifts are still present in varying degrees and there is no contradiction between the church's "spiritual" and "institutional" ministries because it is believed the same Spirit checks and balances both.

Saints Anthony and Paul the Hermit, *who lived in the eastern deserts as anchorites or hesychasts. Icon panel dated 1777 from the monastery of St. Makarios, Cairo.*

EASTERN MONASTICISM

It has been well said that the best way to enter into the spirituality of the Orthodox Church is through the door of monasticism. The origins of the early monastic movement (see pages 44–45) are also the origins of Eastern monasticism. Today, as then, the Orthodox version is recognized by its primitive simplicity. There are no specialized orders such as developed in the West with the Benedictines, Augustinians, or Franciscans: one simply joins a monastery and follows its own particular traditions.

As in fourth-century Egypt and Syria, so today there are three kinds of monastic lifestyles: "hermits" (anchorites or hesychasts) live alone; "cenobites" live in a community; and "semi-eremitics" combine the solitary and communal ways. All monks live under the guidance of a spiritual father or elder variously known as a *geron* (Greece), *starets* (Russia), or *abba*, *abuna* (Arab lands and Ethiopia). Collectively, monasticism

THE "REPUBLIC OF MONKS"

The major centers of Eastern monasticism are in Greece, Russia, and the Middle East. St. Catherine's monastery on Mount Sinai, Egypt, built by the Byzantine emperor Justinian in the sixth century, possesses a rich library of biblical manuscripts, ecclesiastical texts, and icons. Other notable monasteries include St. Sergius-Holy Trinity near Moscow; the monastery of the Caves in Kiev, Ukraine; St. Makarios and St. Bishoy monasteries in Egypt; and St. Sabas near Jerusalem.

However, the most distinguished monastic settlement in the Orthodox world over the past millennium has been Mount Athos in Greece. Known officially as the Autonomous Monastic State of the Holy Mountain, Mount Athos is a self-ruled state housing some 1,500 residents in twenty separate monasteries, as well as a large number of small houses and hermits' cells.

Accessible only by sea, the landscape of the mountain peninsula is breathtaking, with monastic settlements atop jagged precipices, some as high as 7,000ft (2,130m). Mount Athos houses a trove of precious treasures such as medieval icons, vestments, and books.

A portable triptych from Mount Athos *showing Christ in Majesty (top row, center), known in Orthodoxy as Christ Pantocrator—ruler of all—flanked by the Virgin and the Baptist and accompanied by other saints. The side panels depict saints Peter (left) and Paul.*

St. Catherine's monastery *stands in the wilderness of the Sinai Desert, Egypt. Constructed from 527 to 565 around an earlier shrine that was said to mark the spot where Moses encountered the Burning Bush, the remote Greek Orthodox site is among the world's oldest continuously occupied monasteries.*

has shaped the entire life of the Orthodox Church. The monks were often the staunchest defenders of Orthodoxy against heresies; they influenced fasting practices, liturgical cycles, and methods of prayer such as hesychasm (see pages 190–191). Today all bishops of the Eastern church are chosen exclusively from the monastic ranks or celibate clergy.

A LIFE OF PRAYER

The monastic's primary vocation is prayer. The goal of prayer, and of all monastic life, is love for God and neighbor. Some referred to this as "union" with God or "deification" (*theosis*; see pages 190–191) which was the very purpose of the Incarnation. All the disciplines of fasting, prayer, contemplation, worship, good deeds, and manual labor were designed to fertilize the heart for God's love to flourish.

However, these intense ascetical efforts were not to be viewed as a means of "works-righteousness" that earned salvation, as developed in sixteenth-century Western monasticism and was rejected by the Protestant reformers. Mark the Ascetic (fourth century) wrote: "Sonship is a gift given to men through His own blood. Thus the kingdom of heaven is not a reward for works, but a gift of grace prepared by the Master for his faithful servants." Such is the true spirit of Eastern monasticism.

THE *PHILOKALIA*

Next to the Bible, the most widely read spiritual writing in the Orthodox world is the *Philokalia* ("Love of the Good and Beautiful"). Compiled by two Greek monks and published in 1782, it is a five-volume anthology of ascetic writings from the fourth to fifteen centuries. The editors wanted to make the treatises, originally written by monks and for monks, available to laypeople. The *Philokalia* covers many subjects but especially focuses on the Jesus Prayer (see pages 190–191). The work was translated into Russian in the nineteenth century and versions exist in many other languages.

MYSTICAL THEOLOGY

The Transfiguration, *Christ surrounded by Moses and Elijah, an 18th-century icon (detail) from central Russia. The icon illustrates a passage from the gospel of Matthew—"he was transfigured before them, and his face shone like the sun, and his clothes became dazzling white" (Mathew 17.2)—during which Jesus took Peter, James and his brother John up a mountain (Mount Tabor), whereupon the transfiguration, accompanied by a burst of light, took place. Moses and Elijah appeared with Jesus and God spoke to the group, his voice emanating from a cloud.*

In the Orthodox tradition, prayer and theology are interdependent; theology is not merely a discussion of God, it is an extension of spirituality and worship. This connection is captured by an oft-quoted saying of Evagrius Ponticus (345–399): "The theologian is one who truly prays, and one who truly prays is a theologian." Mystical theology is "lived doctrine" and it lies at the heart of Christian dogma in the East. It is the pursuit of deification (*theosis*)—a life fully Christ-like and Spirit-filled.

This experiential approach to the knowledge of God is based on the church's distinction between what are termed the *cataphatic* and *apophatic* ways of knowing. Cataphatic or positive theology (*via positiva*) describes God through affirmative language such as "God is knowable." Apophatic or negative theology (*via negativa*) underscores the limits of human knowledge and the vastness of God's transcendence in negative language such as "God is unknowable" (see sidebar). Yet the negation does not lead to ignorance; it is actually a super-affirmation that leads to a positive encounter with God. Together the two ways reflect the church's view on the role of reason as it relates to the nature of God and the *theosis* of humans.

APOPHATIC WRITINGS

Many Byzantine spiritual writers from the fourth to fourteenth centuries made use of the apophatic approach. Dionysius's massive use of the method widely popularized it throughout Christendom in the Middle Ages. Not only in monastic circles, but also in Orthodox dogma and worship one encounters the prevalence of apophatic language: "For thou art God ineffable, inconceivable, invisible, incomprehensible, ever-existing and eternally the same" (*Anaphora* prayer).

PALAMITE THEOLOGY

The theological underpinnings of how one knows God were developed most eloquently by a monk from Mount Athos, Gregory Palamas (1296–1359), who practiced the hesychast method of prayer (see box). He soon came under attack by another Orthodox theologian, Barlaam of Calabria, who was well versed in Western Scholasticism and the Renaissance. The "hesychast controversy," as it is known, amounted to a disagreement over how the unknowable God can also be known. Barlaam denied the claim that humans can have a direct, personal experience of God, denouncing it as grossly superstitious.

However, the church in Constantinople sided with Gregory and condemned Barlaam in a series of councils. Gregory's book *Triads in Defense of the Holy Hesychasts* gave Orthodoxy definitive answers to questions about the nature of God and the extent of his knowability, synthesizing the preceding thirteen centuries of patristic teaching. The victory of Palamite theology has united the entire Orthodox world since the fourteenth century by giving the church a common spirituality that crosses geographic and cultural boundaries. It confirms that humans can partake of the divine glory in this life. At the same time, however, Palamite theology is just one significant room among many in the larger castle of the church's theology. A balanced spirituality, for example, must also include a variety of emphases from other theologians such as the great saints Cyril of Alexandria and John Chrysostom (see sidebar on page 182).

HESYCHASM: THE "HOLY SILENCE"

For centuries, many monks at places like Mount Sinai and Mount Athos have practiced hesychasm ("holy silence"). Hesychasm is a form of mental prayer, or prayer of the heart, that combined breathing techniques with a short petition known as "The Jesus Prayer": "Lord Jesus Christ, Son of God, have mercy on me" (the words "a sinner" are sometimes added).

By looking at the heart or navel, regulating one's breathing, and reciting the Jesus Prayer continuously, one may experience a vision of the same uncreated light that radiated from Christ when he was transfigured before his disciples on Mount Tabor (Matt. 17.2)—a visible but uncreated light. But Christians who pray the Jesus Prayer are to seek the Giver, not the gift, of the uncreated light. Moreover, hesychasm is not required of all Orthodox Christians, nor is it the only legitimate form of Orthodox mysticism today.

The Holy Mountain *of Aghion Oros, Mount Athos, in Greece. From here the monk and mystical writer Gregory Palamas taught the hesychast technique throughout the eastern Mediterranean.*

ART AND ARCHITECTURE

WINDOWS ON HEAVEN: ICONS

A 14th-century Byzantine icon *of the virgin figure Hodigitria ("she who shows the way").*

From 726 to 843 arguments raged in the Christian East over whether the use of icons (images) in worship and devotion was idolatrous. Thousands died or suffered bodily harm as a result and countless images were destroyed. Icons could take the form of sacred symbols such as the cross, painted images, mosaics, frescoes, or statues (the latter were rare). In the end, the seventh ecumenical council (Nicea, 787) condemned the iconoclasts ("icon-smashers") and concluded that "one may render to icons the veneration (Greek *proskunesis*) of honor, but not true worship (Greek *latreia*) which is due only to God." "Veneration" refers to the bodily act of reverencing icons of Christ or the saints by kissing and bowing down before them. When that happens, "The honor paid to the icon carries over to the one portrayed."

RIGHT *The mandylion of Christ, a 12th-century Novgorod School icon inspired by the portrait of Jesus said to have been sent by him to King Abgar of Edessa.*

OPPOSITE *Andrei Rublev's 1411 icon* The Holy Trinity, *or* Hospitality of Abraham, *illustrates a passage from Genesis 18 in which three angels appeared to Abraham and Sarah. Rublev focused on the angels in order to convey the three persons of the triune God, which was a difficult doctrinal concept for most people to understand.*

Icons are witness to the "Word made flesh" (John 1.14), the deification (*theosis*) of human nature (see pages 190–191), and the transfiguration of this world in the age to come. For these reasons, Orthodox iconography is liturgical and not simply religious art. To be sure, for both East and West, icons are "books for the illiterate," as St. John of Damascus observed. They instruct the faithful and inspire them to imitate the virtues of the saints depicted. Yet unlike naturalistic art, icons seek to convey truth more than realism. They seek to express the faith of the whole church, not the individual artist.

The origins of icon styles lie in late Greco-Roman art, which mixed naturalism with philosophical abstraction—a style taken over by the church of the eastern Roman (Byzantine) empire (330–1453). The church sometimes uses a variety of conventions that were designed to alter the human anatomy in order to emphasize a spiritual truth, such as enlarging the eyes to highlight spiritual vision or minimizing the nose to downplay the senses. Among the best known examples of early Byzantine style are the fifth- and sixth-century mosaics in Ravenna, Italy, and the monastery of St. Catherine on Mount Sinai in Egypt.

Byzantine art survived by passing into Russia, Romania, Bulgaria, and other eastern European cultures. Syrian, Egyptian, Ethiopian, and other Christians of the Mediterranean region often retained a mixture of Byzantine iconographic styles with local variations.

PART 3

THE BIBLE

Symbols of the Evangelists. *Four angels and symbols of the evangelists supporting the Chi-Rho monogram of Christ. Irenaeus of Lyons (ca. 180) identified the four beasts of Ezekiel 1 as the writers of the canonical gospels: the Man (Matthew), the Lion (Mark), the Ox (Luke), and Eagle (John). The Chi-Rho derives from the first two letters of Christ in Greek. Mosaic in the dome of the Archbishop's Palace, Ravenna, 6th century.*

1 THE OLD TESTAMENT

The Christian Bible (Greek *Biblia*, "books") is a collection of writings in two parts: the Old Testament, which is largely the same as the Jewish Bible, and the New Testament, made up of distinctively Christian works (see pages 198–199). The Old Testament was originally written mostly in Hebrew, while the New Testament was composed entirely in Greek.

The Jewish Bible is normally divided into three sections, also known collectively by the Hebrew acronym *Tanakh*: Law (Torah or Pentateuch, the five "books of Moses," Genesis to Deuteronomy), Prophets (Neviim, twenty-one books including works such as Isaiah and Jeremiah), and Writings (Ketuvim, thirteen books including the Psalms, Proverbs, and Job). The most important section is the Torah, containing all 633 commandments of the Jewish law.

The New Testament usually refers to the Jewish scriptures as "the Law and the Prophets," but Luke 24.44 has "the Law, the Prophets, and the Psalms" and New Testament writers also quote from Proverbs and Job This indicates that the third section, the

THE HEBREW BIBLE IN THE NEW TESTAMENT

New Testament authors typically cite the Old Testament in terms such as "thus it stands written in Isaiah the Prophet…." Elsewhere the reference is often vague, for example, "as it stands in the scriptures…." Matthew says that Joseph's move to Nazareth fulfilled "what was spoken by the prophets: 'He [the Messiah] shall be called a Nazarene [or Nazorean]'" (Matt. 2.22–23). However, the source of this quotation is not clear at all.

Similarly, Paul describes Jesus' death and resurrection as "in accordance with the scriptures" (1 Cor. 15.3–4), even though he makes no citation and, again, there is no obvious Old Testament source. As elsewhere, the author may be using a conventional formula to say that events belong to a divine plan.

A shrine for the Law. *This stone carving of ca. 400 depicts a wheeled Torah shrine, in which a synagogue's scrolls of the Law were kept. From the site of the synagogue at Capernaum that replaced the one Jesus knew.*

Writings, had not yet been settled in New Testament times. In fact, the thirty-nine book Jewish canon was probably fixed only in the second century CE.

THE CHRISTIAN OLD TESTAMENT

Jews of Jesus' day actually had two Bibles: one in Hebrew and one in Greek, the Septuagint (see page 204), used by Diaspora Jews. It was essentially the Septuagint that became the earliest Christian Old Testament. It contained fifteen books that were absent from the Hebrew Bible, most originally written in Greek, such as 1 and 2 Maccabees and Tobit. Other books differ in part from the Hebrew: for instance, Esther and Daniel contain additional stories in the Greek. Christians accepted these writings (see box), and some churches also included works from ancient writings known as the Pseudepigrapha (see page 202).

Old Testament passages cited in the New Testament (see sidebar) indicate that Isaiah, the Psalms, and Zechariah were especially important to the early Christians, yielding "messianic" passages said to predict or interpret Jesus' acts. Such passages were included as a proof to outsiders that Jesus was the Messiah, and expressed the Christian conviction that their Lord was the culmination of Old Testament scripture.

THE APOCRYPHA

Judaism later rejected the additional books found in the Septuagint, many of which lacked a Hebrew original. A desire for antiquity also ruled out recent works such as Sirach. When the Christians adopted the Septuagint as their own scriptures, they accepted these works, including Tobit, Judith, and 1 and 2 Maccabees, even if they were not accorded full canonical status. In Catholicism they are known as "deuterocanonical" (secondary or subsidiary to the canon) and in Greek Orthodoxy as *anagignoskomena* ("things which may also be read") and are incorporated in their Old Testament.

Protestants refer to these writings as "Apocrypha" ("things hidden away"), and do not incorporate them in the canon; instead Protestant Bibles (such as the Luther and King James Bibles) often print the Apocrypha in a separate section following the Old Testament.

Tobias and the Angel. *The Apocrypha are the source of popular stories about virtuous individuals, such as Susanna, Judith, and Tobias. Here, the archangel Raphael aids Tobias on his quest to cure the blindness of his father, Tobit. School of Titian (ca. 1488–1576).*

THE NEW TESTAMENT

St. Athanasius, *who in 367 defined the New Testament canon. A 13th-century mosaic in St. Mark's basilica, Venice.*

CODEX AND CANON

The use of the codex (a bound book, as opposed to a number of separate scrolls) helped in defining the Christian canon of scripture since a book, once bound, was difficult to alter. Monumental codices of the fourth century (see page 200) served to publicize the Christian scriptures as then crystallized; in the years after 312, when Christianity was declared a Roman state religion, such visible assertions of the extent of authoritative, canonical texts were timely and important.

It was only gradually that a distinctively Christian canon of scripture, in the sense of an agreed corpus of writings, emerged. The first-century authors of those books that eventually constituted the New Testament certainly did not consider what they were writing as comparable to the Hebrew Scriptures (see page 197). However, the use of early Christian writings in worship and teaching alongside the older scriptures meant that it was not long before Christian works, too, were being described as scriptural. The Church Fathers of the second to fourth centuries (see page 31) assisted the process by frequently introducing quotations from Christian writings with phrases like "as it stands written…," that previously had been used only for the Hebrew Bible.

The main motive for establishing a distinctive Christian canon was primarily to limit the number of texts deemed to be of especial significance, given the increasing growth in Christian writings in the second and third centuries. Gnostic writings and those books now labeled as "New Testament Apocrypha" (see pages 202–203) doubtless served as catalysts, prompting orthodox Christians to list those books which they regarded as authoritative and foundational for the Christian faith, and to separate these from later, sometimes unorthodox, writings.

However, positive criteria were also applied when texts were selected. One was "apostolicity," the recognition that the writing went back to the founders of Christianity. Hence works in the names of Peter, Paul, or John had a strong chance of being listed as authoritative, although that criterion on its own was not sufficient, since numerous apocryphal writings were written under the names of apostles. Another factor was the continuous acceptance and use of a book by all churches; books that had only limited, local support in one geographical area, such as Egypt, were unlikely to be included.

Increasingly, the antiquity of the writing became another essential criterion. There was a suspicion that recently written books were flawed, especially where Montanism, a second-century apocalyptic movement named after Montanus of Phrygia, was prevalent. Mainstream Christians reacted against such works, determined to root their belief on older, foundational documents. Above all, and in addition to any other criteria, the orthodoxy of the contents of each book was of paramount importance.

THE EMERGING CANON

The epistles (letters) of Paul are the earliest surviving Christian writings and they were the first to be accorded special treatment. As early as the composition of 2 Peter, around the end of the first century, Paul's letters were already being spoken of in the same breath as "other scriptures" (2 Peter 3.15–17). Collections of the letters (sometimes including the anonymous Letter to the Hebrews, no longer attributed to Paul) were made, although not all surviving early collections have identical contents.

In the second half of the second century, Irenaeus, bishop of Lyons, approved a four-gospel canon in order to ostracize unwanted apocryphal gospels: Irenaeus accepted only the familiar gospels of Matthew, Mark, Luke, and John as scripture, justifying this number on the grounds that it was divinely ordained. These writings were considered to be four separate accounts of the Christian message, or "gospel" (a word that in origin translates the Greek *euaggelion* or "good news"), hence their titles: "The gospel according to Mark," and so on. Later came manuscript collections that included Acts (Luke's sequel to his gospel) and some, if not always all seven, of the Catholic (or General) Epistles, that is the letters of Peter, James, John, and Jude. From such early collections the full New Testament canon emerged.

NEW TESTAMENT GENRES

Gospels are unique to Christian writing. There are no letters in the Old Testament; in fact, the only genre that both testaments share is "apocalyptic," a term applied to visionary accounts of the end of time, namely Revelation in the New Testament and, for example, Ezekiel and Daniel in the Old. There are also apocalypses in many intertestamental writings, such as 1 Enoch.

ATHANASIUS AND THE FINAL CANON

Whether one argues that the canon is an authoritative collection of writings (meaning that the church bestowed the authority on them) or a collection of authoritative writings (meaning that the church accepted their inherent authority), the final Christian canon became a fixed, immutable historical and theological entity. In the early Christian centuries various lists of approved writings were drawn up, but the most significant was that by Athanasius, bishop of Alexandria (ca. 297–373), in 367. Following the Old Testament books, Athanasius listed the twenty-seven books found today in the New Testament. By the end of the fourth century Athanasius' New Testament canon was generally accepted.

Aided by the use of the codex, or bound book (see sidebar), that canon was eventually recognized throughout the universal church, although Western Christians hesitated over the Letter to the Hebrews (it is anonymous and its apostolic status therefore in doubt) and Eastern Christians had qualms over Revelation (mainly because of its strange contents). The canon has remained largely unquestioned ever since. However, many old Latin Vulgate manuscripts include the apocryphal Letter to the Laodiceans, and Luther queried the inclusion of the Letter of James. Today, some German scholars speak of the need to accept a "canon within the canon," to indicate the preeminence of some works over others.

One of the canon tables *from the Lindisfarne Gospels of ca. 800, setting out parallel passages in the four gospels.*

NEW TESTAMENT MANUSCRIPTS

About five thousand Greek and ten thousand Latin manuscripts of the New Testament are extant. Some have been preserved in monasteries and libraries; others, often the earliest known examples, have been unearthed at archaeological sites comparatively recently. Some are tiny fragments; a few are complete Bibles. The age of these surviving witnesses—obviously a tiny proportion of all those ever transcribed—ranges from the second century up to and beyond the introduction of printing in the fifteenth century. No two manuscripts agree in all particulars. Most variants are small, but several are theologically sensitive, such as the wording of the institution of the Eucharist, and the omission of the Ascension, in Luke, and the endings of Mark and Romans.

THE EARLIEST RECORDS

The oldest extant New Testament manuscript is a tiny papyrus fragment (called P52) of John's gospel in the Rylands Library in Manchester, England. More substantial early papyri are in Dublin (such as P45, which contains parts of the gospels and Acts) and Geneva (P66, John). The relatively few manuscripts of the entire Bible in Greek include two fourth-century manuscripts known as Codex Sinaiticus, the largest part of which is in London, and Codex Vaticanus in the Vatican Library. Probably produced at Origen's famous library at Caesarea in Palestine, they may be among the fifty Bibles that Constantine I commissioned for churches in his new capital, Constantinople. The discovery of Sinaiticus is a fascinating story. During a visit to St. Catharine's monastery on Mount Sinai in 1844, the indefatigable German biblical scholar Constantin Tischendorf (1815–1874) retrieved pages of this manuscript from a wastepaper basket. He pointed out the discarded treasure to the monks, and when he revisited the monastery in 1859 he was shown an even larger portion of the manuscript.

The oldest witness to the New Testament *is this fragile scrap of a papyrus in Greek that came to light in Egypt in 1920. Dated to ca. 125, it contains parts of the gospel of John 18.31–33 on one side and 18.37–38 on the other (shown here), proving it came from a codex. The fragment is 3.5 x 2.5 inches (9 by 6.4 cm).*

Four Dominican Monks at their Desks *by Tommaso da Modena (1325–1376), in the chapterhouse, of the church of San Nicolò, Treviso, Italy. Until the advent of printing in the late 15th century the copying of scripture was entirely in the hands of trained clerical and monastic scribes. Manuscript copies continued to be produced even after 1600.*

Like their Jewish or Muslim counterparts, Christian scribes were perfectly able to copy a manuscript exactly, but that was not their tradition. They incorporated changes into New Testament texts to reflect how those texts were lived and interpreted. Hence, the variants of Mark 1.1 and John 1.18 reflect differing ideas about the nature of Christ, as does the teaching that Jesus died "without God" in some manuscripts of Hebrews 2.9.

Textual criticism tries to trace the origin of any variants and to identify the earliest form of wording. An editor might accept a reading in one trusted manuscript, or a reading in the majority of manuscripts; or seek witnesses over a wide range of time and place. Most editors will accept the "more difficult" reading, or one that most agrees with an author's known style and language. Some apply the rule that the shorter the reading, the more likely it is to be the original, free of additions. However, the opposite may be even more probable, since scribes often accidentally skip words. An example of an editor's difficulties is the longer ending of Mark (16.9–20), which includes appearances of the risen Jesus. This ending is not in all manuscripts, and there are other alternative endings. (See also page 26.)

MANUSCRIPTS AND THE PRINTED TEXT

The first printed Greek New Testament (1516) was edited by the Dutch humanist scholar Erasmus (1466/9–1526), who based it on a dozen manuscripts in Basle. When older manuscripts came to light they were seen in places to differ markedly from the earlier printed texts. Prime among these older witnesses are the codices Vaticanus and Sinaiticus (see box), which had a huge influence on the Greek New Testament and the English Revised Version (both published 1881), and on nearly all subsequent versions. However, some scholars still prefer the text of the majority of manuscripts, commonly called the Textus Receptus, or Majority Text, and close to Erasmus's edition.

OLD TESTAMENT MANUSCRIPTS

Among Jews, the Hebrew Scriptures became more stable, and copying more rigidly controlled, after the sixth century. Before that time the Old Testament in both Hebrew and in Greek (in particular the Septuagint) was less fixed, and thus the situation was the same as for the New Testament. Most of the "Dead Sea Scrolls" are in fact copies of parts of the Bible, and these often differ from later Hebrew manuscripts, showing that at this earlier date a more fluid textual tradition existed. In newer editions of the Bible, the final paragraph of 1 Samuel 10, following verse 27, comes from a Dead Sea manuscript—it is a passage that had not been included in Bibles for two thousand years.

NONCANONICAL WRITINGS

In addition to what was eventually accepted as the Christian canon, Christians were confronted by many other writings from the earliest times. These included a large body of Jewish literature known as the Pseudepigrapha, which means "works written under a pseudonym," because many of them claimed biblical figures as their authors. Most date from the "intertestamental period," between the latest writings of the Old Testament (ca. 200BCE) and the start of the Christian era.

Some of these works were highly influential in the church—hence their survival—and none more so than the First Book of Enoch (1 Enoch). One of several works inspired by a brief but intriguing passage in the Bible (Gen. 5.24), 1 Enoch mainly recounts how the

CHRISTIAN LEGENDS FROM OUTSIDE THE BIBLE

The influence of the Pseudepigrapha is seen in Christian traditions such as the fall of the rebel angels, first found in 1 Enoch, which tells how certain angels had lusted after human women and thereby introduced evil into the world. For this the angels were expelled from heaven and imprisoned under the earth. The Letter of Jude (14–16) cites 1 Enoch's account.

In The Life of Adam and Eve (ca. 1st century), the angels are expelled for pride, because they refuse to worship Adam as the image of God. These and other variants of the story reflect a postexilic Jewish interest in angels and the causes of evil.

Apocryphal Christian writings inspired many popular legends. The Protevangelium of James (ca. 150) tells of the birth and early life of Mary and names her parents, Joachim and Anne (Anna), who became popular saints. The Infancy Story of Thomas, of similar date, recounts episodes from Jesus' childhood, also filling a perceived gap in the gospels.

Perhaps to counter Gnostic speculations about Jesus as a spiritual being, he is portrayed as a normal child, helping Joseph in his workshop. But at the same time he is also clearly a *Wunderkind* who performs miracles, as in a story where he brings clay birds to life. Some of the stories show Jesus as destructive, even killing other children who annoy him.

The Boy Jesus Brings Clay Sparrows to Life, *in the church of Zillis, Switzerland, 14th century. The Gospel of Pseudo-Matthew (ca. 800) drew together numerous apocryphal stories about Jesus, adding details of its own such as the ox and the ass at the crib. In this form the tales were widely popular and often represented in art.*

patriarch Enoch was taken up to the heavens to receive revelations on the cosmos, evil, and the final age. The Letter of Jude quotes it (see box) and it is part of the Ethiopic Bible. Other Christian authors also allude to 1 Enoch and to other pseudepigraphical writings.

NEW TESTAMENT APOCRYPHA

Alongside what became the New Testament was a vast body of Christian literature now commonly known as the "Apocryphal New Testament." These works tell stories of Jesus' family and followers, particularly the apostles, who were seen as Christian role models. Many works reflect canonical genres: there are apocryphal gospels, acts, letters, and apocalypses. Typically they fill in gaps in canonical writings, satisfying the curiosity of believers (see box). The earliest such texts are dated to the second century, although some scholars argue that a few, including perhaps the Gospel of Thomas (see sidebar), may be contemporary with canonical works. Although the church rejected these—on the whole theologically orthodox but often superstitious and naïve—writings from the canon, they were popular among ordinary Christians and continued to be written up to the Middle Ages (see box).

Christian Gnosticism produced its own literature, often highly introspective and concerned with how, through secret knowledge (*gnosis*), initiates can uncover their inner spirituality and attain redemption. It was partly the proliferation of Gnostic writings that spurred proto-orthodoxy to define its own canon of authorized texts, the New Testament.

THE GOSPEL OF THOMAS

Gnosticism was known mainly from the writings of its Christian opponents until the mid-1940s, when a cache of Gnostic texts was unearthed at Nag Hammadi, Egypt. These included the Gospel of Thomas, with its intriguing sequence of sayings of Jesus. Some are very close to canonical sayings, but others are strangely new, such as "Become passers by." However, scholars are uncertain to what extent one may recover Jesus' authentic words from any source, Gnostic or orthodox.

Saint and Angels, *a detail from Debre Birhan Selassie church in Gondar, Ethiopia, 17th century. The Ethiopian canon includes 1 Enoch and other Pseudepigrapha.*

TRANSLATIONS

The Old Testament was originally composed in Hebrew and Aramaic, and the New Testament entirely in Greek. The Jewish scriptures had already been rendered into Greek—the lingua franca of the eastern Mediterranean—by ca. 200BCE to meet the needs of Diaspora Jews who no longer used Hebrew in daily life. This version is known as the Septuagint (from the Latin *septuaginta*, "seventy"), after a legend that the translation was undertaken in Alexandria by seventy-two translators, six from each of the twelve Jewish tribes (see also pages 196–197).

As Christianity spread to different lands the Greek Old and New Testaments were soon translated into other languages. In Syria, Mesopotamia, and Asia Minor versions appeared in the local Semitic language, Syriac, from as early as the second century. A common Syriac edition, the Peshitta, appeared in the fourth to fifth centuries and became dominant in the Syriac-speaking churches. Christianity reached Egypt by the second century and parts survive from many early Bible manuscripts in Coptic, the ancient Egyptian language. The Bohairic Coptic dialect remains the liturgical language of Egyptian Orthodoxy,

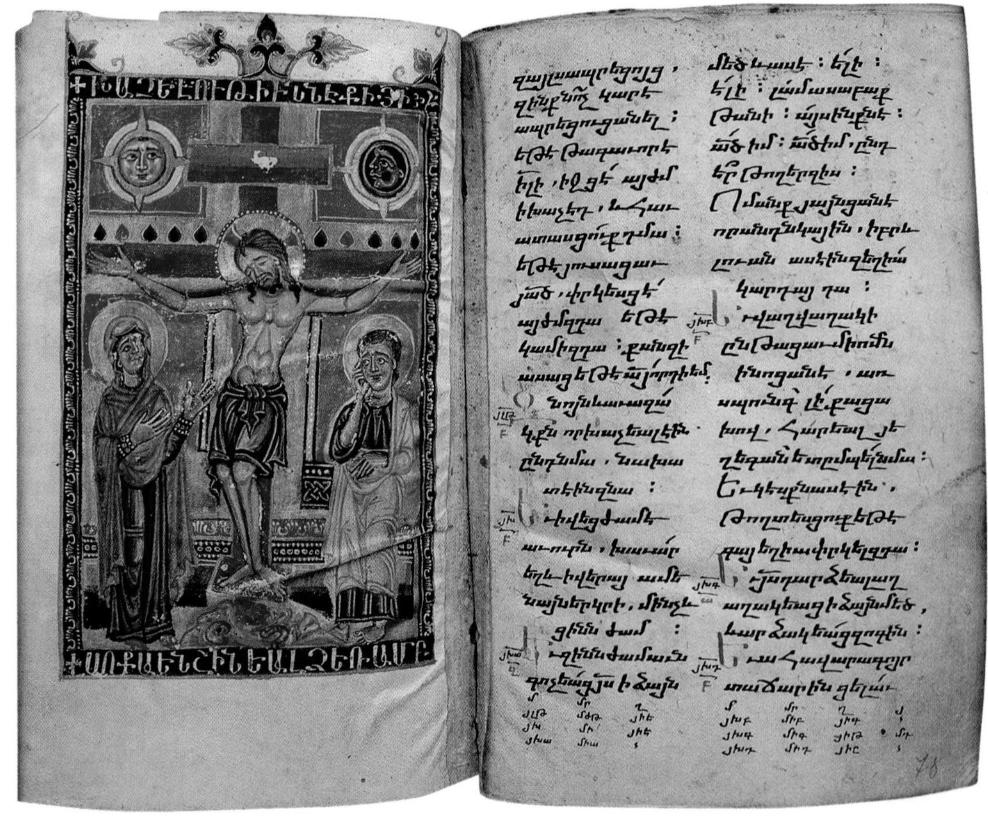

The Crucifixion, *illustrating a 12th-century manuscript of the gospels in Armenian. Armenia was the first state to adopt Christianity as its official religion (in 303; see page 29), and translations of scripture into Armenian soon followed. For the purposes of such translations the monk Mesrop Mashtots created a new Armenian alphabet in 405.*

although Coptic itself is no longer spoken. The Bible was also translated into Ethiopic, Christianity having spread to Ethiopia by the fourth century if not earlier (see page 29).

Scriptures were translated into both Armenian and Georgian soon after the founding of churches in these countries, probably in the 300s and 400s respectively. Many manuscripts survive in both versions, for which new alphabets had to be devised.

WESTERN BIBLES

Unsurpringly, there were various attempts to translate the Bible into Latin, the language of the western Roman Empire, and in 382 Pope Damasus commissioned the scholar Jerome (ca. 347–420) to give some uniformity to the proliferation of Latin translations. The result was Jerome's Versio Vulgata, ("common standard translation"), or Vulgate, which remained the standard Bible of the Roman Catholic Church until modern times.

The translation from Greek into Gothic by the Visigothic bishop Wulfila (ca. 310–383) is the earliest Western version apart from the Latin, and the first in a Germanic language. Portions of this version make up the splendid sixth-century Gothic Codex Argenteus (ca. 500), now in Sweden, written in gold and silver on purple parchment.

The first extant English version is a gloss of the Latin text of the Lindisfarne Gospels (ca. 800). But this is a rare case. Although the common people did not understand Latin, the medieval Western church, unlike those of the East, was reluctant to allow translations lest it lose control over biblical interpretation. Translations that did appear (such as the Wycliffite English versions of the 1380s) were unauthorized and vigorously suppressed by the church.

Christianity reached the Slavs by the ninth century at the latest. Alongside versions in the ancient liturgical dialect known as Old Church Slavonic, there are numerous manuscripts in regional languages such as Serbian and Bulgarian. The Latin alphabet was adopted in Catholic areas (such as Poland and Bohemia), while Orthodox Slavs (for example in Serbia, Bulgaria, and Russia) acquired new alphabets based on Greek (see page 40).

The fifteenth and sixteenth centuries brought two great watersheds in the form of printing and the Reformation. The first printed Bible was the Vulgate of 1453–1455 published in Mainz, Germany, by Johannes Gutenberg, the pioneer of moveable type. The Hebrew Old Testament was first printed in 1488, followed in 1516 by the first printed Greek New Testament, edited by Erasmus. The Complutensian Polyglot, a massive multilingual edition of the Greek, Latin, and Hebrew texts, was printed in 1520 at Alcalá in Spain. In making the scriptures readily available in its original languages, these printed versions naturally encouraged the production of vernacular Bibles. This fact, combined with the Protestant emphasis on preaching and Bible-reading, prompted a wave of new translations. Luther's German Bible first appeared in 1522, and it was not long before Bibles in English (see sidebar), French, and other northern European languages were in use.

The earliest translations met with resistance from the Catholic Church, but printing enabled both mass production and wide circulation, as well as a reduced cost. Nowadays the Bible is available, in total or in part, in around two thousand languages.

TYNDALE AND THE ENGLISH BIBLE

In 1523 the reformist priest William Tyndale (1494–1536) was refused permission to translate the Bible into English, so fled abroad. His New Testament was printed at Worms in 1526 and, later, parts of his Old Testament in English also appeared. These had a Protestant bias, for example "priest" and "bishop" became "elder" and "overseer." Tyndale invented new words such as "Jehovah," "Passover," "scapegoat," and "atonement" for terms in the Hebrew Bible; and coined phrases such as "let there be light," "it came to pass," "a law unto themselves," and "the powers that be."

Declared a heretic, Tyndale was executed near Brussels. But in the wake of the English Reformation, his work underpinned later English translations, above all the Authorised (King James) Version of 1611. This enduring pinnacle of English literature served public worship for centuries and also shaped popular speech and secular literature. It was toppled from its preeminent position only by the Revised Version of 1881–1885. Since then there has been a plethora of English versions, of which the Revised Standard Version (1946–1957), Jerusalem Bible (1966), New English Bible (1970, 1989), and New Revised Standard Version (1990) are among the most significant.

THE BIBLE AS BOOK

Almost without exception the surviving manuscripts of the New Testament are in codex format, that is a bound book with writing on both sides of the pages, which are gathered and stitched together. This applies even to manuscripts from the earliest Christian centuries, when Jews continued to use rolls (scrolls) and secular literature was only slowly changing to the codex.

It is unclear why Christians almost exclusively and from the outset preferred the codex to the roll. The ease of cross-referencing with pages and the economy of using both sides of a page have been suggested as motives, as has the book's supposed greater portability for travelling missionaries—though by the fourth century, the production of large-scale Bibles suggests that ease of carriage was no longer a key consideration in all cases. It was certainly true that the bound codex format lent itself to presenting a selection of texts as an authorized, canonical collection (see page 198). A roll rarely exceeded 45 feet (13.7m), which obviously limited the number of texts a single scroll could include. A desire to be different from surrounding religious cultures may also have been a factor in the choice of a conspicuously "Christian" format.

The Sion Gospels *are adorned with a spectacular cover of wood, gold,* cloisonné *enamel and semi-precious stones. In the center Christ sits enthroned in majesty. German, ca. 1000.*

Another distinctive feature of Christian texts was their use of *nomina sacra* ("sacred names"), the convention of contracting names of theological significance (such as "Lord," "Spirit," "Christ"), usually to their first and last letters, and overlining them to denote the abbreviation.

The earliest papyrus manuscripts of New Testament texts in Greek are functional and without decoration. Usually the block of text is justified, with margins on all sides. Punctuation was not common until the eighth century. Following the conventions of the time, the Greek script is "epigraphic," written in what we now call capital letters with no divisions between words. Such a style persisted until the ninth century, though from the 600s onward an easier, cursive ("running") hand developed which eventually replaced the older form. In this cursive writing words are separated from each other and individual letters are joined up.

A similar phenomenon occurs in Latin manuscripts, where the various scripts in use in the post-Roman period gave way in the late 700s to a more rounded and legible script ("minuscule"), with features such as clear breaks between words. This is usually referred to as "Carolingian" because it was introduced as a standard Latin script at the instigation of the emperor Charlemagne and became widespread throughout western Europe after ca. 800.

LUXURY BIBLES

In the medieval period luxury editions of complete Bibles (pandects) were produced for public display and for use in processions; the bindings of these were often covered in ivory and decorated with gems. But alongside such magnificent productions of iconic status, by the thirteenth century came relatively cheap, functional study editions of the complete Bible for use in universities. These usually contain such reading aids as chapters, headings, and verses (see box). They often had wide margins and much interlinear space so that students could insert comments.

WRITING MATERIALS

By ca. 300 papyrus was giving way to the more durable parchment (sheep or goat hide) or vellum (calf hide) as the preferred writing material for biblical manuscripts. Surviving texts vary in page size from small manual (literally "hand") editions, possibly for private reading, to large manuscripts like Codex Sinaiticus (see page 200), intended for church use. By ca. 800 paper had reached the Middle East from China, where it was invented. It began to be used from the ninth century, but became the norm

CHAPTER AND VERSE: DIVIDING THE TEXT

The original biblical authors wrote their text continuously, without paragraphs or section beginnings. However, some early manuscripts of the gospels and Acts are divided into sections: in Codex Vaticanus, for example, Acts has two sets of capitulation (chapter-division), one of thirty-one chapters, the other of sixty-nine, compared to the present twenty-eight. The epistles were often similarly divided.

Bishop Eusebius of Caesarea (ca. 275–339) devised a numbering system in the margins of gospel manuscripts to enable easy cross-referencing to parallel passages. But it was another 900 years before the familiar system of chapters and verses was introduced. Stephen Langton (ca. 1150–1228), archbishop of Canterbury, is credited with creating the chapter divisions, which were subdivided into verses by Robert Stephanus (or Etienne, 1503–1559), in his printed New Testament of 1551 and his complete French Bible two years later. These are the divisions still in use today.

The Evangelist Matthew (center) with Abraham and Isaac *illustrate the first page of Matthew's gospel in this Byzantine manuscipt of ca. 1060 from Constantinople (Istanbul). The Greek text contains no text divisions apart from the heading of the gospel itself.*

ART AND ARCHITECTURE

ILLUMINATED MANUSCRIPTS

The Talbot Hours, *a book of hours (prayer manual) belonging to John Talbot, 1st earl of Shrewsbury. On this dedication page the owner and his wife are shown venerating the Virgin and Child. French school, ca. 1424.*

OPPOSITE **The title page to Matthew's gospel** *from the Book of Kells, one of the most splendid examples of the Celtic (Insular) style of illumination. Both this and the above manuscript are on vellum (calfskin). Irish, ca. 800.*

Very few early Greek biblical manuscripts are illuminated or illustrated, even though the flat surfaces of a book page obviously lent themselves to decoration. Ornamentation was introduced from the time of the emperor Constantine I, and Greek gospel manuscripts sometimes contain a portrait of each evangelist preceding his gospel. Some manuscripts have key words, such as the divine titles, picked out in red letters. Others have decorated initial capitals of each new paragraph. Sometimes crosses are worked into the lettering. In the early centuries and certainly by the sixth century lavish Bibles written in gold or silver ink on purple pages were produced; these were possibly imperial commissions.

Once the age of iconoclasm (see page 192) had passed, from the eighth century onward, images were reintroduced to enliven manuscript pages. Wherever the Bible was used not only as a book to be read from but also as an artifact for veneration, its text was often enhanced not only by splendid calligraphy but by artistic lettering and elaborate decoration. Illuminations were also added to the pages of text: these served a pedagogical purpose to educate the unlettered but also enhanced the visual impact and value of the book itself. "Miniatures" were originally small pictures in red-lead pigment, or *minium*.

The expansion of Christian Europe led to a growth of Bible production, especially in Latin. In fact, the majority of surviving illuminated manuscripts are Western, medieval, and Latin. The early medieval period, the so-called Dark Ages, saw the production of sumptuously decorated manuscripts, notably under Irish influence. The distinctive and at times astonishingly intricate decoration of Irish and Irish-influenced manuscripts is seen for example in the Book of Kells, a gospel book dating from ca. 800. It was the lavish illustration in many gospel books, rather than the text itself, that led to their preservation into the age of printing, when manuscript copies were no longer needed or used.

Narrative illustrations of the Psalter were also particularly popular in medieval times, and picture Bibles with a minimum of writing were produced in the late Middle Ages, although there are precedents for picture cycles in Bibles from earlier centuries. Revelation (the Apocalypse) was popular too, prompted by the prevalence of the Black Death and the fear that the end of the world was close.

Throughout the Middle Ages, a book of hours, or daily prayer manual, was the indispensable and intimate devotional accessory of laypeople, and numerous manuscript copies survive, some lavishly illustrated.

The heyday of illuminated Bibles was the thirteenth to fourteenth centuries. With the age of printing came the end of the age of illuminated manuscripts, yet written scriptures continued to be made until the seventeenth century and served as the aesthetic standard for the creators of the first printed Bibles.

2 THE GOSPELS

The twenty-seven Christian writings that form the New Testament canon were composed within two generations of Christ's death, mostly between 50 and 100CE. The collection comprises dramatic narratives with reminiscences about Jesus' career and teachings (the four gospels) and about the spread of the early church (in the Acts of the Apostles), personal and pastoral letters from the earliest missionaries, and one apocalypse (Revelation). This chapter begins with an examination of the four gospels.

Classical antiquity produced numerous stories about famous historical figures; Jewish authors also wrote of the deeds and teachings of famous patriarchs. But there is nothing exactly parallel to the New Testament gospels of Matthew, Mark, Luke, and John. They are concerned primarily with Jesus' earthly career as he travels through Judea and Galilee. Teachings to his intimate twelve disciples as well as to a wider public are interwoven with narratives including miracles and healings. The duration of that public

OPPOSITE **St Luke the Evangelist** *from the church of San Vitale, Ravenna, 6th century. He is depicted in this mosaic with his traditional symbol, the ox (see page 195).*

DATING THE GOSPELS

There is a scholarly consensus that Mark, the earliest gospel, was composed at least a generation after the events it relates. Although Mark 13.2 and possibly 13.14 have Jesus predict the downfall of the Temple and with it Judaism as then practiced, it seems to contain no allusion to the actual fall of Jerusalem in 70 during the First Jewish War (66–70), when the Romans destroyed the Temple, and so may have been written in the mid-60s.

The authors of Matthew and Luke may allude to this event (Matt 22.7; Luke 21.20, 24), but even so it is remarkable, given the obvious propaganda value to Christian apologists of the destruction of the Temple—the center of Jewish life and religious practice—that so little, if anything, is made of that catastrophe in the New Testament. One might compare this with the Jewish historian Josephus, writing in the late 70s, who describes the fall and desecration of Jerusalem in considerable detail in his *Jewish Wars*. Hence some scholars consider that all four gospels may have been completed before the year 70.

St. Mark Writing Down the Words of St. Paul *by Fra Angelico (1387–1455). The gospel of Mark was traditionally said to be based on the teachings of apostle Peter, but its character displays a greater affinity to the teachings of Paul (see page 212).*

ministry was comparatively short, at most three years, and Jesus is portrayed as constantly on the move. Matthew and Luke alone recount the circumstances of Jesus' birth but all four refer to John the Baptist and to Jesus' own baptism, and all devote several chapters to Jesus' last week and the Passion—his arrest, trial, and crucifixion.

WHAT IS A GOSPEL?

The gospels are unique. Librarians may be tempted to classify them as "history," but this seems not to be their prime *raison d'être*. "Biography" is not an ideal description either, since many moments in Jesus' life are absent from the gospels. One-third of Mark's short gospel covers just one week in Jesus' career, and it says nothing about his birth. Even Matthew and Luke, which do contain nativity stories, leave great gaps in his early years, which were filled by apocryphal texts (see pages 202–203).

The best classification for the gospels is "theology." Their authors drew on historical reminiscences, but their motive was to evoke faith, as John 20.31 makes clear: "These things are written that you may believe that Jesus is the Christ, the Son of God, and that believing you may have life in his name." Mark similarly describes itself as "the gospel of Jesus Christ, the Son of God" (Mark 1.1), both "Christ" and "Son of God" being theological terms. The end of Matthew ("Go therefore and make disciples of all nations...," Matt. 28.19–20) is, quite literally, a mission statement for would-be followers of Jesus. In each gospel, the teachings of Jesus are in effect addressed to all readers or hearers of the gospel, from whom a response is constantly demanded. When the gospels ask questions such as "What manner of man is this?" they are addressing the reader.

The gospels were originally produced anonymously as if to emphasize that the accounts were not intended to be the author's own view of the Christian message, even though in practice this is what each gospel actually is. The four evangelists (gospel-writers) were not compiling journals of record, nor did they intend their books as scripture—for them, "scripture" was the Old Testament (see page 198). The later gospels drew on earlier written sources but these were

THE GOSPELS AND THE JEWS

One can often plot how stories originating with Mark developed as they were retold by the three later evangelists. For instance, Jesus' death is increasingly blamed on the Jews as a whole; by contrast, the Romans are increasingly exonerated, with Pilate seen only as a weak ruler, unwilling to sentence Jesus to death until coerced by the Jewish mob. Such a development running from Mark through to John reflects the historical developments within a church whose expansion increasingly depended on Roman goodwill and which, by the time John was writing, was no longer a Jewish sect but a predominantly Gentile movement.

not treated as sacrosanct: the authors changed sequences of stories, altered details, and made "corrections" (see sidebar, left). Essentially, the evangelists wrote Christian interpretations of scriptural prophecies and predictions. They believed that the Old Testament anticipated the arrival of Jesus, who thus fulfilled those scriptures. Only after many decades were the gospels deemed to be equal (and, later, superior) in status to the Old Testament (see sidebar). It is unlikely that any of the evangelists was an eyewitness to the events they wrote of. However, nothing within the gospels reveals precisely the identity of their authors or gives explicit indications as to where or when they were written (see box on page 210).

The scribe who first added the name Mark to this gospel possibly had in mind a man called John Mark, a companion of Barnabas (Acts 15). Mark's gospel was probably composed in Rome—it contains Latinisms and its theology, especially its pro-Gentile stance, matches the outlook of Paul, who was in Rome in the mid-60s, when Mark may have been written. The gospel's strong Pauline character contrasts with the ancient tradition that Mark was in fact based on Peter's reminiscences.

Matthew was the name of one of the disciples; he is mentioned in Mark and Luke but Matthew's gospel alone makes a point of his profession of tax gatherer (Matt. 9.9–10, 10.3), perhaps suggesting a particular interest in him. The tradition is that this gospel was originally composed in Hebrew and was associated with Antioch in Syria, reputedly where the term "Christians" was coined (Acts 11.26). It is the most "Jewish" of the gospels, with many references to the Old Testament; some have claimed that it is modeled on the Pentateuch, with the Sermon on the Mount paralleling Moses' giving of the Law.

Luke was a travelling companion of Paul, and the eyewitness of some of the events in Luke's sequel, the Acts of the Apostles (see page 216–217). Tradition, based on Colossians 4.14, claims that Luke was a physician and a Gentile, and some see his two works as pro-Gentile books that also happen to display a medical interest.

The author of John, the fourth and latest gospel, is usually identified as one of the two sons of Zebedee, and one of the inner core of Jesus' disciples (see pages 214–215).

THE "SYNOPTIC PROBLEM"

The gospels of Matthew, Mark and Luke share much material and have a similar view of Jesus' person and ministry. Hence they are often called the "Synoptic Gospels," "synoptic" deriving from Greek words that imply a common viewpoint, as opposed to the somewhat differing portrayal in John. The three gospels are the focus of "the Synoptic Problem"—the difficulty in accounting for their many similarities and differences.

When two or more writings share material, one may seek to explain the parallels as resulting from collusion, copying, or the use of common sources. In addition the artistic freedom of creative authors to reshape their raw materials must also be borne in mind—not everything needs to be explained exclusively in terms of written sources.

Once Mark's priority was accepted in the twentieth century, the normal "solution" to the "problem" was to say that Matthew and Luke independently used Mark's gospel.

They each chose what they needed from Mark, sometimes omitting sections, adapting here, copying exactly there. These activities account for many of the similarities and differences between the two later Synoptics and Mark.

Material found in both Matthew and Luke (much of it teachings by Jesus) but not in Mark could be explained in a similar way, namely that Luke had used some of Matthew's contents. But most scholars argue that such non-Markan material is best explained by Matthew's and Luke's use of a lost source, known as "Q" (from the German *Quelle*, "source"), perhaps a collection of Jesus' sayings similar to the Gnostic Gospel of Thomas (see page 203). However, belief in the hypothetical Q is not unanimous.

The consensus is that Mark was a source of Matthew and of Luke and not an epitome of them. There are many places where Matthew and Luke, independently, seem to have altered or improved on Mark's language and style. Mark's relatively simple theology, especially his picture of Jesus, is also said to agree with an early date, as does his often unflattering portrayal of the disciples. Mark's colloquial Greek compared with the more "correct" language of the other gospels also argues in favor of his primitiveness.

THE ANOINTING OF JESUS

In order to understand the gospels' distinctive characteristics and theology it is fruitful to compare how they recount the same episodes. For example, all four recount a story in which a woman anoints Jesus while he is eating a meal (Matt. 26.6-13; Mark 14.3–9; Luke 7.36–50; John 12.1–8). Her gesture arouses the hostility of those accompanying Jesus, who in contrast accepts her action. Three gospels (Matthew, Mark, and John) locate the story in Bethany shortly before Jesus' Passion, and three name the host as a man called Simon ("the leper" in Matthew and Mark, "the Pharisee" in Luke).

But there are important differences. In Matthew and Mark, the woman anoints Jesus' head, perhaps to show Jesus as a king—the Messiah ("Anointed One"). However, like John, they also wish to show Jesus' awareness of his imminent death and burial. In Luke and John, the woman anoints Jesus' feet, a polite gesture to a welcomed guest. Luke, who places the story during Jesus' Galilean ministry, focuses on Jesus as the forgiver of sins. He even incorporates a parable into his account. In John, after the woman anoints Jesus' feet, Judas complains that the ointment could have been sold for the poor. Thus Judas alone receives the rebuke from Jesus, who says that the woman should keep the ointment to anoint Jesus' body after his death.

Christ in the House of Simon the Pharisee. *Jesus blesses the woman who anoints his feet, traditionally identified as Mary Magdalene. A fresco of Sant' Angelo in Formis basilica (1072) near Capua, Italy.*

THE GOSPEL OF JOHN

Even a cursory look at the four gospels reveals significant differences in character between the three Synoptics (Matthew, Mark, and Luke) and John, which is often referred to simply as the Fourth Gospel. Broadly, the Synoptics contain many short episodes, while John has fewer, longer stories. The Synoptics present Jesus' teaching in brief aphorisms or in "parables," ranging from pithy proverbs to extensive allegories; parables were useful for conveying moral lessons or difficult concepts like the kingdom of God. In John, Jesus delivers long metaphorical discourses; there are no aphorisms and only two passages that resemble allegorical parables (John 10.1–18, 15.1–10). In the Synoptics the teachings focus on God's coming kingdom and the people's behavior, whereas John's main emphasis is on the person and work of Christ.

THE BELOVED DISCIPLE

A distinctive feature of John's gospel is the appearance of a follower of Jesus who is referred to several times only as the disciple "whom Jesus loved." Since early times Christian tradition has generally identified this "beloved disciple" as John, son of Zebedee (Matt. 4.21), whose name the gospel bears, but in the gospel there is no hard evidence for this. Indeed, since he is unnamed, it has been speculated that the disciple may not be one of the Twelve at all. One theory is that he is not a particular individual but an idealized disciple of Jesus, created in contrast to the Twelve with their failings.

John 21.24 describes the beloved disciple as the gospel's author and a witness to its events, a verse clearly added by a later hand. It is not impossible that John, in its earliest form, drew upon the eyewitness account of this anonymous disciple. Certainly, the gospel does seem to display a close knowledge of Jewish practices and festivals as well as of Palestine and Jerusalem. Perhaps it was originally written within, and for, the disciple's own circle, who would naturally emphasize their mentor's privileged access to Jesus.

The Crucifixion, *by Rogier van der Weyden (ca. 1399–1464). The left hand panel shows the figures of Mary and the beloved disciple (John 19.26). The disciple appears at other poignant and intimate moments in John, such as the Last Supper (13.23) and the empty tomb (20.2).*

The Wedding Feast at Cana *by Giusto de' Menabuoi (ca. 1320–1391), a fresco in the baptistery of Padua cathedral, Italy. The story of Jesus turning water into wine, the first of his "signs," is recounted only in John's gospel (2.1–11). It is among the gospel's lengthy and unique episodes that are recognized as pearls of early Christian literature: others are the tale of Nicodemus (John 3), the story of the Samaritan Woman (John 4), and the bizarre story of the raising of Lazarus (John 11). All bear the hallmarks of the gospel's author.*

THE "MYSTICAL" GOSPEL

In John the teachings of Jesus at times appear more meditative, enigmatic, or mystical than in the other gospels. John includes such unique and disturbing pronouncements by Jesus as "No one comes to the Father except through me" (John 14.6), as well as Jesus' potent "I am" sayings, such as "I am the light of the world" (8.12); his long and unique "Farewell Discourses" (chs. 15–17) are also unique to John. Throughout the gospel, Jesus is depicted as God's emissary to a hostile world, aware of his relationship to his Father and of his own destiny and mission. Also famous because of its beauty and profundity is the gospel's opening prologue ("In the beginning was the Word . . .", John 1.1–18) which, echoing the first words of Genesis, describes Jesus as preexistent, part of the Creator who then becomes incarnate. This hymn reflects many of the conclusions reached by Christians about the nature of Christ by ca. 90–100CE, when the gospel was most likely written.

However, the differences between John and the Synoptics should not be overstated. Gnostics and others doubtless found in John's rather mystical Messiah a precedent for their own spiritualized Jesus, who possessed only a phantom body. But John's gospel leaves no doubt that he became flesh and suffered physically on the cross—in other words that, counter to Gnostic teachings, he was quite as fully human as the Jesus of the Synoptics.

John's gospel is associated with Ephesus, one of the largest cities in the Roman world, and there was a strong tradition that its putative author, the disciple John (see box), lived there in old age. The author possibly also wrote the First Letter of John (1 John), and some would even say 2 and 3 John as well. But it is unlikely to be the John who wrote Revelation.

SIGNS AND WONDERS

The Fourth Gospel prefers to describe Jesus' wonder-workings, healings, and nature miracles—some of which also appear in the Synoptics—as "signs." This implies that the evangelist sees Jesus as more than a mere itinerant miracle-worker of a type that was well known in the ancient world. For John, Jesus' actions are no crowd-pleasing magic but indeed signs or distinguishing marks of his divine origins and messiahship. John's message is this: Jesus accomplishes his Father's work and the miraculous powers of God are in him.

THE ACTS OF THE APOSTLES

OPPOSITE SS. Peter (right) and Paul, *a mosaic in the baptistery of the Arians, Ravenna, 5th century. Acts does not report the fate of either apostle, but traditions found in later apocryphal works claim that both were executed in Rome, probably during the persecutions of Nero (ca. 64–65).*

The Acts of the Apostles, often called Christianity's first history book, is the second half of the two-volume work of which Luke's gospel is the first. The gospel covers roughly the first thirty years of the first century, up to Jesus' death and resurrection; Acts covers the following thirty or so. Despite the title, the book concentrates on just two of the apostles—first Peter, then Paul.

Acts tells the dramatic events of Christianity's speedy expansion throughout the Mediterranean, beginning with Peter in Jerusalem and ending with Paul in Rome. On the way, many short and often exciting episodes introduce a vast array of characters, many miraculous deeds, and a few significant speeches. Paul's three famous missionary journeys

PETER IN ACTS

While Paul is clearly the dominant apostle in Acts, Peter is certainly presented as a remarkable church leader. There are fascinating parallels between the portrayals of both apostles. They are the focus of similar events and the teaching attributed to both is also close. Each begins his ministry by healing a lame man (Acts 3.2ff.; 14.8ff.); each encounters a magician (8.9ff; 13.6ff.); each raises the dead (9.36ff.; 20.9ff.); each is a popular miracle-worker (5.15ff.; 20.9ff.); and each escapes from prison through miraculous intervention (12.7ff.; 16.26ff.).

Peter, the former fisherman, also serves in Acts as a very human figure with whom ordinary converts could readily identify. In the gospels, he is often impulsive. His failure to understand Jesus' teachings reaches its climax when he famously denies Jesus three times after Jesus' arrest in Jerusalem. The gospels' portrayal of Peter, warts and all, results in a credible picture of an early disciple who would then serve as a model for later generations of faltering Christians. His "rags-to-riches" career makes him a noteworthy example to others, and that is how he is used in subsequent Christian writings, beginning with Acts.

St. Peter Denies Christ, *a mural by Philip Goul in the church of the Holy Cross at Platanistasa, Cyprus. 15th century. During the high priest's examination of Jesus (top), Peter—as Jesus predicted—three times denies knowing him before the cock crows. On hearing the cock, Peter remembers the prediction and weeps in shame (top left).*

to Asia Minor and Greece, founding or encouraging new churches, take up most of the book. However, like the gospels, Acts is primarily a work of theology, not a factual chronicle. God and the Holy Spirit are its real heroes: God's message spreads through divine intervention and the apostles are merely the human agents who carry the message.

As a consequence, the story is told in a contrived and structured way that suggests editorial planning. The message begins in Jerusalem, the heart of the Jewish faith, and advances from Palestine to Antioch, through to Asia Minor, then into Europe and finally, and significantly, to Rome, the capital of the Gentile world. Acts does not report the conversion of the Romans, probably because the author wishes to name no apostle other than Paul, the pro-Gentile missionary, as reaching Rome. A strong ancient tradition credits Peter with having founded the Roman church, but in Acts he merely "goes off elsewhere" (Acts 12.17).

While Peter plays an important part in Acts (see box), it was arguably Paul who played the key role in turning Christianity from a Jewish cult into a worldwide phenomenon. Paul began as a Pharisee who persecuted Christians with great fervor (Acts 9.1–2), but his conversion on the Damascus road (9.3ff.) made him an even more fervent apostle of the church. He is presented as an idealized figure, a model of endurance and a successful leader of the pro-Gentile movement. The author possibly repeated stories about Peter but replaced him with Paul as the hero, in order to emphasize that Paul was building on Peter's foundations—but with greater success.

APOSTOLIC RIVALRY

Paul's letters pre-date Acts and show the rivalry between himself and apostles such as Peter and James, who insisted that new converts had to follow Jewish practices such as circumcision. But for Paul, the Jewish Law had been superseded and he argued that converts from Gentile backgrounds were not obliged to follow such requirements. Acts downplays the rivalry between Peter and Paul, and shows the two sides agreeing that Gentile converts need not abide by Jewish practices.

THE LETTERS

Within thirty years of its establishment Christian communities were to be found in important centers of the Mediterranean world like Thessalonica, Ephesus, and Rome. Communication between the travelling preachers who had founded those churches and their often fragile and vulnerable communities was maintained either through emissaries or letters. Surprisingly, several of these letters (or epistles, from Latin *epistola*, letter) survived to be incorporated in the New Testament. Many of the latter were composed to meet an immediate local problem, but it was soon recognized that their teaching and authority transcended their original purposes. Their spiritual merit encouraged their circulation and preservation in the early church, and collections of letters were assembled within Christianity's first two centuries.

Most of the twenty New Testament letters were written to churches and the bulk are by the apostle Paul or composed in his name (see sidebar). Nine are to seven named churches in Corinth, Philippi, Galatia, Rome, Ephesus, Thessalonica, and Colossae. The rest were written to individuals (the so-called "Pastoral Letters" to Timothy and Titus,

The Temple of Apollo *and view across the agora (marketplace) of Corinth, where Paul preached. His two letters to the Corinthians were addressed to the fledgling church in this important city of southern Greece.*

and the Letter to Philemon) or are addressed to a general audience (the "Catholic Letters" of James, Peter, John, and Jude). The Letter to the Hebrews, no longer ascribed to Paul, is in effect an anonymous homily and not really a letter at all. The letters are presented in descending order of length, beginning with Romans and ending with Jude.

Paul was a prolific correspondent and his writings are the earliest extant Christian documents. He began writing in the late 40s and continued until the early 60s. The apostle was from Tarsus in southeastern Asia Minor and his mother tongue was most likely Aramaic, but he wrote in Greek—the language of the educated classes—even to the Christians in Rome, knowing that he would be understood.

PAUL'S LETTERS AND THE EARLY CHURCH

Among Paul's remarkable surviving output, the long Letter to the Romans is more of a theological treatise than most of his other letters. This is probably because Paul had not founded the church in Rome (see page 217) and therefore sent his theological manifesto in advance of his planned visit to the city. In Romans he sets out his distinctive theological concerns, especially about the role of Gentiles in the divine plan and their relationship to the Jews, to Jewish history, and to the Jews' former privileges, especially their status as God's chosen people. The universalism of Christianity is his key theme (Rom. 9–11 and elsewhere).

Many of the letters give first-hand insights into the problems of setting up and maintaining a church, its structures, hierarchy, and organization. A sense of urgent and relentless mission shines through all the letters, as do the pastoral concerns and authoritarian manner of church founders like Paul. The birth pangs of the new religion, with Jewish converts reluctant to abandon Jewish practices and Gentile converts tempted to revert to pagan ones, are graphically evident. The letters also contain much about practical aspects of Christian living, such as marriage, communal eating, ethical behavior, and common worship.

Although Paul's letters were written relatively soon after Jesus' life, it may seem surprising that they scarcely refer to the events later recounted in the gospels, apart from Jesus' death and resurrection. On the other hand, Jesus' life and teachings were not Paul's primary concern, certainly in these letters. His main aim was to teach that Christ's death and resurrection had inaugurated a new relationship between man and God: as a consequence of Christ rising from the dead, the age-old cycle of death and decay inaugurated at the Fall had been broken and those who were incorporated into Christ through baptism would share with him in a similar resurrection (Rom. 6).

Much of Paul's teaching is rabbinic in style. He is steeped in Jewish literature and culture and his arguments often rely on his own interpretation of the Hebrew Scriptures, which he cites extensively. The extent to which Gentile audiences would have appreciated such sophisticated argumentation is questionable. Some would have begun as Gentile converts to Judaism who were already familiar with the Jewish scriptures and faith. But complete outsiders would have required a thorough course in biblical theology, although fellow converts with a Jewish background could have explained basic aspects.

PSEUDONYMITY

Most modern scholars agree that Paul did not write all the letters attributed to him. Paul himself was aware of letters purporting to be from him (2 Thess. 2.2). The apostle's popularity and influence were such that others, out of modesty and in recognition of his inspirational leadership, wrote under his name, sometimes incorporating fragments of his genuine teaching. Such pseudonymity may seem dishonest or plagiaristic today, but it was common in the ancient world and often an act of homage.

The Pauline letters that differ most in theology, style, and language from those universally acknowledged to be by Paul—such as Romans, 1 and 2 Corinthians, and Galatians—are dubbed "deutero-Pauline," for example Ephesians and 1 and 2 Timothy. However, some scholars argue that the differences may be better explained not by denying Paul's authorship but by recognizing either that Paul sometimes made freer use of an amanuensis to transcribe his ideas (see Rom. 16.22), or that his style and language changed as he matured.

REVELATION

THE NUMBER OF THE BEAST

Revelation famously refers to two "beasts," agents of Satan who control the earth in succession. According to the author, the name of the second beast may be reckoned from the number 666 (Rev. 13.18). In both Greek and Hebrew, letters were also used as numbers, creating a practice called *gematria*. The Greek word "beast" transliterated into Hebrew has the numerical value 666. So too do the Greek words *Kaisar Neron*—"Emperor Nero"—written in Hebrew script. Nero (ruled 54–68) was notorious for his savage persecution of Christians; for the author of Revelation, Nero's very name revealed his bestial character.

Nero was dead when Revelation was written (ca. 95), but a widespread legend held that he would one day return. So who was Revelation's "second Nero"? The most likely candidate is the emperor Domitian (ruled 81–96), who at the time was initiating his own persecutions of Christians.

Revelation is the final book of the New Testament and one of the most distinctive. As its name suggests, it claims to be a revelation (Greek *apocalupsis*) of the end of time, in the course of which occur many striking images such as the four horsemen of the apocalypse, the Whore of Babylon, and the beast "666" (see sidebar).

The author of Revelation, also called the Revelation to John and the Apocalypse of John, is traditionally held to be the disciple John, son of Zebedee, writing in exile on the Greek island of Patmos. John's gospel is also traditionally ascribed to this disciple, but despite the parallels between the two writings—not least their use of titles such as "Word of God" and "Lamb of God"—the differences in language and style, and the general tone of Revelation, together with its eschatological themes, strongly suggest two different authors with a common theology. Both works were written toward the end of the first century, and perhaps both authors belonged a church that looked to the apostle John as its founder.

Revelation is a dramatic and poetic book, full of literary devices and strange imagery. It opens with letters to seven churches then becomes an apocalyptic book proper, with

sequences of "visions" where the symbolically significant number seven recurs. The opening of a book sealed with seven seals leads to a series of trumpet-calls presaging disasters. After the seventh trumpet comes the preaching of God's and Christ's realm. There are two further visions: the woman persecuted by a dragon and the war between the archangel Michael and Satan. Among later scenes is the judgment on "Babylon" (a bitterly hostile reference to Rome) and on the world. Satan is bound for a thousand years. The book ends with the resurrection of the faithful dead and the last judgment of souls. The author then anticipates, possibly in the near future, a changed order—a new heaven, a new earth, and a New Jerusalem.

The Four Horsemen of the Apocalypse *by Albrecht Dürer (1471–1528), a woodcut illustrating the famous vision of the scourges of humankind who appear in Revelation 6 (left to right): Death, Famine, War, and Pestilence.*

APOCALYPTIC WRITING

There was much argument before Revelation became part of the Christian canon and even today, Orthodox lectionaries exclude it—there are no readings from Revelation in Orthodox liturgy. The churches in the East had problems with it probably because of its strange character: Revelation is the only purely apocalyptic text in the New Testament and its style and content are in marked contrast to the other canonical books. Yet the latter do include apocalyptic passages (notably in Mark 13 and its parallels in Matthew and Luke), while "apocalyptic" as a genre was very popular (see page 199) and indeed survived for centuries.

On one level Revelation and apocalyptic writing in general give the impression that they are interested in foretelling future events, usually doom-laden and foreboding. In this way Revelation conforms to Jewish literary tradition, and is a natural development from Old Testament prophetic literature. Famous prophets like Ezekiel and Isaiah assessed what they saw was wrong in society and warned about the dangers of pursuing false paths. When they project their warnings into an indefinite future (possibly to disguise hostile references to contemporary events), their imagery becomes increasingly flamboyant and colorful and their writing is more properly described as apocalyptic rather than simply prophetic.

Because of Revelation's cryptic imagery and poetry, many fringe groups over the centuries have taken its visions literally and have applied its prophecies to their own times. Such groups have all too often seen Revelation as a secret "code book" for the future, to which only certain insiders have the key. This is to miss the work's essential purpose. It foretells, in extraordinary vivid language and imagery, the overthrow of evil and the triumph of God's kingdom. The original, yet enduring, aim of its coded messages is to reassure readers of divine sovereignty, and to persuade Christians to remain constant in their faith.

OPPOSITE **The Woman Fleeing the Dragon** *by Nicolas Bataille (fl. 1363–1400), from the tapestry known as the Apocalypse of Angers. It illustrates the vivid imagery of Revelation 12.14. The seven-headed dragon is Satan; the woman is variously interpreted as the Virgin Mary, the church, and God's people.*

PART 4

CHRISTIANITY TODAY

St. Mary's cathedral in Urakami, Nagasaki, *was close to the center of the atomic blast that destroyed the city on August 9, 1945. The cathedral was East Asia's largest Roman Catholic church when it was dedicated in 1914, after Japan had ended its prohibition of Christian worship. Its congregation was estimated at around 14,000 in 1945. Rebuilt in 1959, it is both an active church and a memorial to the horrors of nuclear war.*

1 EVANGELISM

From the late fifteenth century evangelism outside Europe went hand in hand with European colonialism, led by the Spanish in the New World and the Portuguese in Africa and Asia; following their establishment in 1540, Jesuits were at the forefront of Catholic missionary activity outside Europe. Protestant missions accompanied the establishment of English and Dutch colonies and global trade networks in the seventeenth century. European mission often involved a form of cultural imperialism; in the "Praying Towns," villages established from ca. 1650 in Massachusetts by John Eliot (1604–1690), Native American converts ("Praying Indians") were expected to acquire English language and customs.

Missions to Africa and to India, China, and Japan, had mixed success. In Far Eastern nations with advanced literate civilizations and existing scriptural religions of considerable

A Celtic cross at Iona abbey, *Scotland. When St. Columba landed on Iona in 563 on his mission to evangelize among the Gaels and Picts, mission could still be on the initiative of "spirit-led" individuals. But the norm was to evangelize within the framework of institutional approval, as with Augustine's mission to the English in 597.*

sophistication (such as Islam, Buddhism, and Hinduism), Christianity never achieved more than small minority status. But in regions of sub-Saharan Africa and the Pacific islands, for example, where European mission followed in the wake of military subjugation, the impact on animistic native religious practice was often considerable.

As in the first Christian centuries, it was sometimes difficult to persuade converts that Christianity was an exclusive religion. However, the Jesuits made headway in China by accepting traditional ancestor rites as a social and not a religious practice until the Dominicans persuaded the pope in 1715 to forbid such rites as heresy. This was a major setback to the Catholic mission and points to one issue in evangelism even today: the rivalry of different missionary groups, even within the same branch of Christianity (see sidebar).

In the twentieth century, instead of "converting the heathen," Christians began to talk seriously to those of other faiths in a climate of mutual respect (see pages 230–231). At the same time, revivalist preachers such as Billy Graham (see box) sought to revitalize the faith in traditionally Christian lands. In the postcolonial era, African Christianity became particularly vigorous, both within established groups (such as the various African Anglican churches) and new ones. In some regions, such as modern China, the growing number of conversions has at times encountered official hostility (see page 238).

PROSELYTISM

The term "proselytism" is often used for attempts by Christians to win converts from other churches. Today ecumenical bodies condemn the practice but recent years have seen inter-church tensions arising from the activities of Protestant missionaries in traditionally Roman Catholic Latin America and Orthodox Russia; and the Russian Orthodox Church has accused Rome of "proselytism" over its support for Eastern-Rite (Uniate) and other Roman Catholics in the former USSR (see also page 233).

BILLY GRAHAM AND MODERN EVANGELISM

Christian evangelism took on a new energy in the second half of the twentieth century with preachers such as Dr. Billy Graham (born 1918), of the Southern Baptism Convention. Graham began a series of "Revival" meetings in 1949, won support and publicity from the politically conservative newspaper magnate William Randolph Hearst, and subsequently preached to enormous crowds in the US and London. Later, Graham also began to preach in eastern Europe, where other US missionaries followed him in the 1990s after the fall of communism, ironically evangelizing in areas that in some cases had had the faith for many centuries already. The arrival of Protestant evangelism has sometimes met with resistance from local traditional churches, such as the Orthodox Church in Russia and the Roman Catholic Church in Latin America (see sidebar).

Present-day missions, especially those originating in the US, take full advantage of modern technologies, such as the Internet, to reach as large an audience as possible. The phenomenon of "televangelism" is reflected in US-based Christian channels such as The God Channel and Trinity Broadcasting Network (TBN), which broadcast worldwide.

Billy Graham preaches *at Oriole Park at Camden Yards in Baltimore, Maryland, on July 9, 2006 during a three-day program of music, prayers, and gospel messages led by his son Franklin Graham.*

EVANGELICALISM

British historian David Bebbington has suggested four chief characteristics of modern Evangelical Christianity: the belief in personal spiritual renewal or being "born again," involving repentance of sins and acceptance of Christ as savior and lord; putting the gospel into action, for example through social reform and mission work; revering the Bible as the Word of God and final authority for all belief and morality; and emphasizing Christ's death on the cross as an act of atonement for human sinfulness. While many Evangelicals would view themselves as living gospel-based lives similar to that of the early church, modern Evangelicalism traces its roots more directly to the Reformation. Lutherans saw themselves as "evangelical" from the first, relying on

EVANGELICALS AND POLITICS

Evangelical Christians have historically campaigned on social issues. The Anglicans William Wilberforce (1759–1833) and Thomas Clarkson (1760–1846) were among prominent British Evangelicals in the movement against slavery, and Evangelicals were also at the forefront of the temperance movement of the nineteenth century. Today's Evangelicals campaign on comparable modern issues in the general area of protecting "family values" and living a good Christian life. On issues such as same-sex marriages, the ordination of homosexuals to ministry, and abortion, Evangelicals typically take conservative positions derived from what they see as their literal reading of scripture. Evangelical opposition in these areas can be vigorous and outspoken.

In the US Evangelicals exercise a considerable political influence by virtue of their numbers and their consistent position on these and other issues. The positions taken by various candidates on such questions can therefore feature prominently in elections. For example, Mike Huckabee, an ordained Southern Baptist minister and former governor of Arkansas who ran as a Republican in the 2008 presidential primaries, was "pro-life" (anti-abortion) and against embryonic stem cell research, though less conservative on some other issues. Evangelical political preference in the US is typically conservative, to match their conservative approach to theological questions.

A member of a German-Russian Pentecostal group *is baptized in a lake at Tokmok. German-Russian Pentecostalists suffered persecution in the old USSR, and there is legal discrimination against Evangelicals and other recently established Christian groups in Russia today.*

A Bible study group *in Mappe, Sierra Leone, 2003, made up of Liberian ex-soldiers who had fled a brutal civil war raging in their home country. Evangelicals place great emphasis on personal study of the scriptures.*

scripture alone and trusting to justification by faith. The Pietism of the seventeenth and eighteenth centuries (see page 169) developed a focus on the importance of a personal relationship with God, particularly with Christ. Calvinists emphasized conversion experiences with a moment of metanoia, or change of heart, and a conviction of being "saved." Later, a sense of being "Spirit-led" arose among Methodists and others (see sidebar).

EVANGELICAL GROUPS

Evangelicalism can manifest itself within a wide range of ecclesial bodies. The Southern Baptist Convention in the US is Evangelical, as are Pentecostalists and Arminian-Holiness churches (see pages 176–179). Other Evangelicals belong to churches organized on Presbyterian or Congregational lines, or to independent "house churches" that meet in domestic and other nontraditional settings. While the common ground shared by Evangelicals is the primacy of scriptural authority over that of institutional churches, there are Evangelical groups within the Anglican (Episcopal) churches and in modern Lutheranism, for example the Lutheran Church-Missouri Synod in the US. The Charismatic Renewal movement is a strand of Roman Catholicism with features resembling those of Pentecostal and Evangelical worship, such as lively services that may include "speaking in tongues" (glossolalia).

Evangelicals tend to rely on "local fellowship" rather than institutional unity. In search of a form of organized unity, an international meeting of Evangelicals set up the Evangelical Alliance in 1846, and today interdenominational ministries such as the InterVarsity Christian Fellowship (founded 1941) and the Campus Crusade for Christ International (founded 1951) encourage a missionary and revivalist activism.

THE INDWELLING SPIRIT

The notion of being directly led by the indwelling Holy Spirit became important among the Methodists (see pages 62–63) and later in Pentecostalism, a movement especially strong in, but by no means unique to, African-American churches in the US (see pages 176–177). During the Reformation, and indeed earlier, this trust that the Holy Spirit would guide the individual had been important in encouraging calls for versions of the scriptures in the vernacular so that people could understand the text (see pages 200–201). As literacy spread, it also motivated churches to promote a regular habit of independent personal Bible-reading.

ECUMENISM

DIALOGUES FOR UNITY

The WCC (see main text) conducted a multilateral dialogue about baptism, Eucharist, and ministry. Most other dialogues of the period after the Second Vatican Council, independently entered into by the participating churches, were bilateral, with the disadvantage that two partners might agree on a technical theological point in terms that were not necessarily acceptable to other churches. The Anglican–Roman Catholic dialogue looked at Eucharist, ministry, and authority, especially the question of universal primacy. There were also Orthodox–Roman Catholic, Lutheran–Roman Catholic, Orthodox–Lutheran, Anglican–Orthodox, Anglican–Methodist, Oriental-Orthodox dialogues, and dialogues involving churches or ecclesial communities that lack the overall institutional structure to identify representatives very easily, such as Pentecostals.

"Ecumenism" is the name given to the movement to bring the church to the unity proper to one "flock" with one "shepherd" of John 10.16. The modern ecumenical movement began in the nineteenth century with the Anglican idea of "Home Reunion," an attempt to reunite in a single communion all churches, including the Orthodox, but excluding the Roman Catholic owing to Anglicanism's rejection of papal primacy and other doctrinal differences. The 1888 "Lambeth-Chicago Quadrilateral" set out four things Anglicans considered essential to unity: the scriptures, the creeds, the sacraments instituted by Jesus himself (baptism and Eucharist), and the "historic episcopate," with its inherent arrangements for ensuring institutional unity. Conferences emphasized the problem of including Presbyterians and other groups that did not have the episcopate.

The Edinburgh Missionary Conference of 1910, convened by Protestant denominations active in mission, agreed to found a "World Council of Churches" (WCC) to further the ecumenical process. Delayed by two world wars, the WCC began work in 1948. Many of the dialogues conducted under its auspices continue and promising reports and agreements have resulted. Bilateral dialogues (see sidebar) have also borne fruit, such as the Porvoo agreement (1994) establishing a communion of Anglican and Nordic-Baltic Lutheran churches—though none has yet resulted in Christian unity. Some groups have

Taizé brothers *at midday prayers. Founded in 1940 by Brother Roger, the ecumenical community at Taizé in Burgundy, France, is made up of over a hundred brothers from Catholic and various Protestant backgrounds. It attracts many young adults and has grown into an international organization.*

stood away from this process, particularly Pentecostalists and Baptists, and fundamentalists tend to be unenthusiastic. There have been some successes, in the form of "uniting churches," usually bringing together previously Congregationalist and Presbyterian bodies.

A key problem is the difficulty of designing structures to form and mark an agreement. Ecclesial authority does not lie in the same place for all Christians. Even the Catholic Church, with its clear procedures and structures, took a decade to respond to the final report (1982) of the first Anglican–Roman Catholic Commission, which proposed agreements on Eucharist, ministry, and authority in the church, with particular reference to papal primacy.

What would successful ecumenism achieve? Could there be a future united church and would it be stable and enduring? Could "eucharistic hospitality" (welcoming one another's members to communion) go one step further to create a single church? The 1952 "Lund Principle"—that churches should act together in all matters except those in which deep differences of conviction compel them to act separately—has proved a lasting practical way forward in what has become, since the 1980s, a troubled period for ecumenism, when hopes prompted by Vatican II (see box) did not materialize and disillusion set in.

ECUMENISM AND THE SECOND VATICAN COUNCIL

The Roman Catholic Church has eschewed membership of the WCC (see main text) because it believes itself already to be the "catholic," or universal, church. However, it sends observers and members to WCC working parties, and it was from the Roman Catholic Church that a new thrust for ecumenism arose in the later twentieth century. *Unitatis redintegratio*, the decree on ecumenism of the Second Vatican Council (Vatican II, 1962–1965) distinguished between "full communion" with the Catholic Church and an "imperfect" or incomplete communion, which was shared by Catholics and Christians in other ecclesial communities. All those, said the decree, "who believe in Christ and have been truly baptized are in communion with the Catholic Church even though this communion is imperfect. The differences that exist in varying degrees between them and the Catholic Church … do indeed create many obstacles, sometimes serious ones, to full ecclesiastical communion. The ecumenical movement is striving to overcome these obstacles. But even in spite of them it remains true that all who have been justified by faith in baptism are members of Christ's body, and have a right to be called Christian, and so are correctly accepted as brothers by the children of the Catholic Church."

The resulting emphasis on defining and realizing the ideal of "communion" was central to the ecumenical dialogues of the second half of the twentieth century (see sidebar).

Roman Catholic bishops *from around the world, gathered for the second Vatican council (Vatican II) called by Pope John XXIII, attend Mass in St. Peter's basilica in the Vatican, Rome, in September 1963.*

INTERFAITH DIALOGUE

FAITH TO FAITH

Christians have sought common ground with Jews and Muslims, but also with other faiths. Rooted in universal compassion, Buddhism traditionally accommodates itself generously to the beliefs of others. Sikhism has always called for mutual respect among religions. Hindu philosophers would argue that Hinduism and Christianity share an essential monotheism. Baha'i stresses interfaith cooperation.

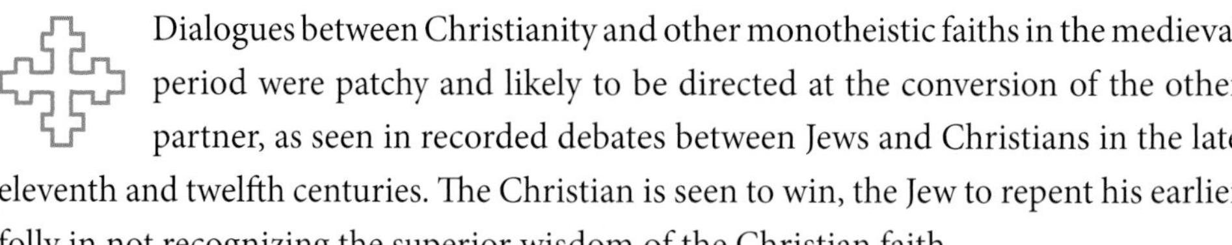

Dialogues between Christianity and other monotheistic faiths in the medieval period were patchy and likely to be directed at the conversion of the other partner, as seen in recorded debates between Jews and Christians in the late eleventh and twelfth centuries. The Christian is seen to win, the Jew to repent his earlier folly in not recognizing the superior wisdom of the Christian faith.

The objectives of Christians who seek dialogue with other faiths today are fundamentally different from those of mission or ecumenism. They modify the earlier Christian assumption that it was a Christian duty to convert others to the Christian faith, and while ecumenists seek church' unity, interfaith dialogue can look only for mutual tolerance and acceptance, and for cooperation among adherents of the world religions.

One reason why interfaith dialogue cannot lead to "unity" is that there is no common structural or institutional basis that Christianity can share even with the other two

HEALING OLD WOUNDS: CHRISTIANS AND JUDAISM

Historical relations between Christians and Jews have often been fraught and characterized at times by terrible violence toward Jews. Christian anti-Judaism was rooted in the notions of deicide ("God-killing," the murder of Christ) and supercessionism (God's rejection of the Jews in favor of the church). But many Christians have also deplored anti-Jewish excesses, and in the wake of the Nazi Holocaust the Roman Catholic Church in particular made substantial moves to heal historic wounds. Vatican II's 1965 declaration *Nostra Aetate* formally absolved Jews of deicide, renounced supercessionism, condemned anti-Semitism, and called for "mutual understanding and respect" between Catholics and Jews. In 1986, in Rome, John Paul II became the first pope to visit a synagogue, where he addressed Jews as "our dearly beloved brothers; in a certain way, indeed, ... our elder brothers."

John Paul II at the Western Wall, *Jerusalem, March 26, 2000. On this visit to Israel the pope—an eyewitness to the Holocaust—put a note in the Wall asking forgiveness for "those who in the course of history have caused [Jews] to suffer."*

principal monotheistic "Abrahamic" religions, Judaism and Islam, and all three have their own internal divisions on exactly this point. Even if Christianity itself were able to speak with one voice, it would be difficult to reach an agreement with "Islam" that would necessarily command the consent of Sunni and Shia alike. Similarly, unanimity on anything which either Islam or Christianity might propose for interfaith agreement is unlikely from a divided Jewish community, with its Orthodox, Reformed, and Conservative parties. Nor has the fact that the Christian and Jewish Bibles and the Quran share many events and figures in common—including Moses and Abraham—encouraged a sense of fellow-feeling among the three religions.

The Expulsion of Adam and Eve from Paradise, *a miniature from Kalender Pasa's* Falname or Book of Divination; *Turkish, 1610. Christian dialogue with Muslims finds common ground in shared "Abrahamic" roots. As the 1994 Roman Catholic catechism puts it, Muslims "profess to hold the faith of Abraham, and together with us they adore the one, merciful God, mankind's judge on the last day."*

Dialogue is, therefore, a more realistic aim than unity. Modern interfaith dialogue had fresh beginnings. In the nineteenth century the Algerian Ahmad al-Alawi (1869–1934), founder of an influential Sufi community, urged dialogue with those of other faiths. However, the main Christian interest in such dialogue arose when the ecumenical movement was becoming active, especially after the Second Vatican Council (see pages 228–229). In 1965 the council agreed to take a more constructive view of talking to those of other religions. The interfaith activists of the 1960s began to have social consequences: in the US, for example, they pressed for equal opportunities and equal civil rights for African Americans. One other historic outcome of Vatican II was a transformation in official Roman Catholic attitudes toward Judaism (see box).

CHRISTIANITY AND ISLAM

In recent years relations between Christianity and Islam have become enmeshed with concerns about radical Islam and one of its offshoots, militant activism or even terrorism. At the present time there is a new urgency to ensure that interfaith dialogue is mutually illuminating in order to avoid misunderstandings or perceived offense to what a particular religion holds sacred. One such case arose in September 2006, with reports that then recently installed Pope Benedict XVI, at a meeting of scholars, had quoted a fourteenth-century Byzantine emperor's criticism of the "warlike" behavior of Islam. There was no suggestion that the pope himself shared such a view, but the popular furor in Islamic countries was considerable and demonstrated the degree of sensitivity required when talking of different faiths.

2 GOVERNMENT AND POLITICS

Early Christians were intermittently victims of oppressive policies of the Roman empire and mainly stayed aloof from the political order. From the fourth to the eighteenth centuries, in both the East and the West, churches—whether Orthodox, Roman Catholic, or Protestant—tended to play some role in government, to a greater or lesser extent, alongside secular authorities. Modernity, in the forms which began and have evolved most fully in the West since the eighteenth century, meant a separation of church and civil power, even where one church nominally retained a position of some privilege. In most cases this has meant that religion cannot be established by law, but must make its way among voluntary forces.

RELIGIOUS AND INDIVIDUAL FREEDOM

However, modernity also meant freedom of worship and the autonomy of the individual, so that in much of western Europe and North America church-state separation has not produced political apathy among Chrisitians. Instead, they have often drawn freely on

Desmond Tutu *(born 1931) at the opening session of the South African Council of Churches Triennial National Conference in Johannesburg, 2007. The 1993 Nobel Peace Prize laureate and, as archbishop of Cape Town (1986–1996), the first black primate of the Anglican church of South Africa, Tutu was an outspoken and courageous critic of the former apartheid regime. However, he vigorously opposed the use of violence as a means to end apartheid and advocated a policy of reconciliation among all sides. Tutu chaired the Truth and Reconciliation Commission (1995–1998), which is credited with easing his country's largely peaceful transition to democracy.*

biblical and traditional resources to press for political change. In the US, for example, Dorothy Day (1897–1980), cofounder in 1933 of the Catholic Worker Movement, was explicit about her faith as she campaigned for social justice, while Rev. Martin Luther King, Jr., (1929–1968) invoked the prophets and Jesus to promote human rights. Throughout much of postcolonial Africa, Latin America, and Asia—precisely where Christianity is prospering most in the twenty-first century—Christian leaders such as Dom Hélder Câmara in Brazil (1909–1999) and Desmond Tutu (born 1931) in South Africa drew on biblical themes to gather Christian energies which worked for political freedom.

While many Christians like to claim that they "invented" religious freedom and democracy, it must be said that much of the breakthrough to the idea of free choice was made possible by the eighteenth-century Enlightenment and other philosophies (see pages 54 and 170–171). However, within a generally less oppressive political setting, many Christians retrieved from their traditions hitherto neglected accents on freedom, human dignity, and the responsibility for making wise and humane choices in civil society.

The very fact of religious diversity, which is a characteristic of modernity, tends to keep any single branch of the church from easily gaining a political monopoly. Thus Christians are called to be inventive and adaptive as they draw on divine commands to be responsible in the civil order. In the free societies that they helped produce, modern Christians have to contend for their own choices, while being open to the choices of others, Christian and non-Christian alike. (See also pages 112–113.)

FAITH AND NATION: RUSSIA

After 1917 the Russian Orthodox Church suffered restrictions and persecution along with all other religious groups in the USSR. This ended with a 1990 law guaranteeing religious freedom, and the church—with which most ethnic Russians self-identify, at least culturally—has since seen a great revival in its fortunes. A new law in 1997 acknowledged the church's "special contribution" to Russian culture, and imposed various bureaucratic difficulties on the operation of newer, foreign-based Christian groups such as Jehovah's Witnesses, Mormons, and Protestant denominations. Indeed, the wider Christian community has claimed that the Orthodox Church under presidents Boris Yeltsin and Vladimir Putin—the latter a devout church member—acquired an unfair degree of state support, at the expense of other groups. **(See also page 225.)**

Vladimir Putin *(center) with Patriarch Alexei II, head of the Russian Orthodox Church, and Metropolitan Laurus (left), head of the Russian Orthodox Church Outside Russia, at a service in May 2007 ending the 80-year split between the two branches of Russian Orthodoxy. The service was held in Moscow's Cathedral of Christ the Savior, demolished in 1931 but rebuilt in the 1990s.*

SOCIAL ENGAGEMENT

In few areas of life have Christians had more influence on the surrounding "secular" world than they have in extending works of justice and mercy. At their best, they serve fellow Christians and followers of other faiths or none with equal passion and attentiveness. In such engagement Christians are more frequently involved personally with non-Christians than they can be when either at worship or in prayer, which believers also consider to be acts of service.

Many Christians have used their faith to avoid engaging with problems and issues affecting wider society, perhaps in the belief that the alteration that comes with religion affects only the inner life of the individual, or the life to come. Christians who take such a passive course might point out that Jesus himself stated that the kingdom he sought to bring about was not an earthly one, and that he denied being a military or political leader.

However, others would point to Jesus' "active compassion" toward the oppressed and marginalized as grounds for social engagement. Moreover, Christianity is also a prophetic faith: following the Hebrew prophets of the Old Testament, it may be argued that Christians are not to restrict themselves to prayer and fasting but are also to care for their neighbor and for all people in need, be they poor, hungry, ill-clad, or victims of injustice. Those Christians

MISSIONARY OF CHARITY: MOTHER TERESA

One of the best-known exemplars of Christian engagement with the poor, irrespective of their faith, is Mother Teresa of Calcutta (1910–1997). Born in what is now Macedonia of Albanian parents and raised a Catholic, Agnes Gonxha Bojaxhiu left home aged 18 to join the Sisters of Loreto, a missionary order. She arrived in India in 1929 and taught in a mission school in Calcutta (Kolkata) until 1946, when she felt herself called by God to exchange her simple but relatively comfortable conditions for a life helping and living alongside the poor.

With Rome's permission, in 1950 Mother Teresa established a new order of nuns, which she named the Missionaries of Charity (MC). In addition to the common conventual vows of chastity, poverty, and obedience, nuns of Mother Teresa's order pledge "wholehearted and free service to the poorest of the poor." At present the MC has more than 4,500 nuns (compared with twelve in 1950) and is active in most countries of the world. Mother Teresa described her mission as the provision of help to "the hungry, the naked, the homeless, the crippled, the blind, the lepers, all those people who feel unwanted, unloved, uncared for throughout society, people that have become a burden to the society and are shunned by everyone." In 1963 the Missionaries of Charity Brothers was founded, and a branch for priests, the Missionaries of Charity Fathers, followed in 1984.The order also has associations for laity.

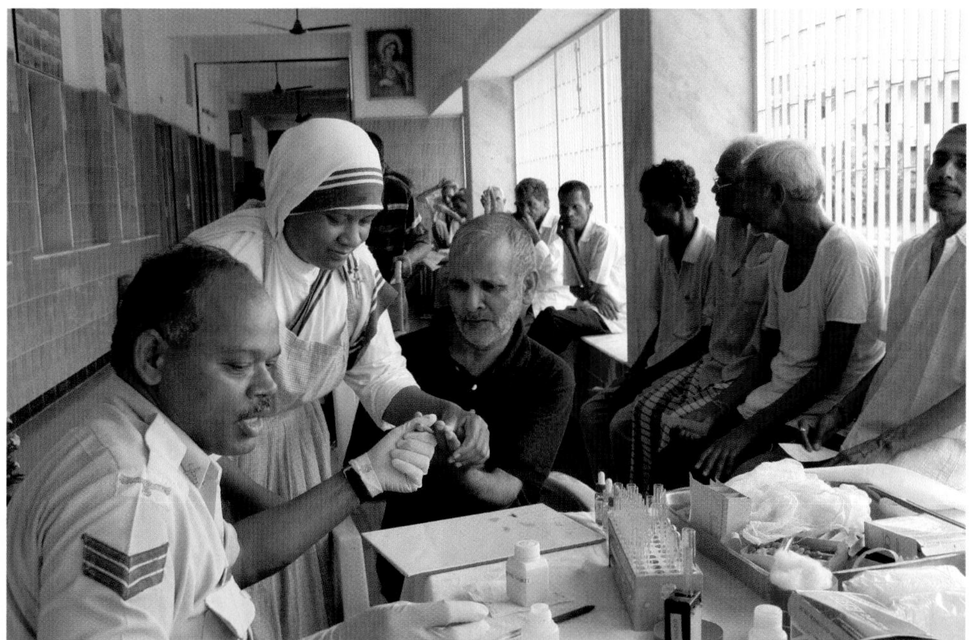

An Indian Air Force medic *examines a resident at the Shanti Nilaya Home for the Dying Destitute managed by the Missionaries of Charity (see box) in Ahmedabad, India, in September 2007. In India the overwhelming majority of those who have benefited from the Missionaries of Charity's homes, hospitals, and schools have been non-Christians. The Missionaries aim to lead "each sister to the perfect love of God and neighbor" and to make "the church fully present in the world of today."*

who become socially active may do so in response to the law of God, which commands such engagement, but more often they will say with the apostle Paul that the love of Christ urges and motivates them. They aim to be a Christ to their neighbor.

In earlier eras social engagement may have followed specific forms dictated by church leadership, whether by the papacy among Catholics, hierarchs among the Orthodox, or a variety of church leaders among Protestants. However, in modern times, personal freedom and liberty of conscience make possible individual and voluntary responses on the part of free believers. The latter may aim to utilize government as the chief agent for social engagement, and will seek to influence it through democratic actions. They will also work to set priorities, provide funds, and establish organizations to work in conjunction with government agencies.

Other Christian activists may prefer to support voluntary forms of social engagement. The latter tend to be less controversial than those which rely on political choice, though partisans of the former strategy argue that only governments can amass resources that even begin to be commensurate with need. Worldwide, however, the voluntary groups—sometimes called "para-churches"—tend to prevail among Christian models. These groups draw upon the law of God and the gospel to inspire believers to become aware of social need, organize to confront it, raise funds, and inspire others.

Most Christian agencies (see sidebar) focus on development issues, addressing physical circumstances associated with poverty, disease, hunger, and lack of shelter. But Christian voluntary agencies may also seek to improve wider human rights, race relations, to develop means of promoting peace. The overwhelming majority offer aid to suffering humanity regardless of the religion of those in need.

CHRISTIAN AGENCIES

Christian voluntary agencies may have an ecumenical or broad Christian base, such as Christian Aid (founded in 1945) and Habitat for Humanity (founded 1976). Other may be associated with particular groups, such as the more than 160 Catholic relief and development groups worldwide that operate under the umbrella of Caritas Internationalis (founded 1897), and Save Africa's Children (founded 2001), a charity operated from the US by a group of African American churches. Christians have also frequently been involved in the foundation or operation of many secular-based charities, such as Oxfam (founded 1942).

THE ROLE OF WOMEN

Paul, the author of the earliest Christian writings, proclaimed that "there is no longer male and female; for all of you are one in Christ Jesus" (Gal. 3.28). For males and females, his "oneness" was seldom realized. Through most of Christian history women served in many roles, as abbesses, nuns, mystics, nurses, deaconesses, teachers, and of course as mothers and wives who influenced children and husbands. Women like Hildegard of Bingen and Teresa of Avila achieved great prominence and indeed sainthood; yet they worked within the parameters of the mainstream church, and for the most part Christian women were obliged to act within a structure of faith which taught them to be passive, submissive, and content with secondary roles.

Hildegard of Bingen *(1098–1179) was a German abbess, polymath, artist, and mystic who founded two monasteries and dealt with male secular and church officials on an equal footing. This page from her own manuscript of her work* Scivias *(*Know the ways of the Lord*) shows God's Presence at Birth (left) and The Stages of Life (right).*

If the eighteenth-century Enlightenment, with its accents on reason, science, and progress, helped advance political freedoms for men, little was said or done by male leaders to help women enlarge their roles or to make room for women to do so on their own.

Long pushed to the margins by "respectable" Christianity, women were, however, often inventive in forming new groups, particularly within Protestantism: Quakers, Shakers, Adventists, Christian Scientists, then, more near to orthodoxy, Holiness and Pentecostal movements, were either founded or led by women.

The roles of Christian women were also somewhat enlarged through their participation in dramatic social movements such as the abolition of slavery or, like the Quaker Elizabeth Fry (1780–1845; see page 115), prison reform. Some abolitionists were also early pioneers for women's rights, such as Elizabeth Cady Stanton (1815–1905), whose *Woman's Bible* interpreted the scripture from a women's perspective. For example, she posited a Trinity of "Father, Mother, and Son."

The continental, British, and American revival movements of the mid-eighteenth and nineteenth centuries, while they did not allow for the ordination of women, were often settings for women's expression, and many became missionaries and educators as western Christians spread their word and works in Africa, Asia, and elsewhere. They led voluntary movements that did not demand ordained clerical leadership, and often set the pace for gathering of funds and recruiting leadership for moral and missionary causes.

WOMEN'S ORDINATION

The issue of female ordination emerged during World War II in Europe and has proved to be particularly troublesome in some churches, notably in Roman Catholicism, Eastern Orthodoxy, and conservative Protestant churches, where biblical and theological arguments have been advanced to reject such a new role for women. Most Protestant churches, however, have come to support the ordination of women, some only after fierce controversy. Not that ordination is the only mark of women's freedom to be fulfilled and to be of full service in the church. However, it has significance not only for potentially doubling the numbers of Christian leaders, and its advocates argue that it is also symbolic for what it says about women in the light of scriptures, tradition, and faith.

CHRISTIAN FEMINISM

After the middle of the twentieth century, stirrings associated with the concept of modernity finally took explicit, sometimes even militant, forms in Christian feminist versions of "women's liberation" movements. Scholarly women revisited biblical texts and demonstrated that in the Hebrew Scriptures and the New Testament women had roles which were under-reported or even intentionally obscured by men in power.

In the US and many other parts of the modern world movements designed to increase women's dignity, rights, freedom, and opportunities arose in and after the 1960s. Critics of Christian movements tried to dismiss them as imitators of secular feminism, but biblical scholars and theologians such as Dorothee Sölle (1929–2003) in Germany, Rosemary Radford Ruether (born 1936) and Elisabeth Schüssler Fiorenza (born 1938) in the US, Chung Hyum Kyung in Korea, and Rigoberta Menchú (born 1959) in Guatemala, while acknowledging the influence of local cultures and international feminism, insisted that their real resources were Christian. They all sought to make a direct impact on churches and, through them, on the wider world.

Rigoberta Menchú Tum, *Guatemalan 1992 Nobel Peace Prize laureate, poses next to a painting during the quadrennial Universal Forum of Cultures in Monterrey, Mexico, in October 2007.*

THE SECULAR CHALLENGE

For most of Christian history, the "secular" and the "sacred" were not seen as things in opposition: they simply described two coexisting spheres. Land, for example, might be in sacred (ecclesiastical) or secular (non-ecclesiastical) ownership. The word "secular" itself comes from the Latin *saeculum*, meaning "of this age," and sometimes it was applied to the "this-worldly" majority over against the "other-worldly" religious, who cared for the life to come more than for the present world and time.

Modernity, in the eyes of most historians and social thinkers, exaggerated the division between "secular" and "sacred" and gave the secular primacy, or even a monopoly, in human affairs. Such an accent did not necessarily mean that the secular was always opposed to faith. Thus when some nations such as the new United States sought to separate "church" and "state," they were advancing legal secularity. It did not

CHRISTIANITY IN CHINA

Following China's communist revolution of 1949, the new and determinedly atheist regime made extreme efforts to extinguish Christian churches, which have had minority presences in China in recent centuries. It is impossible to measure the number of Christians there early in the new millennium, because the legally permitted (and highly controlled) churches like the "Chinese Patriotic Catholic Association" do not hold the loyalty of the vast majority of believers. Government censuses might acknowledge fifteen million Christians, but the illicit "underground" congregations that meet covertly in houses and elsewhere may number from fifty to over one hundred million believers.

Foreign missionaries are banned, but Christians find ways to circulate Bibles and devotional literature and to educate their young. Protestant organizations in particular, being very varied and flexible, find ways to perpetuate ministries. Some observers speak of their unofficial churches as booming, even in the face of continued harassment and persecution.

A Chinese Catholic *carries a crucifix at Shizishan (Calvary, literally "Cross Mountain"), a Catholic shrine in Meixian County, Shaanxi Province, China, on May 2, 2007. The state-supervized Chinese Patriotic Catholic Association is China's only legal Catholic Church and forbids loyalty to Rome; but many Roman Catholics are believed to worship clandestinely.*

Stem cell research. *Liquid is dripped into pots containing cultures of stem cells, the precursor cells from which all the body's specialized cell types develop. Scientists believe it may be possible to employ human embryonic stem cells for therapeutic purposes. However, because the process can involve destroying or cloning human embryos, this field of research has prompted much ethical debate and also vigorous opposition among some Christian groups. It is a central issue in present-day "science versus religion" arguments.*

mean that the secular was anti-God or anti-faith but was simply a representation of another sphere of life. "Secularism," however, is a more defined and militant expression of secularity that is expressly in opposition to the sacred or the religious.

Modernity, with its acceptance of diversity, also in matters of faith and religious governance, included the breaking up of large spiritual monopolies, leaving people free to act and think without reference to what churches or their leaders said. Religious law became ever less effective and church attendance became voluntary, so it often declined. In many dimensions of life, particularly in the developed states of the traditionally Christian West, the secular came to be the main characteristic of governance and social relationships: reason ruled where divine revelation had once been dominant. Science took the place of faith in determining what mattered and made a difference, for example, in healing the sick, a field in which religion had once dominated.

FUNDAMENTALISM AND ANTIMODERNISM

At the same time, in many cultures historic religions took on "anti-modern" and "anti-secular" forms that are often called "fundamentalist." Exuberant and ecstatic religious movements such as Christian Pentecostalism seem, by most definitions, to be countersecular, but they also have their place in modernity. So strong are these new religious forces that some social thinkers question what they call "the secular hypothesis"—the idea that the basis of human society tends ever more toward the secular and nonreligious—itself. It is evident that in recent times what are broadly understood as the "secular" and the "religious" are both prospering and contending for attention and support.

"SECULAR" TOTALITARIANISM

Twentieth-century totalitarian ideologies such as Soviet Communism, Fascism, Nazism, and Maoism were all opposed to traditional religion to a greater or lesser degree and all avowedly "secular." However, in their leadership cults, demands of strict obedience, and elaborate pageantry, such ideologies themselves became quasi-religions, pseudo-religions—or anything but simply "secular" in the post-Enlightenment sense of permitting citizens the liberty to think and act how they wished (see also box).

GLOSSARY

Allegory Interpretation of biblical passages that finds their real meaning not in a literal reading.

Anabaptists Sixteenth-century Protestant groups that affirmed adult baptism.

Anglo-Catholics Members of the Anglican Church who view their tradition as essentially Catholic.

Antitrinitarian Opposed to the doctrine of the Trinity; compare **Unitarians**.

Apostasy Forsaking the Christian faith after having previously affirmed it.

Apostolic Pertaining to the apostles or the era in which they worked.

Apostolic Succession The notion of unbroken continuity between the apostolic church and the present.

Archbishop Bishop overseeing several dioceses.

Archdeacon Head of the College of Deacons; also, senior cleric supporting the bishop in administrative matters.

Arianism The belief, enunciated by Arius in the fourth century, that Jesus, while God, is a created being.

Arminianism Belief named after the Dutch Calvinist theologian Jacobus Arminius, who rejected predestination and held that humans have free will.

Asceticism The commitment to bodily self-denial as an expression of Christian faith.

Atonement The teaching of the meaning of Jesus' death on the cross.

Baptists Seventeenth-century Protestant churches that affirmed the baptism of adults upon their confession of faith.

Beatification Second step in the Roman Catholic canonization process.

Canon Law The collection of the laws of the Roman Catholic or Anglican churches, for example, concerning marriage.

Canon (1) The Old and New Testament writings officially in the Christian Bible.

Canon (2) A priest who aids the local bishop in carrying out specific tasks.

Canonization Final step in the Roman Catholic process to establish officially the sainthood of an individual, allowing the faithful to venerate them and name churches after them.

Cardinal Highest position in the Roman Catholic hierarchy after the pope; advises the pope or has important administrative functions in the Vatican.

Cathars Medieval renewal movement declared heretical by the Catholic Church in the thirteenth century.

Catholic Universal; often used as short form of Roman Catholic.

Chalcedonian Related to the Council of Chalcedon, which affirmed the full humanity of Jesus.

Charismatic Individuals and communities claiming special gifts, such as speaking in tongues (glossolalia).

Christology Study of the person and work of Christ.

Church Fathers The name given to a number of eminent early Christian churchmen and theologians.

Classes Small group gatherings, for example in **Methodism**.

Congregationalism Church polity that places authority in the local congregation.

Consistory Calvinist church body supervising faith and morals.

Consubstantiation Teaching, sometimes associated with Lutheran theology, that the substance of bread and wine remain alongside the substance of the body and blood of Jesus. Compare **Transubstantiation**.

Council Assembly of bishops to determine positions on faith and morals; the Roman Catholic Church affirms, in addition to the first six **Ecumenical Councils**, some 14 more.

Deism Belief in a supreme being without an affirmation of a divine revelation to humankind.

Dialectic Theology Twentieth-century Protestant theological movement that stressed the categorical difference between God and humans.

Dissenters English Protestants who left the Church of England because of its retention of Catholic practices.

Docetism Belief in early Christianity that Jesus was an ethereal spirit.

Doctors of the Church In the Roman Catholic Church, some 30 men and women who made pivotal theological contributions to the church.

Donatism Early movement in North Africa favoring high moral standards, including not accepting Christians who had lapsed during persecution.

Ecumenical Pertaining to the relationship of churches with each other as well as with other religions.

Ecumenical Councils The first six councils of the church, from Nicea I (325) to Nicea II (787).

Eschatology The teaching in theology of the "last things"—the end of history and the return of Jesus.

Eucharist (also Lord's Supper, Last Supper, Communion) Christian rite performed in response to Jesus' exhortation at the Last Supper.

Evangelical (1) Pertaining to the gospels or to Evangelicalism.

Evangelical (2) An adherent of Evangelicalism or similar groups within other churches.

Evangelicalism Especially in the US, a conservative form of Protestantism.

Filioque Latin "and from the son," a phrase about the relationship of the Holy Spirit to the other two persons of the Trinity found only in the western version of the Nicene Creed, and a source of schism with the Eastern Church.

Fundamentalism Theological movement beginning in the twentieth century that affirmed orthodox Christian teaching.

Great Schism (1) The division between western (Latin) and eastern (Orthodox) Christianity.

Great Schism (2) The division in western Christianity relating to the two papacies in Rome and Avignon.

Heretic Individual whose belief or teaching is condemned by the church.

Historic Episcopate Teaching that the divinely instituted order of bishops forms an unbroken continuity from the apostles to the present.

Holiness Churches Protestant churches, mainly in North America, emphasizing personal holiness of their members.

Hussites Anti-Catholic movement triggered by Jan Hus in Bohemia.

Iconoclasm The destruction of religious images on the grounds that they are forbidden by the Bible.

Indulgence The Roman Catholic practice of allowing, in return for a good deed, the remission of punishment for sin.

Liberalism Theological movement, beginning in the late eighteenth century, that sought to harmonize Christian teaching and the modern world-view.

Liturgy A manner in which Christian worship is conducted.

Mennonites Dutch and North German Anabaptists influenced by Menno Simons.

Messianic Of or pertaining to the Messiah, the prophesied savior of Israel.

Methodism Renewal movement founded in eighteenth-century England by John and Charles Wesley.

Metropolitan Bishop or archbishop responsible for an ecclesiastical province.

Modalism Theological view, declared heretical by the early church, that the three persons of the Trinity are different "modes" of God's manifestation.

Monarchian Modalism Theological view that there is no differentiation within the triune Godhead, who appears as Father, Son, and Holy Spirit.

Monophysitism Belief that Jesus had only one (divine) nature.

Montanism Position held by Montanus in the second century favoring an ascetic Christianity.

Nestorianism Position held by Nestorius in the fifth century that Jesus was two persons with two natures.

Nicene Creed The creed adopted by the first Council of Nicea affirming the full deity of Jesus.

Nonconformist Of or pertaining to the the non-Anglican Protestant churches of England.

Oecumenical Councils *see* **Ecumenical Councils.**

Patriarch (1) One of the patriarchs of Israel (Abraham, Isaac, Jacob); in the New Testament, Jacob's sons and King David are also called patriarchs.

Patriarch (2) Originally, a bishop of one of the five leading sees in the Roman empire: Rome, Constantinople, Antioch, Alexandria, Jerusalem. The term came to denote various types of senior bishop across the churches.

Pelagianism Teaching of Pelagius, that humans are free to do good.

Pentecostal Churches Protestant churches that affirm the fruits of the spirit, such as healing and speaking in tongues.

Pilgrimage Travel to holy sites that are characterized by spiritually important qualities, such as the relics of a saint.

Predestination Teaching that God decreed both salvation and damnation of all humans.

Presbyter Greek, "elder," an ecclesiastical position of varying identity in different churches.

Presbyterianism A form of Reformed Protestantism characterized by the office of "elder."

Puritanism Historical movement in the Church of England striving for a "pure," more biblical religion, more radically removed from Catholicism.

Reformed Term used for Calvinism and Calvinist churches from the second half of the sixteenth century onward.

Relics Remains of saintly persons that the Roman Catholic tradition views as devotional aids and objects.

Sacraments Practices that are vehicles of divine grace, such as **Eucharist**.

Sainthood Catholic teaching that identifies individuals whose good works and miracles bestow on them a special status that allows the faithful to venerate them.

Sect Mainly a pejorative term to denote a small religious grouping with a strong focus on a specific teaching.

Spirituals Franciscan friars who affirm absolute poverty.

Transubstantiation Roman Catholic teaching, promulgated formally in 1215, that the substance of bread and wine are literally changed into the substance of the body and blood of Jesus.

Unitarians Movement with roots in the sixteenth century rejecting the notion of the Trinity and affirming a strict monotheism.

Vows Formal promises made to God, for example when entering a monastic order.

Waldensians French followers of Peter Waldo, a medieval figure declared a heretic by the Roman Catholic Church.

TIMELINE

- **63BCE** Roman occupation of Judea
- **ca. 30CE** Crucifixion of Jesus
- **ca. 50s** Paul's first letter to the Corinthians
- **ca. 64** Apostles Peter and Paul suffered martyrdom
- **98** Emperor Trajan establishes policy for how Christians should be treated
- **130** Conversion of Justin (Martyr)
- **144** Marcion rejects the Hebrew Scriptures (Old Testament) and is excommunicated in Rome
- **ca. 156** Montanus advocates ascetism
- **ca. 165** Justin martyred
- **225** Tertullian dies
- **251** Anthony, a key figure in Western monasticism, is born
- **ca. 254** The Novatian schism over the treatment of the lapsed
- **284–305** Reign of Emperor Diocletian; great persecution of Christians
- **ca. 297/300** Athanasius born
- **ca. 311** Donatist Controversy begins
- **312** Constantine defeats Maxentius at the battle of Milvian Bridge to become emperor of the western Roman empire
- **313** The Edict of Milan gives Christians equal status with other religions of the empire; crucifixion abolished
- **316** Constantine rules against the Donatists
- **325** First Council of Nicea condemns Arianism and Monarchianism
- **337** Emperor Constantine dies
- **ca. 340** Eusebius of Caesarea, bishop of Caesarea and first church historian, dies
- **345** John Chrysostom born
- **361–363** Persecution under Emperor Julian the Apostate
- **373** Athanasius of Alexandria dies
- **379** Basil the Great of Cappadocia dies
- **379–395** Under Emperor Theodosius Christianity becomes the sole official religion of the Roman empire
- **381** Council of Constantinople affirms creed of Council of Nicea (Nicene Creed)
- **386** Conversion of Augustine
- **393** Council of Hippo recognizes the biblical canon.
- **395** Augustine becomes bishop of Hippo
- **411** Pelagian controversy begins
- **451** Council of Chalcedon affirms creed of Nicea and declares full humanity of Jesus; beginnings of Monophysite controversy
- **525** Boethius, author of *The Consolation of Philosophy*, executed
- **547** Benedict of Nursia dies
- **560** Isidore of Seville born
- **597** Gregory the Great sends Augustine of Canterbury to convert the English
- **604** Pope Gregory the Great dies
- **613** Augustine of Canterbury dies
- **615** Columbanus (Columban), Irish missionary to the continent, dies
- **622** Muhammad's flight from Mecca to Medina: the beginning of Islam
- **635** Nestorian Christians reach China
- **636** Isidore of Seville dies
- **ca. 680** Boniface, English missionary to Germany, born
- **787** Second council of Nicea
- **800** Charlemagne crowned "Emperor of the Romans" by Pope Leo III
- **909** Founding of Cluny monastery
- **988** Christianity brought to Russia
- **1014** *Filioque* inserted into the Nicene Creed in the Western church
- **1054** Metropolitan of Constantinople excommunicated by Pope Leo IX; division of Eastern and Western churches
- **1073** Gregory VII excommunicates Holy Roman Emperor Henry IV
- **1075** Investiture Controversy begins
- **1096–1099** The First Crusade takes Jerusalem and establishes Christian "crusader states" in the Near East
- **1109** Anselm of Canterbury, father of Scholasticism, dies
- **1147–1149** The Second Crusade.
- **1153** Bernard of Clairvaux dies
- **1184** Waldensians are declared heretical
- **1187** Turks take Jerusalem
- **1189–1192** The Third Crusade
- **1202–1204** The Fourth Crusade; Constantinople sacked by the crusaders
- **1209** Pope Innocent III proclaims a "crusade" against the Waldensians
- **1210** The Franciscan order recognized
- **1212** The Children's Crusade
- **1215** Fourth Lateran Council affirms doctrine of transubstantiation
- **1216** The Dominican order recognized
- **1219–1221** The Fifth Crusade
- **1221** Dominic de Guzmán dies
- **1226** Francis of Assisi dies
- **1229** The Sixth Crusade
- **1248** The Seventh Crusade
- **ca. 1300–ca. 1400** Bubonic plague, or Black Death, ravages Europe
- **1309–1377** The pope moves to Avignon
- **1378** The Great Schism: Pope Gregory XI returns the papacy to Rome; France declares Clement VII pope in Avignon
- **1381** John Wycliffe is banished from Oxford (dies in 1384)
- **1415** Council of Constance condemns Wycliffe and burns Jan Hus (John Huss)
- **1417** The Council of Constance deposes the rival popes and ends the Great Schism
- **1492** Muslims expelled from Spain
- **1507** Martin Luther ordained as a priest

- **1509** Henry VIII is king of England
- **1513** Leo X elected pope
- **1517** Martin Luther posts his Ninety-Five Theses
- **1519** Charles V elected Holy Roman Emperor; Leipzig Disputation
- **1521** Luther excommunicated
- **1521** Diet (parliament) at Worms declares Luther a political outlaw
- **1524–1525** German Peasants' War
- **1525** Luther's controversy with Erasmus
- **1525** Rise of Anabaptism in Zurich
- **1526** Edict of Worms suspended
- **1529** Diet at Speyer reintroduces Worms edict; reformers called "Protestants"
- **1529** The Colloquy of Marburg
- **1530** Diet at Augsburg; Lutheran "Augsburg Confession"
- **1531** Huldrych Zwingli, reformer, dies in battle at Kappel
- **1534** Parliament in England declares the monarch "the only supreme head ... of the Church of England"
- **1535** Dissolution of the English monasteries begins
- **1536** Erasmus dies; Calvin in Geneva
- **1536** William Tyndale burned at the stake
- **1536** First edition of Calvin's *Institutes*
- **1540** Society of Jesus is approved
- **1545** Council of Trent opens
- **1546** Luther dies
- **1549** *Book of Common Prayer* published in England
- **1552** Forty-Two Articles in England
- **1553–1558** Mary I of England fails to restore Catholicism
- **1555** Peace of Augsburg
- **1556** Emperor Charles V abdicates
- **1558** Elizabeth I is queen of England
- **1559** First French War of Religion
- **1580** Lutheran *Book of Concord*
- **1560** Scottish parliament approves the *Scots Confession*
- **1563** Last sessions of the Council of Trent
- **1564** John Calvin dies
- **1567–1568** Vestments Controversy
- **1572** John Knox, Scots reformer, dies
- **1572** St. Bartholomew's Day massacre of Protestant Huguenots in Paris
- **1582** General Assembly in Scotland ratifies *Second Book of Discipline*
- **1598** Edict of Nantes
- **1609** Jacobus Arminius dies
- **1611** The Authorized (King James) Version of the Bible is published
- **1612** First Baptist congregation
- **1618–1619** The Synod of Dort
- **1620** Puritans found Plymouth Colony
- **1633** William Laud becomes (anti-Puritan) archbishop of Canterbury
- **1642–1651** English Civil War between Royalists and pro-Puritan parliament
- **1647** George Fox establishes the Religious Society of Friends (Quakers)
- **1649** Puritan republic led by Oliver Cromwell begins in England
- **1658** Oliver Cromwell dies
- **1660** Charles II is restored to the English throne
- **1661–1663** John Eliot publishes the Bible in Algonquian
- **1675** Phillip Jakob Spener's *Pia Desideria*
- **1685** Edict of Nantes revoked; thousands of Huguenots emigrate
- **1695** August Hermann Francke establishes the "foundations" at Halle
- **1734–1737** The First Great Awakening
- **1738–1739** John Wesley's Aldergate experience inspires Methodism
- **1736** Joseph Butler's *Analogy of Religion, Natural and Revealed*
- **ca. 1773–1775** The first black Baptist church in America founded at Silver Bluff, South Carolina
- **1784** Thomas Coke, first North American Methodist bishop
- **1792** "Particular Baptist Society for Propagating the Gospel among the Heathen" founded
- **1799** Church Missionary Society founded
- **1799** Schleiermacher's *On Religion: Speeches to its Cultured Despisers*
- **1816** African Methodist Episcopal Church founded by Richard Allen
- **1830** *Book of Mormon*; founding of the Church of Christ of Latter-day Saints (Mormons)
- **1833–1841** The Oxford Movement
- **1854** Catholic doctrine of the Immaculate Conception promulgated
- **1864** Catholic Syllabus of Errors
- **1870** First Vatican Council; dogma of papal infallibility promulgated
- **1876** Bible Student Movement (later Jehovah's Witnesses) established
- **1879** John Henry Newman, an Anglican convert to Catholicism, made cardinal
- **1890** Cardinal Newman dies
- **1900** "What is Christianity?" lectures by Adolf von Harnack
- **1909** Scofield Reference Bible
- **1930** Adolf von Harnack dies
- **1934** Barmen Declaration of German Protestants (against Nazi church policies)
- **1939–1958** Papacy of Pius XII
- **1940** Taizé community begins
- **1941** Reinhold Niebuhr's *The Nature and Destiny of Man*
- **1942** William Temple, archbishop of Canterbury
- **1945** Dietrich Bonhoeffer, Lutheran pastor and opponent of Hitler, executed by the Nazis
- **1948** World Council of Churches established
- **1950** Catholic doctrine of Mary's bodily assumption into heaven is promulgated
- **1958–1963** Papacy of John XXIII, who convenes second Vatican Council (Vatican II)
- **1962–1965** Second Vatican Council, great reforming council of the Roman Catholic Church
- **1963–1978** Papacy of Paul VI, who implements reforms of Vatican II
- **1968** Karl Barth, theologian, dies
- **1968** Medellín Conference of Catholic bishops supports "liberation theology"
- **1978–2005** Papacy of John Paul II (Karol Jozef Wojtyla, the first non-Italian for centuries)
- **2005** Cardinal Joseph Ratzinger, a German, is elected Pope Benedict XVI

FURTHER READING

GENERAL

Achunike, Hilary C. *What is Church History? An African Perspective.* Rex Charles and Patrick Ltd: Nigeria, 1996.

Cambridge History of Christianity. (Series: 9 Vols.) Cambridge University Press (CUP): Cambridge, 2006.

Chidester, David. *Christianity: A Global History.* Allen Lane: London; HarperCollins: San Francisco, 2000.

Cook, Chris. *The Routledge Companion to Christian History.* Routledge: London, 2007.

González, Justo L. *The Story of Christianity, Volume 1: The Early Church to the Dawn of the Reformation.* HarperCollins: New York and London, 1984.

González, Justo L. *The Story of Christianity, Volume 2: The Reformation to the Present Day.* HarperCollins: New York and London, 1985.

Hastings, Adrian. (ed.) *A World History of Christianity.* Wm. B. Eerdmans: Grand Rapids, Michigan, 2000.

Herrin, Judith. *Byzantium: The Surprising Life of a Medieval Empire.* Princeton University Press: Princeton, New Jersey, 2008.

Herring, George. *Introduction to the History of Christianity.* NYU Press, New York, 2006.

Irvin, Dale T. *History of the World Christian Movement: Earliest Christianity to 1453.* (Vol 1.) T. & T. Clark: London and New York, 2002.

Jedin, Hubert., et al. *Atlas zur Kirchengeschichte: Die christlichen Kirchen in Geschichte und Gegenwart.* Herder: Freiburg, 2004.

Kee, Howard C., et al. *Christianity: A Social and Cultural History.* (2nd ed.) Prentice Hall: New Jersey, 1998.

Lindberg, Carter. *A Brief History of Christianity.* Wiley-Blackwell Publishing: Oxford, 2005.

MacCulloch, Diarmaid. *Groundwork of Christian History.* Epworth Press: London, 1987.

Noll, Mark A. *Turning Points: Decisive Moments in the History of Christianity.* (2nd ed.) Baker Academic: Ada, Michigan, 2001.

Norris, Frederick W. *Christianity: A Short Global History.* Oneworld Publications: Oxford, 2002.

Shelley, Bruce L. *Church History in Plain Language.* (2nd ed.) Thomas Nelson: London, 1996.

PART 1 CHAPTER 1

Brown, Raymond E. *The Birth of the Messiah: A Commentary on the Infancy Narratives in Matthew and Luke.* Doubleday: New York, 1979.

Brown, Raymond E. *The Death of the Messiah: From Gethsemane to the Grave: A Commentary on the Passion Narratives in the Four Gospels.* Doubleday: New York, 1994.

Ehrman, Bart D. *The New Testament: A Historical Introduction to the Early Christian Writings.* Oxford University Press (OUP): Oxford and New York, 2007.

Goodacre, Mark. *The Synoptic Problem: A Way Through the Maze.* Continuum: London, 2001.

Johnson, Luke T. *The Writings of the New Testament: An Interpretation.* (rev. ed.) Augsburg Fortress: Minneapolis, 1999.

Porter, J.R. *Jesus Christ: The Jesus of History, the Christ of Faith.* OUP: New York; Duncan Baird Publishers: London, 1999.

Rowland, Christopher. *Christian Origins: The Setting and Character of the Most Important Messianic Sect of Judaism.* SPCK: London, 2002.

Sanders, E.P. *The Historical Figure of Jesus.* Penguin: London, 1993.

Sanders, E.P., and Davies, Margaret. *Studying the Synoptic Gospels.* SCM: London, 1989; Trinity Press International: Philadelphia, 1990.

Theissen, Gerd. *The Shadow of the Galilean: The Quest of the Historical Jesus in Narrative Form.* Augsburg Fortress: Minneapolis; SCM: London, 1987.

PART 1 CHAPTER 2

Brown, Peter. *The Rise of Western Christendom.* (2nd ed.) Wiley-Blackwell: Oxford, 2003.

Chadwick, Henry. *Heresy and Orthodoxy in the Early Church.* Variorum: Burlington, Vermont, 1991.

Dowley, Tim. (ed.) *An Introduction to the History of Christianity.* Augsburg Fortress: Philadelphia, 2002.

Duffy, Eamon. *Saints and Sinners: A History of the Popes.* Yale University Press (YUP): New Haven, Connecticut 1997.

Hillerbrand, Hans J. (ed.) *The Oxford Encyclopedia of the Reformation.* (4 Vols.) OUP: New York and Oxford, 1996.

Hussey, J.M. *The Orthodox Church in the Byzantine Empire.* OUP: Oxford, 1986.

Knowles, David. *Christian Monasticism.* McGraw-Hill: New York, 1969.

Lynch, Joseph H. *The Medieval Church: A Brief History.* Longman: New York and London, 1992.

McManners, John. (ed.) *The Oxford History of Christianity.* OUP: New York and Oxford, 1994.

Neill, Stephen. *A History of Christian Missions.* Penguin: New York, 1986.

White, James F. *A Brief History of Christian Worship.* Abingdon: Nashville, Tennessee, 1993.

PART 2 CHAPTER 1

Braaten, Carl and Jenson, Robert. (eds.) *Christian Dogmatics.* (2 vols.) Augsburg Fortress: Philadelphia, 1984.

Gunton, Colin E. (ed.) *The Cambridge Companion to Christian Doctrine.* Cambridge University Press: Cambridge, 1997.

Guthrie, Shirley C. *Christian Doctrine.* (rev. ed.) Westminster John Knox: Louisville, Kentucky, 1994.

McGrath, Alister. *Christian Theology: An Introduction.* Blackwell: Oxford, 2006.

Musser, Donald W. and Price, Joseph L. (eds.) *A New Handbook of Christian Theology.* Abingdon Press: Nashville; Lutterworth Press: Cambridge, 1992.

Peters, Ted. *God: The World's Future: Systematic Theology for a New Era.* (2nd ed.) Fortress: Minneapolis, 2000

Schwarz, Hans. *Christology.* Wm. B. Eerdmans: Grand Rapids, 1998.

Schwarz, Hans. *Eschatology.* Wm. B. Eerdmans: Grand Rapids, 2000.

Schwarz, Hans. *Evil: A Historical and Theological Perspective.* Academic Renewal Press: Lima, Ohio, 2001.

PART 2 CHAPTER 2

Bradshaw, Paul. (ed.) *The New Westminster Dictionary of Liturgy & Worship.* Westminster John Knox Press: Louisville, Kentucky, 2002 (published in the UK under the title *The New SCM Dictionary of Liturgy and Worship.* SCM Press: Norwich, 2002).

Farhadian, Charles E. (ed.) *Christian Worship Worldwide: Expanding Horizons, Deepening Practices.* Wm. B. Eerdmans: Grand Rapids, 2007.

Johnson, Maxwell E. *The Rites of Christian Initiation: Their Evolution and Interpretation.* Liturgical Press: Collegeville, Michigan, 1999.

Jones, Cheslyn., et al. (eds.) *The Study of Liturgy.* SPCK: London; OUP: New York, 1992.

Kieckhefer, Richard. *Theology in Stone: Church Architecture from Byzantium to Berkeley.* OUP: New York, 2004.

Senn, Frank C. *Christian Liturgy: Catholic and Evangelical.* Augsburg Fortress: Minneapolis, 1997.

Stuhlman, Byron D. *A Good and Joyful Thing: The Evolution of the Eucharistic Prayer.* Church: New York, 2000.

Wainright, Geoffrey., et al. (eds.) *The Oxford History of Christian Worship.* OUP: New York, 2006.

White, James F. *A Brief History of Christian Worship.* Abingdon: Nashville, 1993.

Wybrew, Hugh. *The Orthodox Liturgy: The Development of the Eucharistic Liturgy in the Byzantine Rite.* SPCK: London, 1989.

PART 2 CHAPTER 3

Barth, Karl. *Church Dogmatics.* T. & T. Clark: Edinburgh, 1961.

Bonhoeffer, Dietrich. *Ethics. (Dietrich Bonhoeffer Works,* Vol. 6.*)* Augsburg Fortress: Minneapolis, 2005.

Boulton, Wayne G., et al. (eds.) *From Christ to the World: Introductory Readings in Christian Ethics.* Wm. B. Eerdmans: Grand Rapids, 1994.

Hauerwas, Stanley. *The Peaceable Kingdom: A Primer in Christian Ethics.* University of Notre Dame Press (UNDP): Notre Dame, Indiana, 1983.

Lammers, Stephen. *On Moral Medicine.* Wm. B. Eerdmans: Grand Rapids, 1987.

MacIntyre, Alistair. *A Short History of Ethics: A History of Moral Philosophy from the Homeric Age to the Twentieth Century.* Routledge: New York, 1967.

Montford, Angela. *Health, Sickness, Medicine and the Friars in the 13th and 14th centuries.* Ashgate Publishing: London and Burlington, Vermont, 2004.

Niebuhr, Reinhold. *Christ and Culture.* Harper & Row: New York, 1951.

Niebuhr, Reinhold. *An Interpretation of Christian Ethics.* Harper & Brothers: New York, 1935.

O'Donovan, Oliver. *The Desire of the Nations.* CUP: Cambridge, 1995.

Ramsey, Paul. *Basic Christian Ethics.* Scribner: New York, 1950.

Ramsey, Paul. *The Just War: Force and Political Responsibility.* Scribner: New York, 1968.

Yoder, John Howard. *The Priestly Kingdom* UNDP: Notre Dame, Indiana, 1985.

PART 2 CHAPTER 4

Brown, Peter. *The Cult of the Saints: Its Rise and Function in Latin Christianity.* SCM: London, 1981.

Congar, Yves. (trans. Donald Attwater.) *Laity, Church and World.* Helican: Abingdon, 1960.

de Ste. Croix, Geoffrey. *Christian Persecution, Martyrdom and Orthodoxy.* OUP: Oxford and New York, 2006.

Frend, W.H.C. *The Rise of Christianity.* Darton, Longman & Todd: London, 1984; Augsburg: Minneapolis, 1986.

Hillerbrand, Hans J. *The Division of Christendom: Christianity in the Sixteenth Century.* Westminster John Knox: Louisville, Kentucky, 2007.

Kyrtatas, Dimitris *The Social Structure of Early Christian Communities.* Verso: London, 1987.

Lane Fox, Robin. *Pagans and Christians.* Penguin: London, 1988.

McLeod, Hugh, and Ustorf, Werner. (eds.) *The Decline of Christendom in Western Europe, 1750–2000.* CUP: Cambridge, 2003.

Moorhouse, Geoffrey. *Against All Reason.* Weidenfeld & Nicolson: London, 1969.

de Ridde-Symoens, Hilde. *A History of the University in Europe: Volume 1: Universities in the Middle Ages.* CUP: Cambridge. 1992.

Ward, Graham. *True Religion.* Blackwell: Oxford, 2003.

Williams, Rowan. *Teresa of Avila.* Continuum: London, 2000.

PART 2 CHAPTER 5

Bokenkotter, Thomas. *Concise History of the Catholic Church.* (rev. ed.) Image: New York, 2005.

The Catholic Church. *Catechism of The Catholic Church.* (2nd ed.) Doubleday: New York, 2003.

Gillis, Chester. (ed.) *The Political Papacy: John Paul II, Benedict XVI and their Influence.* Paradigm: Boulder, 2006.

Hellwig, Monica K. *Understanding Catholicism: 1480–1522.* (2nd ed.) Paulist Press: New Jersey, 2002.

Küng, Hans. *The Catholic Church, A Short History.* Modern Library: New York, 2003.

McBrien, Richard. *Lives of the Popes: The Pontiff from St. Peter to John Paul II.* HarperOne: San Francisco, 2006.

Norman, Edward. *The Roman Catholic Church: An Illustrated History.* Thames and Hudson: London, 2007.

O'Collins, SJ Gerald and Farruquia, SJ Mario. *Catholicism: The Story of Catholic Christianity.* OUP: Oxford and New York, 2003.

Parravincini, Giovanna. (ed.) *Mary Mother of God.* Liguori: Liguori, 2004.

PART 2 CHAPTER 6

Bouyer, Louis. *The Spirit and Forms of Protestantism.* World: Cleveland, 1964.

Chadwick, Owen. *The Reformation (Pelican History of the Church).* Penguin: London, 1964.

Clasen, Claus Peter. *Anabaptism: a Social History 1585–1618.* Cornell University Press: Ithaca, 1977.

Dillenberger, John, and Welch, Claude. *Protestant Christianity Interpreted Through Its Development.* Macmillan: New York, 1988.

Flew, R.N., and Davies, R.E. (eds.) *The Catholicity of Protestantism.* Muhlenberg: Philadelphia; Lutterworth: Cambridge, 1950.

Hillerbrand, Hans J. *The Protestant Reformation.* Harper Torchbooks: New York, 1968.

Hollenweger, Walter J. *Pentecostalism.* Hendrickson: Peabody, 1997.

Léonard, Émile G. *A History of Protestantism.* Bobbs-Merrill: Indianapolis, 1968.

MacCulloch, Diarmaid. *The Reformation: A History.* Viking: New York, 2004.

Marty, Martin E. *Protestantism.* Holt, Rinehart & Winston: New York, 1972.

Rouse, Ruth, and Neill, Stephen. (eds.) *A History of the Ecumenical Movement, 1517–1948.* World Council of Churches (WCC): Geneva, 1986.

Tillich, Paul. *The Protestant Era.* University of Chicago Press: Chicago, 1948.

Whale, J.S. *The Protestant Tradition.* CUP: Cambridge, 1955.

PART 2 CHAPTER 7

Binn, John. *An Introduction to the Christian Orthodox Churches.* CUP: Cambridge, 2002.

Bradley, Nassif. *New Perspectives in Historical Theology: Essays in Memory of John Meyendorff.* Wm. B. Eerdmans: Grand Rapids, 1996.

Clendenin, Daniel B. (ed.) *Eastern Orthodox Theology: A Contemporary Reader.* (2nd ed.) Baker Academic: Grand Rapids, 2003.

Connor, Carolyn L. *Women of Byzantium.* YUP: New Haven, 2004.

Fairbairn, Donald. *Eastern Orthodoxy Through Western Eyes.* Westminster John Knox: Louisville, 2002.

Hussey, J.M. *The Orthodox Church in the Byzantine Empire.* OUP: Oxford, 1986.

Kruegher, Derek. (ed.) *Byzantine Christianity.* Fortress Press: Philadelphia, 2006.

McGuckin, John Anthony. *The Orthodox Church: An Introduction to the History, Doctrine and Spiritual Culture.* Wiley-Blackwell: Oxford, 2008.

Mango, Cyril. *The Art of the Byzantine Empire, 312–1453.* Prentice Hall: New Jersey, 1972.

Meyendorff, John. *Byzantine Theology: Historical Trends and Doctrinal Themes.* Fordham University Press: New York, 1983.

Meyendorff, John. *Imperial Unity and Christian Divisions: The Church 450–680 A.D.* SVSP: London, 1989.

Parry, Ken, et al. (eds.) *The Blackwell Dictionary of Eastern Christianity.* Wiley-Blackwell: Oxford, 2001.

Roberson, Ronald G. *The Eastern Christian Churches.* (6th ed.) Pontifical Oriental Institute: Rome, 1999.

Schmeman, Alexander. *The Historical Road of Eastern Orthodoxy.* St. Vladimir's Seminary Press (SVSP): New York, 1997.

Ware, Kallistos. *The Orthodox Way.* SVSP: New York, 1995.

Ware, Timothy. *The Orthodox Church.* (new ed.) Penguin: London, 1993.

PART 3 CHAPTER 1

Burkitt, Delbert. *An Introduction to the New Testament and the Origins of Christianity.* CUP: Cambridge, 2002.

Cartlidge, David R., and Elliott, J.K. *Art and the Christian Apocrypha.* Routledge: London and New York, 2001.

Elliott, J.K. *The Apocryphal New Testament.* OUP: Oxford, 1993.

de Hamel, Christopher. *The Book: A History of the Bible.* Phaidon: London, 2001.

Herbert, Edward D. and Tov, Emanuel. (eds.) *The Bible as Book: The Hebrew Bible and the Judaean Desert Discoveries.* OKP: New Castle; BLP: London, 2002.

Van Kampen, Kimberly and Sharpe, John L. (eds.) *The Bible as Book: The First Printed Editions.* Oak Knoll Press (OKP): New Castle, Delaware, 1997; British Library Publishing (BLP): London, 1999.

McDonald, Lee Martin. *The Biblical Canon: Its Origin, Transmission and Authority.* Hendrickson: Peabody, 2007.

McKendrick, Scot and O'Sullivan, Orlaith. (eds.) *The Bible as Book: The Transmission of the Greek Text.* OKP: New Castle; BLP: London, 2003.

Porter, J.R. *The Illustrated Guide to the Bible.* OUP: New York; Duncan Baird Publishers: London, 2007.

PART 3 CHAPTER 2

Aune, David E. *Word Bible Commentary: Revelation.* (3 Vols.) Word: Dallas, 1997–1998.

Barrett, C.K. *Acts (International Critical Commentary Series).* (2 vols.) T & T. Clark: Edinburgh, 1994, 1998.

Barton, John, and Muddiman, John. (eds.) *The Oxford Bible Commentary.* OUP: Oxford and New York, 2001.

Burkitt, Delbert. *An Introduction to the New Testament and the Origins of Christianity.* CUP: Cambridge, 2002.

Dunn, James D.G. *The Theology of Paul the Apostle.* T. & T. Clark: Edinburgh, 1997.

Dunn, James D.G., and Rogerson, John W. (eds.) *Eerdmans Commentary on the Bible.* Wm. B. Eerdmans: Grand Rapids, 2003.

Moloney, Francis J. (ed.) *An Introduction to the Gospel of John.* Doubleday: New York, 2003.

Porter, J.R. *The Lost Bible: Forgotten Scriptures Revealed.* University of Chicago Press: Chicago; Duncan Baird Publishers: London, 2001.

Streeter, B.H. *The Four Gospels: A Study of Origins.* Macmillan: London, 1924.

PART 4 CHAPTER 1

Booker, Mike, and Ireland, Mark. *Evangelism: Which Way Now?* (2nd ed.) Church House: London, 2007.

Bowen, Kurt Derek. *Evangelism and Apostasy.* McGill-Queen's University Press: Montreal, 1996.

Conn, Harvie M. *Evangelism: Doing Justice and Preaching Grace.* Zondervan: Grand Rapids, 1982.

Dayton, Donald W., and Johnston, Robert K. (eds.) *The Variety of American Evangelicalism.* Tennessee University Press: Knoxville, 2001.

Drane, John W. *Evangelism for a New Age.* HarperCollins: London, 1994.

Kirby, Gilbert W. (ed.) *Evangelism Alert: European Congress on Evangelism, 1971.* World Wide Publications: Amsterdam, 1972.

Hudson, Darril. *The World Council of Churches in International Affairs.* WCC: Leighton Buzzard, 1977.

Knitter, Paul F. *One Earth Many Religions: Multifaith Dialogue and Global Responsibility.* Orbis: New York, 1995.

Lossky, Nicholas., et al. (eds.) *Dictionary of the Ecumenical Movement.* Wm. B. Eerdmans: Grand Rapids, 1991.

Magnuson, Norris. *Salvation in the Slums: Evangelical Social Work, 1865–1920.* Wipf and Stock: Eugene, Oregon, 2004.

Moorhouse, Geoffrey. *The Missionaries.* Eyre Methuen: London, 1973.

Packer, J.I. *Evangelism & the Sovereignty of God.* InterVarsity Press: London, 1991.

Pollitt, Herbert J. *Inter-Faith Movement: The New Age Enters the Church.* Banner of Truth Trust: Edinburgh, 1996.

Purdy, William A. *The Search for Unity: Relations between the Anglican and Roman Catholic Churches from the 1950s to the 1970s.* Geoffrey Chapman: London, 1996.

Sider, R.J. *Evangelism and Social Action.* Hodder and Stoughton: London, 1993.

PART 4 CHAPTER 2

Berger, Peter L. *The Sacred Canopy: Elements of a Sociological Theory of Religion.* Doubleday: New York, 1969.

Casanova, José. *Public Religions in the Modern World.* University of Chicago Press: Chicago, 1994.

Gutiérrez, Gustavo. *A Theology of Liberation.* (rev. ed.) Orbis: New York, 1988.

Hauerwas, Stanley. *The Peaceable Kingdom: A Primer in Christian Ethics.* UNDP: Notre Dame, Indiana, 1983.

McLeod, Hugh. *Secularisation in Western Europe: 1848–1914.* Macmillan: New York, 2000.

MacHaffie, Barbara J. *Her Story: Women in Christian Tradition.* (2nd ed.) Augsburg Fortress: Minneapolis, 2006.

Malone, Mary T. *Women & Christianity, Vol. III: From the Reformation to the 21st Century.* Orbis: New York 2003.

Martin, David. *A General Theory of Secularization.* Harper & Row: New York, 1978.

Moltmann, Jurgen. *Theology of Hope.* SCM: London, 1969.

Niebuhr, Reinhold. *The Nature and Destiny of Man.* (2 Vols.) Scribners: New York, 1964.

Rauschenbusch, Walter. *A Theology for the Social Gospel.* Macmillan: New York, 1917.

Ruether, Rosemary R. *Womanguide: Readings Toward a Feminist Theology.* Beacon: Boston, 1985.

Tawney, R.H. *Religion and the Rise of Capitalism.* John Murray: London, 1926.

Taylor, Charles. *A Secular Age.* Harvard University Press: Cambridge, Massachusetts, 2007.

INDEX

C

ACKNOWLEDGMENTS AND PICTURE CREDITS

Acknowledgments

The publishers would like to thank Kristin Lanzoni at Duke University for her contributions toward the Art and Architecture feature on Baroque and the Renaissance. In Part 1, Chapter 2: The Story of the Church, Anne T. Thayer contributed up to and including Scholars and Schisms, Hans J. Hillerbrand contributed The Reformation through to The Modern Age.

Picture Credits

The publisher would like to thank the following people, museums and photographic libraries for permission to reproduce their material. Every care has been taken to trace copyright holders. However, if we have omitted anyone we apologize and will, if informed, make corrections to any future edition.

AA	Art Archive, London
ADO	Alfredo Dagli Orti
AFP	Agence France Presse
AKG	akg-images, London
BAL	Bridgeman Art Library, London
Bednorz	© Achim Bednorz, Cologne
BL	The British Library, London
GDO	Gianni Dagli Orti
Lessing	Erich Lessing
ML	Musée du Louvre, Paris
MP	Museo del Prado, Madrid
Monheim	Bildarchiv Monheim, Krefeld
MBAC	courtesy of the Ministero Beni e Att. Culturali, Italy
Scala	Photo Scala, Florence
SHP	Sonia Halliday Photographs, Buckinghamshire
SH&LL	Sonia Halliday and Laura Lushington
V&A	Victoria and Albert Museum/© V&A Images, London. All rights reserved
Vatican	Vatican Museums, Rome
WFA	Werner Forman Archive, London

t = top b = bottom

Page 1 AKG/York Minster/Monheim; **2** Bednorz/St Knuds Kirche, Odense; **3** WFA/Cathedral Treasury, Limburg; **6** Scala/Sistine Chapel, Vatican; **7** Scala/Chigi Saracini Collection, Siena; **8** Corbis/Paul Almasy; **10–11** Scala – MBAC/Galleria degli Uffizi, Florence; **12** SHP; **13** AKG/Lessing; **14** AKG/Archivio Archiepiscopale, Rossano/Lessing; **15** AKG/Johanneshospital, Bruges/Lessing; **16** Scala/Museo dell'Opera Metropolitana, Siena; **17** AA/Episcopal Museum Vic, Catalonia/GDO; **18** AA/National Gallery, London/Eileen Tweedy; **19** SHP; **20** Yale University Art Gallery, Dura Europos Collection; **21** Scala/Musée des Beaux-Arts, Tournai; **22** Art Archive/Real Collegiata San Isidoro, Leon/GDO; **23** Scala – MBAC/Museo di San Marco, Florence; **24** SHP; **25** Alamy/Gianni Muratore; **26** AA/Church of Saint Barbara, Cairo/GDO; **27** AA/Monastery of Santo Domingo de Silos, Spain/ADO; **28** AA/San Gennaro Catacombs, Naples/GDO; **29** Robert Harding/Bruno Barbier; **30** Scala/Church of San Francesco, Assisi; **31** Scala/Museum of East Asian Art, Bath/HIP; **32** Scala/Pierpont Morgan Library/Art Resource; **33** AA/Roger Cabal Collection/GDO; **34** Scala/St Peter's Basilica, Vatican; **35** AKG/Andrea Jemolo; **36** AA/Vezzolano, Italy; **37** AKG/Lessing; **38** Bednorz; **39** V&A; **40** Corbis/epa/Sergei Chirikov; **41** Bednorz; **42** Corbis/Dave Bartruff; **43** Scala – MBAC/Pinacoteca Nazionale, Siena; **44t** Corbis/Godong/Philippe Lissac; **44b** AKG/Monheim; **45** Scala/Church of San Francesco, Montefalco; **46t** Scala/Saint-Sernin, Toulouse; **46b** & **47** Bednorz; **48** WFA/Treasury of St Mark's Venice; **49** Koninklijke Bibliotheek, The Hague; **50** AA/University Library, Prague/GDO; **51** Scala/ML; **52t** Bednorz; **52b** AKG/Monheim; **53** Bednorz; **54** AA/GDO; **55** AA/Nationalmuseet, Copenhagen/ADO; **56** AA/Musée des Beaux Arts, Lausanne/GDO; **57** AKG/Thyssen-Bornemisza Collection/Lessing; **58** AA/MP/GDO; **59** AA/Museo degli Affreschi, Verona/GDO; **60** BAL/Frans Hals Museum, Haarlem/Index; **61** AKG/Lessing; **62** AKG/Christian Alder; **63** BAL/© The Fleming-Wyfold Art Foundation; **64** Getty Images/Daniel Berehulak; **65** AKG; **66–67** Corbis/Vittoriano Rastelli; **68** The Beinecke Rare Book and Manuscript Library, Yale University; **70** AKG; **71** Scala/MP; **72** Scala/Sistine Chapel, Vatican; **73** BAL/Private Collection; **74** BAL/Hamburger Kunsthalle, Hamburg, Germany; **75** © The Trustees of the British Museum, London; **76t** SHP/SH&LL; **76b** SHP/SH&LL/Landesmuseum, Munster; **77** SHP/SH&LL; **78** AA/Episcopal Museum, Vic, Catalonia/GDO; **79** Scala/MP; **80** AA/Anagni Cathedral, Italy/ADO; **81** AA/Palazzo Leoni-Montanari, Vicenza/GDO; **82** Tate Enterprises, Presented by Lord Duveen 1927; **83** Corbis/Digital Art; **84t** Scala/St Mark's Basilica, Venice; **84b** AA/ADO; **85** AKG/Nimatallah; **86** AA/Santa Maria delle Carceri Abbey, Carceri/GDO; **87** V&A; **88** BL; **90** V&A; **91** Getty Images/Robert A Sabo; **92** Corbis/Godong/Fred de Noyelle; **93** AKG/Bibliothèque Publique et Universitaire/Lessing; **94** Scala/Museo dell'Opera del Duomo, Florence; **95** AA/San Carlos Museum, Mexico City/ADO; **96** Getty Images/AFP/Hoang Dinh Nam; **97** Corbis/Andrew Fox; **98** AA/Cathedral Treasury, Aachen/ADO; **99** WFA/Private Collection; **100** V&A; **101** Corbis/Michael Nicholson; **102** Scala/Hospital of the Ceppo, Pistoia; **103** AKG/Sainte-Foy Church, Conques/Lessing; **104** Scala/Metropolitan Museum of Art, New York. Rogers Fund, 1918. (18.70.28)/Photo Bob Hanson; **105** & **106t** Bednorz; **106b** AA/Santo Domingo church, Oaxaca/Mireille Vautier; **107** Bednorz; **108** Scala/Bildarchiv Preussischer Kulturbesitz, Berlin – Gemaeldegalerie, Berlin; **109** Corbis/Richard T Nowitz; **110** BAL/Christie's Images; **111** Corbis/Godong/Phillipe Lissac; **112** Corbis/Flip Schulke; **113** AA/Bibliothèque Municipale, Abbeville/GDO; **114** Scala/ML; **115** BAL/Private Collection; **116** SHP; **117** AA/Suermondt Museum, Aachen/ADO; **118** Bednorz; **120** Getty Images/AFP/Tim Sloan; **121** Scala – MBAC/Biblioteca Laurenziana, Florence; **122** Corbis/Reuters/Tony Gentile; **123** BAL/Natural History Museum, London; **124** Corbis/Reuters/Brian Snyder; **125** BAL/Winchester Cathedral, Hampshire; **126** Corbis/Robert Harding World Imagery/Ellen Rooney; **127** Corbis/Dallas Morning News/David Leeson; **128** Photo Scala Florence/HIP/BL; **129** Corbis/Bohemian Nomad Picturemakers; **130** Getty Images/The Image Bank/Joanna McCarthy; **131** Scala – MBAC/Galleria Sabauda, Turin; **132** AKG/Cathedral Treasury, Aachen/Lessing; **134** Scala/Galleria Comunale, Prato; **135** Corbis/Sygma/Tim Graham; **136** Getty Images/AFP/Sakis Mitrolidis; **137** Corbis/Reuters/Vincenzo Pinto; **138** Scala/MBAC/Pinacoteca di Brera, Milan; **139** AA/Bibliothèque Municipale, Laon/GDO; **140** The National Archives UK (TNA(PRO)E164-25 f222); **141** Corbis/Sygma/Brooks Kraft; **142** Getty Images/AFP/Vincenzo Pinto; **143** © Steve Collins, London/www.smallfire.org; **144** Scala; **145** AA/Museo Civico, Bolzano/GDO; **146** Corbis/Roger Wood; **147** Getty Images/Peter Macdiarmid; **149** AA/Koninklijke Museum, Amberes; **150** Getty images/AFP/Francisco Leong; **151** Scala/Church of Ognissanti, Florence; **152t** SHP/F H C Birch; **152b** V&A; **153** BAL/Santa Maria Gloriosa dei Frari, Venice/Giraudon; **154** Corbis/Paulo Fridman; **155** Corbis/epa/Nic Bothma; **156** Alamy/Philip Scalia; **157** AKG; **158** BAL/Bibliotheque Nationale, Paris; **159** AA/Musée des Antiquités, Rouen/GDO; **160** Corbis; **161** AKG/Woburn Abbey, Bedfordshire; **162** AP images; **163** Corbis/Kulla/Owaki; **164** Photolibrary.com/Steve Dunwell; **165** AA/Museum of Fine Arts, Boston/Laurie Platt Winfrey; **166** Corbis/Bob Krist; **167** Photolibrary.com/The Travel Library; **168** Alamy/Sherab; **169** AKG/ML/Lessing; **170** Corbis/William Manning; **171** BAL/Musées de la Ville de Paris, Musée Carnavalet, Paris/Lauros/Giraudon; **172** BAL/Private Collection/Peter Newark American Pictures; **173** BAL/Brooklyn Museum of Art, New York; **174** Corbis/Michael Freeman; **175** Getty Images/National Geographic/James P Blair; **176** Corbis/David Brabyn; **177** Corbis/Karen Kasmauski; **179** Corbis/Catherine Karnow; **180** Corbis/Bob Krist; **181** AKG/ Skulpturensammlung und Museum für Byzantinische Kunst, Berlin; **182** AA/Hosias Loukas Monastery/GDO; **183** Corbis/Godong/Julian Kumar; **184t** Robert Harding/Gavin Hellier; **184b** AF Kersting, London; **185** SuperStock/Steve Vidler; **187** AA/Coptic Museum, Cairo/GDO; **188** Alamy/IML Image Group Ltd; **189** Corbis/zefa/José Fuste Raga; **190** AA/Palazzo Leoni-Montanari, Vicenza/GDO; **191** Robert Harding/Tony Gervis; **192** Scala/Benaki Museum, Athens; **192** BAL/Tretyakov State Gallery, Moscow; **193** Scala/Tretyakov State Gallery, Moscow; **194–195** Scala; **196** SHP; **197** AKG/Galleria dell'Accademia, Venice/Cameraphoto; **198** Scala/St Mark's Basilica, Venice; **199** BL; **200** Reproduced by courtesy of the University Librarian and Director, The John Rylands University Library, The University of Manchester; **201** BAL/San Nicolo, Treviso; **202** SHP; **203** Corbis/Jon Hicks; **204** SHP; **206** SHP/V&A; **207** AKG/Bibliothèque Nationale, Paris; **208** BAL/Fitzwilliam Museum, University of Cambridge; **209** BAL/© The Board of Trinity College, Dublin; **210** Scala – MBAC; **211** Scala/San Vitale, Ravenna; **213** AA/San Angelo in Formis, Capua/ADO; **214** Scala/The Philadelphia Museum of Art/Art Resource; **215** Scala/Baptistery, Padua; **216**, **217**, **218** SHP; **220** Scala/Musée des Tapisseries, Angers; **221** Scala – MBAC; **222–223** Magnum Photos/Chris Steele-Perkins; **224** Alamy/Robin Nelson; **225** Getty Images/Alex Wong; **226** Corbis/Jim McDonald; **227** Getty Images/Natalie Behring-Chisholm; **228** Corbis/Christophe Boisvieux; **229** Corbis/David Lees; **230** Corbis/Sygma/Ziv Koren; **231** AA/Topkapi Museum, Istanbul/ADO; **232** Corbis/epa/Jon Hrusa; **233** Getty Images/AFP/Dmitry Astakhov; **235** Getty Images/AFP/Sam Panthaky; **236** AKG/Lessing; **237** Getty Images/AFP/Alejandro Acosta; **238** Getty Images/China Photos; **239** Corbis/Andrew Brookes.